PARLIAMENTS

PARLIAMENTS

A Comparative Study on the Structure and Functioning of Representative Institutions in Forty-One Countries

Introduced by Giuseppe Codacci-Pisanelli, former
President of the Inter-Parliamentary Union

Published for the
INTER-PARLIAMENTARY UNION
by
FREDERICK A. PRAEGER, *Publisher*
New York · London

FREDERICK A. PRAEGER, *Publisher*
64 University Place, New York 3, N.Y., U.S.A.
49 Great Ormond Street, London, W.C.1, England

Published in the United States of America in 1963
by Frederick A. Praeger, Inc., Publisher

Printed in Great Britain

PREFACE

On the occasion of its 50th plenary Conference, held in Brussels in September 1961, the Inter-Parliamentary Union submitted to its members, and indeed to everyone interested in present-day political developments, the results of an Inquiry conducted into the different types of Parliament in the world.

This work is being published at a time when the organization has behind it some seventy years of continuous existence which have taken it through one of the most turbulent periods of history and the trials of two world wars. It bears witness to the experience acquired by several generations of parliamentarians who, across continents and notwithstanding differences of nationality and political system, have been united by a common concept of the mission which faces representative assemblies as the interpreters of the hopes and true interests of the people.

The present comparative study is based on information collected from forty-one individual Parliaments in answer to a questionnaire addressed to all member groups of the Union.

The difficult task of analysing and presenting in systematic form the material thus assembled has been carried out by the Inter-Parliamentary Bureau, and more particularly by Mr Ivo Rens, under the guidance of an international committee which included representatives of the major ideologies and political trends of the present day.

This committee, which benefited from the assistance of two experts, Mr Emile Blamont, Secretary General of the French National Assembly, and Sir Edward Fellowes, then Clerk of the House of Commons, was at the outset composed as follows:

Chairman: Professor G. Codacci-Pisanelli (Italy); Members: Sir Herbert Butcher (Great Britain), Mr Pierre Grégoire (Luxembourg), Mr K. A. Goubine (USSR), Mr Elis Hastad (Sweden) and Dr N. M. Perera (Ceylon).

Unanimously approved by this committee in April 1961, the text of the present volume owes much to the author of the preliminary draft, Mr Michel Ameller, a member of the Secretariat of the French National Assembly. The final version was completed in close consultation with the national groups participating in the Inquiry.

v

Naturally, a document of this kind cannot hope to be completely up to date at the time of publication, as the institutions which it sets out to describe are in constant evolution. It would obviously have been impracticable to follow the changes which have occurred by successive addenda to the original material.

Indeed, it would have been impossible to modify the data relevant to any given country, as a consequence of constitutional changes that may have occurred there, without at the same time destroying the comparative basis on which the whole work rests. To attempt to do so would certainly have been a labour of Sisyphus.

It was therefore decided that the study should describe the parliamentary institutions of the countries in question as at a certain date, namely 1 January 1957. In view of this, no account has been taken of any changes which have occurred subsequently. This is particularly regrettable in the cases of such countries as Czecho-slovakia, France and the United Arab Republic, where new Constitutions have since come into force. It is also to be noted that a number of Parliaments to which reference will be found have now ceased to function.

All this is to say that the comparative study as it now stands is already historical in character. The conduct of an international inquiry is time-consuming and demands great tact and caution, as much on the psychological as on the political plane. The published text cannot therefore be fully up to date.

The main purpose of this Inquiry has been to contribute to one of the essential tasks of the Union: that of developing parliamentary institutions and enhancing their prestige. In view of the diversity of such bodies functioning today under the various political régimes, there could be no question of taking any one form of Parliament as a model. The aim has been to provide readers, and especially those who are themselves parliamentarians, with an opportunity to view their own system in the light of others.

Assemblies of longer standing might themselves well profit from such a comparison. For they should not be content to rest com-placently on their past achievements: in politics, as in other fields, the search for truth must be unremitting. The institutions best fitted to represent a people and serve its true interests are not necessarily those developed in a particular period of history. On the contrary, their effectiveness may depend on their ability to adapt themselves to changing circumstances in the light of experience.

For new Parliaments the comparisons provided in the present study are of even greater value. It is important that their members see how other peoples have solved problems similar to those which they in their turn must face, not for the purpose of imitation, but to help them find their own solutions. These should both take into account practices existing elsewhere and also ensure that parliamentary institutions be adapted to the actual conditions existing in each country. Where there is no such adaptation, representative Assemblies have a somewhat artificial character and may well therefore be short-lived. There are not a few recent examples of this.

But the present publication has yet another purpose: that of strengthening throughout the world the idea of Parliament, by describing the methods and procedures of the various assemblies.

There is no doubt that human progress has been fostered by the development of private law, and of such basic concepts as legal title, obligation and contract. These are notions which are now commonly accepted and on which all peoples can agree.

Similarly, humanity will benefit from the gradual perfecting of parliamentary law and procedure, and of the fundamental ideas underlying them. It could be said, for example, that the improved and extended application of such principles of parliamentary life as the procedure governing debates, the prior approval of Bills and of the Budget, the opportunities for interpellation and the duties of objective chairmanship contribute towards improving the parliamentary system as practised in the different countries of the world.

The objection might, however, be raised that in certain countries acceptance of such principles is not genuine. But even if this were true, the final result would be the same. It has been said that hypocrisy is a tribute that vice pays to virtue. Once a nation, no matter how hyprocritically, has begun to experiment with the parliamentary system, it will end, *nolens volens*, by cultivating it and making it genuinely effective; for it will inevitably come to recognize it as the best possible system of government that a democratic community can adopt in pursuance of its intrinsic aims and interests.

Such is the view of those who believe that human society is subject to improvement. Their belief can be sustained by reference to Homer himself for whom civilization implied a system of social organization founded upon assemblies having the power of decision after due deliberation. There was, he said, no more striking evidence of the barbarism of the Cyclops than their very lack of such deliberative assemblies.

' . . . Το ῖ Δ ιν δόῦτ' ἀγυραὶ Βονλμφόροι οὔτε θεμιΔτες. . . '
(*Odyssey*, IX, 112)

It is in the spirit of this conviction, as ancient as the Odyssey but which has lost nothing of its force, that the Inter-Parliamentary

Union presents the results of its Inquiry into the different types of Parliament existing in the world. It does so in the hope that it will contribute to the development of the representative system and, consequently, to the progress of humanity.

G. CODACCI-PISANELLI,
Minister of State,
Member of the Chamber of Deputies

Montecitorio Palace, Rome
May 16, 1962

CONTENTS

Part Three

Part Four

INTRODUCTION

This study on the different types of Parliament in the world is the result of a combined international effort within the Inter-Parliamentary Union by a small group of MP's who, among themselves, represent all the major political trends of the present day.

In a world divided by opposing ideologies, the Union is a forum where men of all political convictions can meet, exchange ideas and seek a basis for common action.

Created in 1889, the Union—which last year held its 50th plenary Conference in Brussels—is the oldest international organization of a political character. It was one of the initiators of the movement which led to the creation of the League of Nations and, later, of the United Nations Organization. Despite the two world wars which for a time compelled it to suspend its activities, the Union has worked unremittingly in the cause of peace and for better understanding among peoples, whatever their political, economic or social systems.

The Union's initial objective lay in the development of inter-national arbitration. Over the years, however, the scope of its activities has broadened, for the problems of peace are indivisible. To secure peace, it is not enough to strengthen the juridical bases of international relations. Economic, social and ideological factors often underlie the tensions arising between states. They have also become the concern of this world organization of Parliaments which is progressively achieving its aim of universality.

The Union's objectives, as laid down in its statutes, are twofold. On the one hand, it must examine 'all questions of an international character suitable for settlement by parliamentary action'. On the other, it has to work for the 'firm establishment of democratic institutions' and to make 'suggestions for the development of parliamentary institutions, with a view to improving the working of those institutions and increasing their prestige'.

As regards the first of these fields of action, the Union's work parallels that of the United Nations and the specialized agencies set up after the last war.

Indeed, the same problems are being discussed: disarmament, international economic relations, assistance to the underdeveloped countries, human rights, the freedom of cultural exchanges, the elimination of colonialism. These are all subjects which, from year to year, reappear on the agenda of the intergovernmental organizations and with which the Union is itself no less concerned.

This does not signify, however, mere duplication. For Inter-Parliamentary meetings have an entirely different character from those of government representatives, bound by formal instructions.

The members of the Union come to conferences uncommitted in this respect. Their debates take place in a completely free atmosphere. Irrespective of nationality, delegates maintain personal relations which are characterized by mutual trust. This factor is not without a certain moderating influence whenever political ideas or interests enter into conflict.

The rigidity of governmental positions is further lessened by the system of voting provided for under the statutes of the organization. The number of votes allotted to each delegation attending the Inter-Parliamentary conferences varies, in fact, from one country to another in accordance with a weighted system based, first, mainly on the size of each country's population. In addition, the vote has an individual character and each delegate can exercise it according to his own convictions. It thus frequently happens that the votes of a particular delegation are divided, the spokesmen for the Opposition adopting a different attitude from that of their colleagues who represent the majority party. This explains why the recommendations made in resolutions adopted by the Union on certain international issues sometimes go further than the positions held by Governments at the United Nations.

It is, indeed, by remaining in the forefront of the international movement that the Union is faithful to the tradition and ideals of the two men—Frédéric Passy of France and William Randal Cremer of Great Britain—who created it and wanted it to become a pioneering force in the struggle for peace.

The statutes define the action to be taken regarding resolutions that have been adopted by Inter-Parliamentary conferences. National groups are obliged to bring such resolutions to the attention of their respective Parliaments and Governments, and to use every means at their disposal for achieving those objectives upon which there has been common agreement.

It is therefore true to say that, while it has no direct sway over the course of political events, the Union does exercise, indirectly, a constructive influence, the importance of which is both recognized and welcomed in many countries.

The second field in which the Union is active—namely, that of parliamentary problems—is one rightfully its own. Here there is no risk of any duplication, for the body which represents the world's legislative assemblies has, in this regard, a mission which no other institution is in a position to fulfil.

Its work in this field is carried out in close liaison with that of the Association of Secretaries General of Parliaments, a body set up under its aegis and which brings together the most qualified experts in matters of legislative procedure.

For both organizations international inquiries, conducted with the assistance of their respondents in the various countries, form the most effective method of studying, on a comparative basis, the problems with which representative assemblies are confronted.

During recent years the Association of Secretaries General of Parliaments has in this way drawn up a number of well-documented reports on various questions of parliamentary law, including, among others, the extent of parliamentary control over the executive, the organization of the work of Parliament, interpellation and like procedures, the role of committees and the powers of the Speaker.

There can be no doubt that the information thus gathered together has been of the greatest service, particularly in a number of new states, which, while adopting the principles and techniques of Western democracy, seek to adapt them to the requirements and conditions of their national life.

In addition, an inquiry carried out some years ago by the Association of Secretaries General of Parliaments led to the publication of a valuable study on European parliamentary procedure.

The Association's objectives complement the work of the Union itself which, naturally, reflects the more pronouncedly political preoccupations of its members.

At Inter-Parliamentary conferences, which are held each year in different countries and continents, the Union generally debates some aspect of the functioning of Parliament. Resolutions were thus adopted in 1957, in London, on the influence of and control by Parliament over the Government; in 1958, at Rio de Janeiro, on the development of representative assemblies in non-self-governing territories; in 1959, at Warsaw, on the role of Parliament in protecting the rights of the individual; and in 1960, at Tokyo, on the future of parliamentary democracy in Asia.

In 1961, at its 50th plenary session, the Union considered a problem of the greatest interest and concern to Western European political circles—that of parliamentary control of international organizations.

Although not always the subject of international inquiries, which entail long delays, the problems for debate at plenary conferences are always well prepared. Some months before the session, the subject chosen is examined by one or other of the study committees, which are established on a permanent basis. Following this exchange of views, a draft resolution is drawn up, a rapporteur appointed and a preliminary report is sent to all national groups. It is therefore in full knowledge of the facts that a debate is held which leads to the adoption of a resolution expressing the wishes and recommendations of the sole world organization of Parliaments.

This brief survey of the aims and working methods of the Union would be incomplete without some reference to the structure of the organization. Its main organs are: the Inter-Parliamentary Conference, which meets annually; the Inter-Parliamentary Council, which is the governing body and is composed of two delegates representing each national group; the Executive Committee, which is the administrative organ of the Union and comprises eleven members, ten of whom are elected by the conference, the President of the Council being *ex officio* both member and President; and, finally, the Inter-Parliamentary Bureau, which has its offices in Geneva and fulfils the functions of an international secretariat.

The members of the Union are 'National Groups constituted in Parliaments functioning as such within the territory of which they represent the population, in a State recognized as a subject of international law'.

At the present moment the following sixty-four countries are represented: Albania, America (United States of), Argentina, Australia, Austria, Belgium, Brazil, Bulgaria, Burma, Canada, Central African Republic, Ceylon, Chile, Czechoslovakia, Denmark, Ethiopia, Finland, France, Germany (Federal Republic of), Ghana, Great Britain, Greece, Guatemala, Haiti, Hungary, Iceland, India, Indonesia, Iran, Iraq, Ireland, Israel, Italy, Japan, Laos, Lebanon, Liberia, Libya, Luxembourg, Monaco, Mongolia, Netherlands, New Zealand, Nigeria, Norway, Pakistan, Panama, Paraguay, Peru, Philippines, Poland, Rumania, Spain, Sudan, Sweden, Switzerland, Thailand, Tunisia, Turkey, United Arab Republic, USSR, Venezuela, Vietnam (Republic of) and Yugoslavia.

Naturally, the hazards of political life affect participation in the work of the Union. For varying reasons certain Parliaments may sometimes suffer eclipse and, temporarily at least, the seats previously occupied by their delegations remain empty. But experience has shown that the idea of democratic legitimacy of power is, today, so firmly rooted in the mind of man that sooner or later representative assemblies are re-established even in those countries where the parliamentary system seemed to have been discredited.

This is, no doubt, one of the reasons why the Inter-Parliamentary Union has endured through the upheavals of the last fifty years. While empires have foundered and authoritarian régimes have collapsed, the ideal of 'government of the people, by the people and for the people' has not lost its force.

Admittedly, parliamentary institutions have in many cases had to modify their methods to meet the changing conditions of life in a modern State. But no doctrine has as yet been advanced which could be substituted for that of popular representation, as the essential basis of governmental power.

By its very nature the Inter-Parliamentary Union is dependent upon the political and constitutional evolution in various parts of the world. Consequently it has had successes and failures, alternate periods of rapid development and of crisis. Based on the voluntary adherence of its national groups and without the security of government support, its juridical structure is as fragile as its material resources are modest. Nonetheless, it represents, morally speaking, a constructive force in the world today. For it embodies a democratic ideal which, in one form or another, is alive in the hearts of all men, whatever their country or political views.

It is hoped that the present study will demonstrate the intellectual honesty which imbues the work of the Union in its search for a measure of common ground so that supporters of the different political systems and rival ideologies may collaborate for better understanding and agreement.

ANDRÉ DE BLONAY,
Secretary General of the
Inter-Parliamentary Union

May 15, 1962

Part One

THE STRUCTURE AND
ORGANIZATION OF PARLIAMENT

THE STRUCTURE AND ORGANIZATION OF PARLIAMENT

It may seem a somewhat rash undertaking to try to strip the Parliament of its aura of mysticism; to disclose what it really is, in forty-one different countries; to describe its inner workings and discover their underlying meaning and those constant factors so often hidden beneath political trappings of one kind or another. The very term 'Parliament' has still to be defined, and its definition is by no means the least of the problems that political science has to face.

Before venturing into and exploring this field in its practical manifestation we must first find out exactly how far it extends. In its broadest sense, embracing all extremes, Parliament may be regarded as a collective part of the government of a country, consisting as a rule of a large number of elected members and representing the interests of an entire population both in legislating and *vis-à-vis* the executive. This is a vague, abstract concept covering a wide variety of representative bodies all over the world, as well as within the Inter-Parliamentary Union itself; but a description of these bodies will help us to place them in perspective and to understand them better.

* * *

THE STRUCTURE OF PARLIAMENT

The diversity of parliamentary institutions in the different states considered is reflected first of all in the way in which the problem of the number of Chambers making up the Parliament has been tackled. The controversy to which this can give rise is one of the major issues of constitutional law. It is not merely a matter of professional wrangling; it actually represents the translation of basic political likes and dislikes into seemingly ordinary every day terms.

Should there be one chamber or two, a unicameral or a bicameral system? The choice seems simple enough. It is the first choice that

3

those who are drawing up a Constitution are called upon to make. In some cases framers of constitutions have been spared the choice, owing to the peculiar structure of the particular State—for the Parliaments of federal states are invariably bicameral. But non-federal states—and this means the majority of states—have had to face the issue and, for reasons we shall try to explain, to opt in favour of either the bicameral or the unicameral system.

I

The Bicameral System in Federal States

Here, as we have already said, the dilemma does not arise. There is no other choice open, since federal states are by definition two-tier in structure. On the one side there is the nation as a complete entity; on the other, the member-states of the federation, with whatever degree of autonomy they possess.

In the Federation's Parliament, this two-tier structure inevitably implies separation into two chambers, the one emanating from the people as a whole, the other made up of delegates representing each of the member-states.

This logical interpretation of the bicameral nature of the federal state—and there is no alternative—is actually the outcome of an entirely fortuitous historical expedient. Federal bicameralism came about as the result of a happy compromise between two schools of thought championed with equal vigour in the Philadelphia Convention of 1787, which had to thrash out the question of how many 'representatives' each state was to have, assuming that there was to be a single chamber.

Usage transformed the compromise into law and, applied in its strictest sense, the underlying principle provides the key to the essential features of the stock type of federal Parliament. It should perhaps be pointed out that these features are found exclusively in the chamber whose membership represents the Federation's member states. The inherent features of this chamber are as follows:

(a) It must be made up of an equal number of representatives from each federated unit, irrespective of its size or population
(b) The powers it possesses must be the same as, or equivalent to, the powers of the chamber representing the people as a whole.

4

Four nations have constitutions which fulfil both these conditions:

First we have the United States of America. The House of Representatives is made up of 435 members, each elected for two years and representing a given proportion of the population. The Senate consists of two senators per state, elected for six years. The powers of the two Houses are not strictly equal; the power of impeachment and the right to initiate revenue Bills are vested solely in the House of Representatives, but these are offset by the Senate's exclusive right to confirm or reject official appointments and to participate in the drafting and ratification of international treaties. Hence it might be said that neither House has a definite superiority over the other.

In Switzerland, there is no question whatever of one House having any superiority over the other. The powers of the National Council, with one member, elected for a four-year term, for every twenty-two thousand citizens, and those of the Council of State, with two members per canton, are strictly equal.

Though in another part of the world from Switzerland and vastly different in size, Brazil is another member of this same group. Here the Senate, consisting of three delegates from each state, has equality of powers with the Chamber of Deputies, except for certain prerogatives enjoyed by the latter in regard to legislative procedure.

The final example is the Soviet Union where, side by side with the representation of the people in the Soviet of the Union, we find the special interests of the territories represented in the Soviet of Nationalities on a strictly equal footing for each type of unit. Twenty-five members are elected to represent each Republic of the Union, eleven for each autonomous Republic, five for each autonomous region and one for each national territory. The two chambers of the Supreme Soviet have identical rights.

In the Australian Parliament, only the second of the two conditions referred to above—equality of powers as between the two Houses and equal representation of the states in the federal Parliament—is fulfilled. Each of the various states does in fact return the same number of representatives—ten—to the Senate, but the position differs from that of the other four countries mentioned above inasmuch as the Senate's power are not so wide as those of the lower House, particularly in regard to money Bills.

When we turn to the Federal Republic of Germany, we are still further away from the stock pattern of the federal Parliament. Here, while each of the Länder is represented in the Bundesrat (Federal Council), their delegates vary in number with the size of the population (admittedly according to a system of weighting). Each Land has a minimum of three delegates, but those with over two million inhabitants are entitled to four, and those with over six million inhabitants have five. Another noteworthy point is that the Bundesrat has no part in the appointment of the Chancellor, cannot pledge the responsibility of the Government and has not the same legislative rights as the Bundestag (Federal Diet), which is elected by universal suffrage.

In Austria, the system is the same—the Diets of the various Länder return to the Federal Council of fifty members a varying number of delegates, between three and twelve, according to size of population. The powers of the Federal Council are less than those of the National Council both in legislative matters and in its relations with the executive.

In the Union of Burma, the Chamber of Nationalities comprises 125 seats, distributed, as in the case of the Federal Republic of Germany and Austria, roughly in proportion to the population of each state and territory. As regards their relative powers, the two Houses are decidedly unequal, only the Chamber of Deputies having competence in regard to the Union's financial affairs.

In India, again, this same power in regard to money matters and, in addition, that of government responsibility, is what marks the supremacy of the House of the People (Lok Sabha) over the Council of States. A further peculiarity here is that, as the majority of the membership of the Council of States is elected by the legislative assemblies of the fourteen states not on a basis of equality, but varying with the population of each state, the usual principles of federal organization do not strictly hold in India.

Although it may be true that in Australia, the Federal Republic of Germany, Austria, Burma and India the balance between the two Houses is not always in accordance with the principles we have tried to define, the fact remains that the bicameral character of their legislatures is due to their federal structure, just as it is in the United States of America, Switzerland, Brazil and the USSR.

Instances do of course occur where it is more difficult to establish so direct a link between a federal state and a bicameral Parliament. In Yugoslavia, for example, the federal structure is not reflected, as it is elsewhere, in the existence of a separate chamber representing the federated territories. The former Council of Nationalities has since 1953 been incorporated into the Federal Council—a body consisting first and foremost of representatives directly elected by the people. This is not to say that it no longer exists. Representatives elected to the Federal Council by the Assemblies of the People's Republics and the autonomous regions have the right to sit apart, as the Council of Nationalities, should the protection of 'the equilibrium defined by the Constitution' be deemed necessary. Thus the operation of this procedue constitutes a special case.

The Second Chamber, or Council of Producers, is not federal in character: it comprises in fact members elected by the manual workers and employees in industry, the members of agricultural co-operatives and self-employed craftsmen and handicraft workers.

It is evident from the ingenious notion hit upon by the Yugoslav Constitution, where the desire for representation of the producers has pushed federal representation into the background, that the choice of the bicameral system is not necessarily dictated by the basic principles of state structure. Frequently, it is the outcome of other equally important factors, especially in non-federal states which have opted for the system.

II

The Bicameral System in Non-Federal States

Quite apart from the special constitutional factors inherent in federal states, the bicameral system is based on a variety of factors which are extremely perplexing and awkward to analyse.

It has its roots deep in past history and, because of the peculiar way in which it has evolved at the whim of geographical and political circumstance, it is difficult to pin down. The fact is that over a long period of time it has developed new and varied facets as a result of theoretical and practical rationalizations which in the end have supplanted the original intention, which has long since been forgotten.

In the history of parliamentary institutions, the earliest example of the bicameral system is to be found in England, where it has its roots in a desire on the part of the King's vassals, the Lords Spiritual and Temporal, to preserve a form of representation distinct from that of the common folk. This is the origin of the House of Lords, a unique phenomenon in contemporary constitutional law, with its hereditary membership, nearly a thousand strong, designated entirely by the Crown. But, although the non-democratic composition of the Second Chamber has managed to survive through the ages, its wings have been clipped, first of all by the creation of 'peers' no longer necessarily of noble birth and, secondly, by a gradual attrition of its powers in favour of the lower House, the House of Commons. The arguments for a bicameral system nowadays are of two kinds:

(a) The concern for a more stable balance between the Executive and the Legislature, the unbridled power of a single chamber being restrained by the creation of a Second Chamber recruited on a different basis.

(b) The desire to make the parliamentary machine run, if not more efficiently, at any rate more smoothly, by having a so-called 'revising' chamber to maintain a careful check on the sometimes hasty decisions of a First Chamber.

In practice, historical explanation and theoretical and practical rationalizations have merged one into another, with the result that the establishent of the bicameral system can nowhere be attributed strictly to any one of these factors. If we are to grasp the true nature of the bicameral system, we must look beyond these rationalizations to the deep political motivation that lies at its root. This, of course, takes us beyond the strict limits of 'description'; but it will help to give us a better understanding of parliamentary institutions.

In non-federal states, the nature of the Second Chamber in some cases reflects the desire, conscious or unconscious, of those who framed the Constitution to curb the democratic aggressiveness of the First Chamber by including in it more conservative elements so as to keep it under control. Assuming that the aim of democracy is to enable the sovereign will of the people to express itself as directly as possible and that the evolution of man towards democratic ideas is linked historically with the growth of universal suffrage, we can assess the strength of the conservative elements in question by applying two complementary criteria in regard to the nature and structure of the Second Chamber:

(a) The way in which its members are appointed.

(b) The relative extent of its powers as compared with those of the lower Chamber.

By taking these two criteria together we can classify bicameral systems in non-federal states as we did for the federal states—though the approach is different. But, however convenient it might be to pigeon-hole each system as neatly as possible, our classification makes due allowance for the hard facts and the complex nature of modern institutions which range from 'conservative' bicameral system to a virtually 'unicameral' bicameral system.

8

An extreme example would be a system in which the Second Chamber was recruited by non-democratic means, but had powers equal to or greater than those of the First Chamber.

There is no instance today where these two conditions are rigorously applied, and to find an example we must go back to the time when the House of Lords in Great Britain was equal in status to the House of Commons. But Parliament in the following countries shows varying degrees of kinship to this type of system.

Laos: Here the National Assembly and the Council of the King have equivalent if not equal rights; all the members of the upper House are nominated by the King, but half their number have previously been recommended by a resolution of the National Assembly. Thus, in the selection of the King's Councillors, universal suffrage is only partially and indirectly applied.

Ceylon: Here the bicameral system is somewhat similar. Of the thirty members of the Senate, fifteen are appointed by the Governor-General on the recommendation of the Prime Minister, the other fifteen being elected, as in Laos, by the House of Representatives. It should be noted, however, that, in financial matters at any rate, the upper House's powers in Ceylon are more restricted than those of the lower.

Sudan: The Sudanese Senate has less power than the lower Chamber, not in financial matters in this case, but politically. The Government is not responsible to the Senate. On the other hand in legislation the Senate has a delaying power, a political weapon which can be effective against the whims of the lower House. Two fifths of the Senate are members nominated by the Supreme Commission, a body with a membership of five who collectively exercise the functions of Head of State.

Ireland: As in Laos, Ceylon and the Sudan, the method of appointment of members of the Seanad does not altogether comply with the principles of universal direct suffrage. Eleven members out of sixty are appointed by the Prime Minister, and six are elected by the universities. Nevertheless, the features of a modern Western European bicameral system are more clearly recognizable here. Forty-three senators are elected by the deputies, outgoing senators and the local authorities, and the supremacy of the Dail over the Seanad, i.e. of the lower over the upper House, in respect of powers is more marked. The Dail has exclusive control over the State budget and over international treaties; it alone is competent to declare war, and it can require the Seanad to adopt legislative measures in the form in which it submits them. Thus, while the method of appointment of members of the Second Chamber is not altogether in keeping with ordinary democratic principles, that is offset by the fact that the powers of the Seanad are considerably curtailed.

In certain democracies of the parliamentary type to be found in Western Europe, the desire to create a balance between the powers has worked the other way; the tendency had been to increase the powers of the Second Chamber, and at the same time to adopt what appears to be a more democratic method of appointment.

This is the case with the bicameral Parliaments of Belgium, France, the Netherlands, Italy and Sweden, where the Second Chamber is appointed by universal suffrage and has powers almost equal to those of the lower Chamber.

This does not mean that the system of 'checks and balances' is no longer in evidence; it is reflected in the various procedures for dealing, *inter alia*, with the appointment of members of the upper House:

Vestiges of autocracy of Belgium, where the King's sons or, if there is no male issue, princes in the direct line of descent are *de jure* members of the Senate at the age of eighteen.

Tribute to eminent citizens in Italy, where the President of the Republic can nominate as life senators five citizens who have rendered distinguished service to their country; in addition, former Presidents of the Republic are *ex officio* members of the Senate. As for encroachment on universal suffrage, this differs according to the country concerned and, though it is unobtrusive, it is nevertheless significant (e.g. raising of the age-limit—for the electorate and the candidate in Italy, for the candidate only in France and Belgium; and the institution of indirect suffrage in France, Sweden and the Netherlands).

On the other hand, in Italy, and to a great extent in Belgium (106 members out of 172), the Senate is elected by direct universal suffrage, though the system of voting differs from that of the Chamber of Deputies. This essentially democratic origin of the two Houses makes it reasonable to give them equal powers. We do not find this equality of powers either in the Netherlands or in France where, because the rules governing the upper House keep it remote from popular sovereignty, for that very reason its rights are substantially restricted in legislative matters and, as far as the Council of the French Republic is concerned, in regard to the responsibility of the Government to it.

A system not unlike the parliamentary régime which, with slight variations, is practised in these five European countries, is found in

10

two other nations, Japan and the Philippines. Here the machinery of Parliament has something of the same appearance, characteristic of a bicameral system—a democratic basis for the upper House (the House of Councillors in Japan and the Senate in the Philippines) and powers slightly less than those of the lower House.

As well as this type of bicameral system, which is based on simple principles (though in practice there are vast differences in points of detail), we get the parliamentary systems of Norway and Iceland which, paradoxical as it may sound, can fairly be called 'unicameral bicameral systems'. Here the existence of a Second Chamber is not based on political considerations, as in the other cases. As far as the structure of both Houses is concerned, democratic evolution has gone as far as it can go, so that the underlying motive is simply one of practical convenience. In these two countries, Parliament is elected as a whole direct by the people and the separation into two takes place only after the elections. The Members of Parliament themselves appoint a certain proportion from among their number (in Iceland one third, in Norway a quarter) to sit in the upper House. The sole purpose of having two Houses is to facilitate the work of legislation. Thus, the method of appointment of the upper House and the fact that its powers are identical to those of the lower House make this theoretically bicameral system in actual fact a form of the unicameral system. This is illustrated by the fact that, in non-legislative matters, in particular for the examination of questions of finance, the Parliaments of these two countries meet in joint session.

III

The Unicameral System in Non-Federal States

Thus, according to contemporary constitutional theory, the unicameral system is more appropriate to democracy, bicameral systems being regarded as essentially designed to restrain and moderate the ebullience of popular sovereignty, which would operate in too ruthless a manner if there were only a single chamber. The single chamber should ideally be elected by direct universal suffrage, and that is in fact the commonest practice. But, as a criterion, it does not fully account for the nature of the unicameral system, since here, more than anywhere else, allowance has to be made for the spirit, the traditions and the economic and social evolution of the particular nation concerned.

11

Thus seventeen of the states included in the Inquiry have a Parliament consisting of a single chamber, and any attempt to group under a single heading the reasons which have led them to make this choice is bound to be somewhat arbitrary. Two of these states, Monaco and Luxembourg, have been able in all probability to cut out one chamber simply owing to their small geographical size, inasmuch as for small nations the problem of the balance of political power is less difficult to solve than it is for bigger countries. The eighteen members of the Monaco National Council are enough to carry on the administration of the Principality, and the fifty-two Luxembourg deputies can administer the affairs of the Grand Duchy with its population of 300,000.

In the case of Denmark, the fact that it is small in size was probably one of the reasons for its recent adoption of the unicameral system. There is in fact a decided movement in all the Scandinavian countries except Sweden towards the institution of a single chamber within the framework of the parliamentary system. Finland was the first illustration of this tendency and is still the best example.

In Turkey, the Grand National Assembly is also a single chamber, and, at any rate in its most recent form, it functions within a constitutional system of the Western type. The same is true of the Knesset in Israel. But these two Parliaments have other points in common—in the first place, their fairly recent establishment and, secondly, the upheavals out of which they emerged, namely, the revolution in Turkey and the founding of a new state in Israel.

Similar factors have played an even more decisive part in the case of states in the Near and Far East, e.g. Egypt, Syria, Indonesia, Pakistan and the Republic of Vietnam, which have recently gained their independence. In all these countries, a unicameral system has had a youthful, modern look, as being an institution where considerations of efficiency are more important than the search for the traditional type of political equilibrium.

Thus, a unicameral system would appear to be the more satisfactory one for peoples in the process of evolution, in countries where the dynamic political situation, which so frequently leads to profound upheavals in old-established institutions, cannot get along with the restraints regarded as being inherent in the bicameral system. It is natural, therefore, to find that the People's Democracies come under this heading—except for Yugoslavia, whose unusual system has already been discussed. Albania, Bulgaria, Czechoslovakia, Poland and Rumania are in a phase of their evolution in which the search for a workable system has produced, as far as Parliament is concerned, a single chamber elected by universal suffrage. In Spain, however, political circumstances have determined the special methods applied to recruit the single chamber. Thus, in the Cortes, corporative representation takes precedence over popular representation. Fifty members are appointed by the Head of State, the rest by the large cities and provincial communities, and by various national corporations such as the syndicates, associations of engineers, barristers, solicitors, doctors, veterinary surgeons, architects, etc.

This rapid survey of the institutions of forty-one countries, from the narrow point of view of the number of Houses in their Parliaments, shows quite clearly that the importance of the choice between the bicameral and unicameral systems is not exaggerated. Frequently it has its roots deep in the country's history, its peculiar characteristics and national spirit; in the main, it involves a fundamental political choice which goes far beyond the sphere of every-day parliamentary practice.

However, if we confine ourselves strictly to the problem in hand and avoid any value-judgment as to the political systems within which Parliament functions, it is evident that a bicameral Parliament is better suited to:

(a) Federal states, by the very fact of their two-tier structure, and irrespective of whether their political system is liberal or authoritarian.

(b) Some non-federal states because of varying circumstances, such as the existence of a long parliamentary tradition.

A unicameral Parliament on the other hand is better suited to the requirements of young states, the political evolution of which is taking place under conditions which are fundamentally different from those which obtained at the birth of parliamentary government in Western Europe.

This fairly rough classification, based on extra-juridical principles, will be elucidated as we examine the practical procedure by which assemblies are appointed.

IV

Membership of Parliament and Elections

In the previous chapter emphasis was placed on the upper Chamber with special reference to its powers and the way in which its members were recruited. The problem of the membership of Parliament relates more particularly to popular chambers, since it tends to coincide with the question of suffrage. In representative systems, the consent of the people, whence all authority emanates, is signified by elections. To get an overall picture of the way in which elected chambers in Parliament come into being, we must therefore look in turn at the three factors—the electorate, the ballot and the elected members—which must be forthcoming in that order, before an election can be regarded as having taken place.

V

The Electorate

The Franchise—Electoral Register—Electoral Constituencies

1. THE FRANCHISE

Democracies incline natually towards universal suffrage. All popular chambers, i.e. those of unicameral Parliaments and the lower chambers of bicameral Parliaments follow this system, with the exception of the Spanish Cortes. In an absolute sense, there is no satisfactory definition of universal suffrage. The only way to grasp what it implies is by comparison with suffrage limited by qualifications of property, social status or ability, such systems which today are merely of historical interest; they were used only to slow up the transition from autocratic government to democratic government. In the course of the twentieth century, universal suffrage has become the 'legitimate' form of power. In actual practice, however, it runs into a number of difficulties when the question arises of determining precisely who shall have the right to vote. In practice, this problem is solved by the establishment of legal rules governing the right to vote, the compilation of electoral registers, and the demarcation of constituencies within which the choice of the elector can operate.

One initial difficulty which arises when the theory of universal suffrage is put into practice is the definition of an elector, since the vote cannot, after all, be granted to everyone indiscriminately. The selection of legislators is too important a matter to be left even partly in the hands of irresponsible elements, and hence electoral theory tends to disqualify these elements on the basis of quite specific factors such as nationality, age, or rectitude of conduct. Thus, the degree of encroachment upon what is theoretically universal suffrage can be measured by the severity of the disqualifications which are imposed in the various countries.

For a long time, the vote was restricted to men, political affairs being regarded as an exclusively male domain. Since the turn of the century, the progress of democracy and the campain in favour of equality of rights for women have prevailed over the efforts of the male sex to maintain its privileged situation.

In Europe, Switzerland and the Principality of Monaco continue to deny women the vote but, the time is surely not far off when women will gain the vote there. Reform will perhaps be longer in coming in certain countries where the privileges of the male are still based on a deeply ingrained historical and religious tradition which will not be easy to overstep.

The primary condition for the exercise of the franchise, adopted by all codes of electoral law, is that of nationality. Before a person can vote, he must be a national of the country; for this reason the vote is nowhere given to aliens. The only practical problem is to decide what to do about aliens who have become nationals by the process of naturalization. This problem is particularly important in countries where there is large-scale immigration and where the influence of the immigrants could have a decisive impact on the conduct of public affairs. Thus, the general rule is to grant the franchise only after a certain length of time, or where the persons concerned can show that they are sufficiently well assimilated in their new surroundings.

In France, naturalized persons can only vote after they have been naturalized for five years. In Belgium, they must have acquired so-called 'full naturalization' which is more difficult to obtain than ordinary naturalization. In the United States, citizenship must have been acquired for a certain length of time. This differs according to the particular state, and in many cases is combined with qualifications based on length of residence as a necessary condition for granting voting rights.

The nationality qualification is not always sufficient. In the majority of countries, only those who have shown some continuity of residence in the district to which they belong are regarded as qualified to take part in political affairs. Where the district in question is the same as the electoral constituency, the period for residential qualification may be fairly short, inasmuch as citizens may have to move from place to place, but will not lose their civic rights by doing so. In other words, the purpose of the residence period is partly to ensure as strict as possible a check on the way in which the elections are carried out. The question of the time-limit

15

is more serious where a whole country is concerned, as in Norway or Iceland. Here the minimum period is five years, which automatically eliminates a sizeable body of citizens. Similarly in the United States, where movements of population take place on a fairly large scale, the residence qualification required by most of the states has the effect of cutting down the number of electors.

In contrast to this, the electoral laws in some countries carry the theory of universal suffrage to its logical conclusion. In Albania, Bulgaria, Czechoslovakia, Israel, Poland, Rumania and the USSR, for example, the domicile or residence qualification is unknown. To ensure that the right to vote is universal, a system of electoral cards is used in Czechoslovakia; this enables citizens who have changed their place of residence after publication of the electoral registers to vote in a constituency other than that where they were registered.

The franchise requires that electors, male and female, should have reached an age at which they are fully aware of their civic duties and are capable of expressing a common sense opinion on political matters. As a rule, this age coincides with that of legal majority. In other words, it varies very little from one country to another, ranging from a minimum of eighteen to a maximum of twenty-three years, the age adopted by the majority of electoral legislations being twenty-one.[1]

New governments or governments of a revolutionary type are the most apt to grant the franchise at an early age, as in the People's Democracies and the nations which have attained independence relatively recently.

Age is not the only factor on which the qualification of the intelligence of the elector is based. To qualify for participation in the political life of the country, a citizen must also be of sound mind. This is a principle which every country recognizes. The difficulty of course is to determine precisely at what point an individual shall be regarded as insane or mentally deficient, in other words, to decide where to draw the line between madness and sanity. Hence, in most instances the disqualification is not insanity or mental deficiency, even where the cases are clear, but their legal recognition, in the form of certification or committal of the person to an asylum. Thus in Czechoslovakia the mentally certified no longer enjoy the right to vote.

[1] Voting age 23: Denmark, Netherlands; 22: Turkey; 21: Australia, Belgium, Ceylon, Finland, France, Federal Republic of Germany, Iceland, India, Ireland, Italy, Luxembourg, Monaco, Norway, Philippines, Spain, Sudan, Sweden, United Kingdom, United States; 20: Austria, Japan, Switzerland; 18: Albania, Burma, Brazil, Bulgaria, Czechoslovakia, Egypt, Indonesia, Israel, Laos, Poland, Rumania, Syria, USSR, Republic of Vietnam and Yugoslavia.

16

In some countries other infirmities or presumptions of infirmity are treated in the same way. In Laos, deaf mutes and blind persons, and in Denmark, Spain and Switzerland, persons who are a charge on public funds are disqualified. In some instances, the mental ability required of electors is measured in terms of a certain level of education. In the Philippines, a person must be able to read and write, and some states of the United States require the ability to read an excerpt from the Constitution and even to comment on it.

Apart from this special case, which in the absence of impartial control can lead to abuse, the loose nature of the regulations governing electoral disqualifications is a measure of the desire to avoid any serious encroachment upon the principle of universal suffrage.

The same concern is also evident in regard to the standard of rectitude required of the elector. In the interests of strict impartiality this tends to be defined in a negative way, i.e. a person is considered fit to be a voter provided he has not a mark against his character in the form of a conviction which incurs automatic disqualification. The essential problem here is to define precisely the scope of such convictions. The principle involved differs from country to country, but in a general way there is an evident desire to pursue a middle course, so that persons who are really depraved can be kept off the electoral registers, without unduly extending the list of disqualifications, since this would strike at the whole principle of universal suffrage.

For this reason, the offence committeed or the penalty imposed must be of a certain degree of gravity before it entails confiscation of the right to vote. In Australia, Belgium, Ceylon, Egypt, France, Indonesia, Japan, Laos, Luxembourg, Monaco, the Netherlands, the Philippines and the United Kingdom, the duration of the term of imprisonment constitutes the determining factor. In some legal systems, the important factor is the nature of the offence committed—treason, in the case of Australia Belgium, Brazil, the Federal Republic of Germany, Ireland and Turkey; matrimonial and domestic misdemeanour in Austria, Belgium, and Egypt; electoral corruption in Ceylon, Finland, the Federal Republic of Germany, India, Ireland and Japan.

Apart from convictions for criminal offences, in countries with a strong middle-class tradition, there may be disqualification on the grounds of lack of moral probity where the person concerned has been guilty of dishonourable conduct in business; e.g. persons declared insolvent or bankrupt are particularly liable to disqualification in Belgium, France, Luxembourg and Monaco, as well as in Ceylon, Egypt and Pakistan.

The fact remains, however, that in the great majority of cases, sentence by a court of law is the criterion. This rules out any political rigging, at any rate in so far as no considerations except the ordinary legal ones are involved. However, at the present time, it would appear that the kind of political sentence which at one time could be applied to entire social categories and could ultimately virtually lead to a restricted suffrage has to all intents and purposes disappeared. Moreover, if we remember that deprivation of voting rights is seldom of a permanent character, that usually, as in Syria and the Federal Republic of Germany, it is concurrent with the length of the sentence or connected with the duration of loss of civic rights, as in Czechoslovakia and that it can be annulled by the process of rehabilitation or amnesty—a common practice in France —it is clear that the severity of the law on disqualification for venial and other offences is gradually being relaxed in favour of universal suffrage. In the USSR and the other People's Democracies there are no restrictions in respect of the rights of citizens, except age and citizenship. In the Soviet Union, the citizen's right to vote is retained even when he is sentenced by a court.

These are the main conditions governing the exercise of the franchise as seen in the various national legislations. So far, only the personal qualifications relating to the invididual voter have been prescribed—sex, nationality, age and rectitude of conduct; there has been no tampering with the democratic principle.

In some countries, however, there are provisions designed to restrict the franchise in respect of membership of a particular social group. The motive underlying such restrictions on the suffrage is the concern to safeguard electoral freedom. The voters affected more particularly are persons whose occupations impose a certain measure of discipline—members of the armed forces in Belgium, Brazil, Syria and Turkey; the police in Ireland, Syria and Turkey; members of religious orders in Burma and Laos. The aim is to prevent professional discipline from jeopardizing the genuineness of the voter's choice and to ensure that electioneering does not make for a slackening of discipline. Other categories not entitled to vote are non-taxpaying students in Laos and peers in the United Kingdom.

2. ELECTORAL REGISTERS

Once the conditions required for the exercise of the vote have been established, the next step is to determine which electors in actual fact shall take part in the voting.

The electoral registers are the tangible aspect of the theory of the franchise. The establishment of registers serves a two-fold purpose: it enables every elector to vote and it ensures that those who are not qualified electors shall not take part in the elections. Thus, it is a matter of the utmost practical importance. It demands the strictest impartiality on the part both of the authorities compiling the registers and of those who will have to decide the issue in the event of the results being contested.

If the full strength of the electorate is to be mustered at the polling stations, it must first be split up in some way. Hence the electoral registers are drawn up by small territorial units, small enough to make a rapid and efficient check of the population practicable. Hence the bodies most competent to undertake this are obviously the local authorities, where they possess civil registers giving at a glance full particulars concerning the local residents. This is the system most frequently found in Western Europe—Austria, Belgium, France, the Federal Republic of Germany, Italy, Luxembourg, Monaco, the Netherlands and Switzerland. Similarly, in Indonesia, Japan, Laos and the Republic of Vietnam, the preparation of the electoral lists is in the hands of the administrative services in the villages and communes.

In countries where British influence has been felt, the system found most satisfactory is to entrust the task to officials of the executive who are completely remote from local affairs and hardly likely to be accused of partiality. The compiling of the electoral registers is done by specially trained civil servants—in Australia the Commonwealth Electoral Officer, in Burma, the Enrolling Officer, in Ceylon, the Commissioner of Parliamentary Elections, in Ireland, the County Registrar, in Israel, the officials of the Ministry of the Interior, and in the Philippines, the Inspection Committee of Elections.

In Spain, the electoral registers are kept by the National Statistical Institute. An even more unequivocal expression of the guarantee that impartiality will be exercised in the application of the often difficult and complex regulations governing the franchise is seen in those cases where the responsibility is placed on judicial bodies, as in Brazil and Syria.

In the USSR and the People's Democracies of Albania, Bulgaria, Czechoslovakia, Poland, Rumania and Yugoslavia, the responsibility for drawing up the electoral registers rests with the Executive Committees of the local People's Councils. The task is made easier by the simplicity of the voting system and by the civic enthusiasm which is characteristic of elections; and the committees would appear to achieve fully the purpose of universal suffrage. The negligible number of abstentions and the absence of complaints would suggest that the electoral registers embrace virtually the whole of the electorate.

Where mistakes are made or unfairness is alleged, the electors have invariably the right of appeal to higher authority. This authority may sometimes be purely administrative, as in Burma and the Federal Republic of Germany; but as a rule it is a judicial authority, since a court of law is the ideal body to settle a conflict in accordance with the Constitution and the law. In spite of the many different methods used for drawing up and keeping the electoral registers, the purpose intended is perfectly clear, namely, to ensure that the maximum possible number of citizens exercise their voting rights.

3. ELECTORAL CONSTITUENCIES

Electoral constituencies are the territorial divisions within which the electors have to elect either a specific number of representatives in the case of voting by lists of candidates, or a single representative, in the case of the ballot for a single place.

It is, generally speaking, impracticable for the entire nation to form a single electoral college and elect *en bloc* all Members of Parliament—in most cases several hundred persons. Such a system would be perfectly in keeping with the theory of national sovereignty which holds that Members of Parliament do not represent their particular constituency, but the country as a whole. In practice, it is only feasible in small states, such as Monaco, which is no larger than a town. It is, nevertheless, in use in Israel, where the 120 members are elected *en bloc* from national lists.

The division into constituencies also serves to bring the elected Member of Parliament into closer contact with the electors and it helps the electorate, first of all, to exercise a choice and, secondly, to keep the system under proper control. However, this practical necessity must not be allowed to impair the fundamental principle of equality of suffrage, which presupposes that every elected member shall represent an equal portion of the population. Hence the business of determining the size of constituencies is of vital importance and, for that reason, the principles governing it are invariably laid down, if not in the Constitution itself, as is the case in Ceylon, Iceland, Luxembourg, Norway and Switzerland, at any rate in the electoral laws.

Sizes of constituencies are as follows:

Albania	10,000 inhabitants
Switzerland	24,000 „
Bulgaria	30,000 „
Rumania	40,000 „
Laos	50,000 „
Republic of Vietnam	55,000 „
United Kingdom	50,000 to 60,000 „
Yugoslavia	60,000 „
Federal Republic of Germany	100,000 to 150,000 „
Brazil	150,000 „
Indonesia and USSR	300,000 „

In those states where the ballot is for a single place, the method of determining the number of inhabitants to be included in each constituency is to divde the total population of the country by the number of seats in the Chamber. In those states where each constituency sends several members to Parliament, a similar system is used, but this is less exact, for account must be taken of the 'remainders' which are in this case inevitable. Thus in Italy each constituency has a right to one deputy per 80,000 inhabitants or per 'remainder' exceeding 40,000.

Once a figure has been established, the next question is to determine the geographic boundaries of the constituency itself. This requires, first of all, very precise figures of the local population and, secondly, absolute impartiality, since the operation of dividing up the population may comply with the strict letter of the law and yet do outrage to its spirit if there is any political influence at work. The operation is conducted by different authorities, according to the state. In the USSR it is the responsibility of the Presidium of the Supreme Soviet. In Australia, Ceylon, the Federal Republic of Germany, India, Pakistan and the United Kingdom it is carried out by technical bodies. In certain countries, it is the right of Parliament itself.

In most countries, as in France, Norway and Switzerland, the electoral constituencies are identical with the administrative or political divisions of the country, so that there is relatively little opportunity for party manoeuvre. But the spontaneous concentra-

21

tion of population does not always coincide with the grouping of the inhabitants into administrative divisions. Hence there are certain inequalities which it is practically impossible to get rid of. Examples of this can be found in France in particular. In so far as these inequalities in the representation of the people derive from technical necessities, their influence on election results may be regarded as negligible.

The problem of electoral constituencies is twofold—it has both political and technical aspects. The method of dealing with the first aspect is to have the country divided up by technical experts independent of both the executive and the legislative, who will aim at ensuring that the proportional rule is observed with mathematical precision, so that every citizen has an equal share in the selection of representatives.

This equality of representation is less absolute, even in principle, where dependent territories are concerned. Events in our time have considerably reduced the number of such territories, but it is still interesting to discover how the problem of representation of their populations has been solved. Recent developments have brought most of them to the stage of internal self-government, so that they possess legislative councils of their own, though they do not necessarily have a say in the general policy of the country whose dependent territories they are. This is the situation, for example, in the Belgian Congo and in some of the British and Dutch possessions. Liberal participation in policy matters is enjoyed by the representatives of the dependent territories of the United States and Australia, but in the first place these territories are of very minor importance and, secondly, their delegates do not enjoy all the prerogatives of Members of Parliament. With regard to the right to vote, for example, in the United States they do not possess it at all. In Australia, they are entitled to vote only on a motion for the disallowance of an ordinance concerning their respective territories. In this respect, France is in a special position. It is the only state still responsible for a large number of overseas territories which provides for their representation in the national Parliament. Representatives of the French overseas territories, elected by universal suffrage, sit in the French Parliament and enjoy the same rights as members representing metropolitan France. It should be pointed out, however, that in this matter more than in any other the trend of events follows so closely on the trend of ideas that even the most enterprising innovations are soon obsolete.

VI

The Ballot

*Voting Procedure—Special Conditions of Voting—
Compulsory Voting—Voting by Proxy and by Post—Plural
Voting—Secrecy of the Vote—Polling—Voting Papers—
Collections and Count—Fraud at Elections—Disputed
Returns*

The actual operation by which the electorate selects its representatives is determined by regulations and practical procedures which govern the voting method used, the nature of the vote and the organization and supervision of the ballot.

1. VOTING PROCEDURE

The choice of an electoral system seems, at first sight, to raise only one technical problem, namely, how the parliamentary seats are to be allotted on the basis of the voting as expressed by the voters. There are two main voting systems—the simple majority vote, by single or successive ballot, in which the candidate or candidates obtaining most votes are elected, and proportional representation, by which the seats are divided up among the lists or parties in proportion to the number of votes obtained by each.

The common feature of the various majority systems is that they give minorities only an indirect and approximate representation and, even then, only when minorities at national level become the majority in certain constituencies; on the other hand, proportional representation theoretically guarantees minorities a representation corresponding to their precise strength as shown by the elections. The result is that the choice between these two systems, far from being purely technical, is frequently based on political considerations, which can make the whole question of the validity of the election controversial.

For a long time, the problem of the voting method did not give rise to any query. Parliamentary tradition, especially that of the Anglo-Saxon countries, managed perfectly well with the simplest system of all—the single ballot vote—until the time when the theories of the supporters of proportional representation were actually carried into effect. The system of proportional representation was adopted in some of the Swiss cantons as early as 1891 and 1892, in Belgium in 1899, in Finland in 1906 and in Sweden in 1908.

Gradually, it has caught on in Europe, especially in connexion with the changes in political systems brought about by wars. Outside Europe, the system has not achieved anything like the same success.

This brief historical outline largely explains the geographical distribution of the various methods of voting:

The majority system with a single ballot has always been used in the United Kingdom; hence it is hardly surprising that it is found also in most of the countries which have systems based on that of Great Britain, especially among members of the Commonwealth and those states which at one time or another have been politically influenced by Great Britain: Burma, Ceylon, Egypt, India and the Sudan. The same system is in force in the United States and the Philippines; Laos and the Republic of Vietnam have also adopted it.

In the USSR and the People's Democracies the candidate who has obtained the absolute majority of votes in one constituency is declared elected, but the electoral law in these countries allows for a second ballot in the event of a candidate not obtaining an absolute majority of the votes the first time. This system, which was used for a long time in France, has in Eastern Europe a different character in view of the practice of the single list of candidates. Throughout the rest of Europe, proportional representation has gradually become the rule. The system is the basis of the electoral methods of all the Scandinavian countries (Denmark, Norway, Sweden and Finland) and also of Austria, Belgium, France, the Federal Republic of Germany, Italy, Luxembourg, the Netherlands and Switzerland. The system does not always function in the same way in these countries and this illustrates the difficulty of applying a principle which is theoretically very simple. Sometimes, as in France, proportional representation is combined with the majority system by the alliance of lists of candidates; elsewhere the two systems exist side by side, as in the Federal Republic of Germany and Iceland.

Outside Europe, proportional representation exists in Brazil and in Israel.

The question whether balloting is by lists of candidates or by individual candidates is less important than the question whether the system is the majority vote or proportional representation. The two questions are closely linked, since in actual fact the majority voting system frequently coincides with the individual candidate system as practised in the Anglo-Saxon countries.

Majority voting for lists of candidates is very rare. It is, however, the system applied in the election of the Council of the Republic in France and in most of the French Departments, and in the election of the National Council in Monaco.

Voting for individual candidates rules out in principle proportional representation. Nevertheless, some ingenious theorists have tried to combine the systems, particularly by the use of the so-called 'single transferable vote'. This is the system applied in Australia for the Senate, in Ireland, in India for the Council of States, and for one of the constituencies in the Sudan. Under this system, the elector casts his vote for a particular candidate, and then indicates his preference for one or more others, where the constituency comprises several seats. Once a candidate has obtained the electoral quota, he is elected. The additional votes he obtains are passed on to the second-choice candidate, and so on. This highly complicated system has the effect of breaking down the rigidity of the party system by using proportional representation to enable a vote to be cast for individuals.

Not unlike this system is the one practised in Japan, which is even more unusual, although it derives from the single-candidate British system. The constituencies are required to elect several members in a single ballot, but each of the electors votes for a single candidate only, the candidates at the head of the list being elected. Thus the problem for each party is to calculate precisely how many candidates to present. If they put up too many, the votes may be split up among them in such a way that none is elected. If they put up too few, each candidate elected will have a number of extra votes which might well have elected another candidate of the same party.

These two examples show how far the imagination of legislators has gone in devising electoral systems and also how the principle of equality of suffrage has been distorted. All electoral systems, whether based on majority vote or on proportional representation, have the effect ultimately of weighting the election, i.e. giving the votes cast by the electors an influence which does not correspond exactly to their numerical strength. In actual practice, however, the discrepancy is generally less than might be expected, since the inequalities tend to balance out among all the constituencies in a given country, and it is rare for parliamentary representation not to reflect approximately the main currents of opinion in the electoral body.

The electoral system reflects each country's politics, of which it is both cause and effect. Those countries which are most at home with the majority vote and the single ballot as a rule have only two parties, whereas proportional representation is the system characteristic of countries with a large number of parties. In a word, the object of electoral systems should be to ensure the smooth running of the parliamentary machine, while at the same time safeguarding the representation of minorities which is the true basis of democracy.

2. SPECIAL CONDITIONS OF VOTING

(a) Compulsory Voting

Theoretically, there are two ways of regarding the franchise—as a right or as a duty.

The first is bound up with the theory of the sovereignty of the people; every citizen is entitled to the vote on the strength of his share in that sovereignty. The second way of regarding the franchise is linked with the theory of national sovereignty; the nation needs organs through which to express its will, and the elector is one such organ. In other words, he is performing a duty.

If the franchise is a right, voting is optional since no one can be forced to exercise a right. If it is a duty, voting may be made compulsory. Few legislative systems have adopted this latter theory, and those which have done so have based their action mainly on practical considerations. Theoretical hair-splitting apart, the main point has been to prevent a part of the electorate from staying away from the polls and to ensure that the selection of legislators is not exclusively in the hands of the professional politicians.

In Spain, the obligation to vote is restricted, since the Cortes are not elected by universal suffrage. But for this reason the penalty for not voting is all the more severe—the names of abstainers are published; they are taxed more heavily; and, in the case of civil servants, an adverse report is placed on the personal file of those who do not vote and there may even be a deduction from their salaries. In Austria, voting is compulsory in only one or two of the federal Länder, and in Switzerland only in certain cantons. But compulsory voting is general in Australia, Belgium, Brazil, Egypt, Italy and Luxembourg. In the Netherlands electors are not in fact obliged to vote, but they are bound to go to the polling station unless they are prevented from so doing for certain reasons.

The trickiest question is to decide what sanctions shall apply to reinforce the obligation to vote. If they are severe, they are intolerable; if they are light, they are ineffectual. The golden mean, which might be described as 'encouragement' to exercise the right to vote, consists mostly of the payment of a fine. This fine imposed for failure to vote is never very high—five guilders, as in the Netherlands, or £2 in Australia, seems to be about the largest amount. Moreoever, excuses on reasonable grounds are accepted.

It is easy to gauge how effective the compulsion is from the size of the poll recorded in elections in the various countries. The conclusion would appear to support compulsory voting. In Australia Austria, Belgium, Egypt, Luxembourg and the Netherlands, the proportion of non-voters to the total electorate is not higher than 10 per cent. Where it is high—say 30 per cent as in Brazil—the reason is partly the insignificant nature of the penalties.

The percentage of non-voters in countries where the vote is optional shows the other side of the picture. Apart from Iceland, where the electorate gives evidence of a particularly strong sense of public duty, in most of the Western-type democracies the proportion is in the neighbourhood of 20 per cent. This means that, for example, in the Nordic countries—Denmark, Finland, Norway and Sweden— where participation in the elections may be regarded as 'normal', one elector in five does not exercise the vote. The percentage is roughly the same in France, the Federal Republic of Germany, Indonesia, Israel, Monaco, the Philippines, Turkey and the Republic of Vietnam, and slightly higher in Ceylon, Ireland, Japan, Laos, the United Kingdom and the United States.

Failure to vote constitutes a serious problem in India (40 per cent), Burma (53 per cent), Syria (58 per cent) and the Sudan (60 per cent). This would appear to indicate that the electors are not yet sufficiently aware of their newly acquired political responsibilities. In the USSR, on the other hand, and in the People's Democracies, even though voting is not compulsory, failure to vote is practically non-existent— 0.22 per cent in the USSR and Albania, 0.52 per cent in Bulgaria, 0.82 per cent in Czechoslovakia, 0.84 per cent in Rumania.

(b) Voting by Proxy and by Post

Voting is a personal act; it calls for the physical presence of the voter at the polling station. It must also be secret if it is to be free; no one should come between the elector and the ballot box. In practice, owing to this twofold requirement, those who through sickness or because of their work cannot be present in person at the polling station may be deprived of their right to vote. To cater for such cases and to ensure that the principle of universal suffrage is really genuine, methods have been devised by which persons who cannot attend at the polls can nevertheless cast their vote. The main methods are voting by proxy and voting by post. However, in view of the difficulty of organization and supervision, these methods are rarely used.

Only eleven of the countries covered by the Inquiry—Austria, France, Japan, Laos, Luxembourg, Monaco, the Netherlands, Sweden, Switzerland, the United Kingdom and Yugoslavia—allow voting by proxy, which is regarded as highly dangerous to the principle of the freedom and secrecy of the ballot; and the law in these countries has invariably been careful to impose strict limits on the classes of voters to whom this concession is made. In all cases, the first on the list are invalids, the sick and the blind. In Japan, Monaco and Yugoslavia, illiterate persons also qualify, and in the United Kingdom, members of the armed forced in certain circumstances. In France, army and navy personnel may vote by proxy where they are serving a long way from the polling station. The Swedish law grants the same privilege where the wife or husband is absent.

The fact that the classes of voters who qualify are restricted and that the procedure is complicated makes the practical use of the vote by proxy somewhat difficult. Postal voting seems to offer less difficulty, and it is more widespread, both geographically and in its legal application; in other words, it embraces both more countries and more electors. In Australia, Denmark, the Federal Republic of Germany, Sweden, and the United States, there are no restrictions attached to postal voting. The mere fact of being away from the polling district entitles the citizen to vote by post.

In other countries, the conditions are stricter; absence is only accepted as a qualification if the person belongs to one of certain strictly defined social categories—in Burma these are students, and members of the armed forces and the foreign service; in India and Yugoslavia, members of the armed forces and the foreign service; in Ireland and France, members of the armed forces; and in Norway members of the foreign service. In the United Kingdom and, to a lesser degree, in France, infirmity, sickness or old age constitute adequate grounds. As the list indicates, a postal vote, like a proxy vote, is available to only a very restricted number of electors, and even these often think twice about taking advantage of it owing to the trouble involved.

(c) Plural Voting

Nowadays, plural voting, or the right of one elector to cast more than one vote, is of merely historical interest. Along with franchise by property qualification, it was designed to increase the electoral power of the more well-to-do. Under one of its most recent forms—the family vote—heads of families were entitled to extra votes on the grounds of their social responsibilities. But the principle of equality of the vote finally ousted plural voting everywhere. It disappeared in Belgium in 1921 when the Constitution was revised. It has also been eliminated in the United Kingdom, where certain electors were previously entitled to vote in more than one constituency (e.g. the Universities, and the City of London). Today, every elector has one vote and one only.

(d) Secrecy of the Vote

It is generally considered that a public ballot tends to hamper the freedom of the elector, making him more vulnerable to official and social pressure or to reprisals from his political adversaries. The secrecy of the vote, as a corollary to freedom of the vote, is largely a matter of practical arrangement, and most legislative systems have taken ample precautions in this direction.

In the first place, with the introduction of the individual polling booth, the elector can choose whichever ballot paper he wishes or mark his paper (as the case may be) with no possibility of being spied on. As a rule, it is compulsory to go into a polling booth. In Monaco, it is optional; in Burma where, as will be seen below, the voting procedure is of a special nature, the room where the various ballot boxes are situated is cut off from the rest of the polling station, and the voters are allowed in one by one.

The second safeguard of the secrecy of the vote is the rule that the ballot paper shall either be placed in an envelope or folded so that the elector's choice is not disclosed. In addition, the paper must not bear any writing or any special mark by which the person using it could be identified. This provision is in practice a difficult one to enforce. Perhaps the most satisfactory system in this respect is that used in Belgium; the ballot paper gives a list of candidates; at the top of the list, and also opposite each name, is a black square with a white dot in the centre. The elector votes by blacking in completely either the square at the top if he wishes to vote for the entire list, or one or more of the squares opposite the names if he wishes to split his vote. In Czechoslovakia, as in a number of other countries, the ballot papers are not numbered and they are so designed and made as to render identification of the electors who have used them impossible, either at the time of voting or later.

The third formality consists in requiring the elector to place his ballot paper in the box with his own hand. Exceptions to this are found in Austria and Egypt where he must hand it to the President of the Polls, who himself deposits it in the box.

In Ceylon, if an elector is unable, because of disability of any kind, to fill in his voting slip himself, the President may do it for him, provided he does so in an individual polling booth. A similar provision is made in Poland and Rumania, where electors who are sick or illiterate may be replaced by any other person. Egypt allows this in the case of blind and infirm persons and, in fact, goes even further—it is possible to cast the vote orally, in such a way that only the polling officers can hear.

A final point of importance is that everywhere the ballot boxes are sealed until the time comes for counting the votes. In Spain, the ballot papers are destroyed once the election is over.

The principle of the secret vote is thus recognized by all countries, though in its actual application, some countries are more strict than others. One of the most effective safeguards is the use of computer voting machines which are becoming more common in the United States.

3. POLLING

(a) Voting Papers

To enable the elector to cast his vote, voting papers with the name of each individual candidate or with each list of candidates on them are placed at his disposal. He chooses one of these papers and, after making his choice, he deposits the slip in a ballot box. This, at any rate, is the normal procedure.

In Burma, a different system has been introduced; the voting slips are replaced by identical voting tokens which the voter places in whichever box he chooses. The method of choosing between the various candidates is to have a number of separate boxes, each of a different colour and bearing the name of the candidate concerned. In practice, this would appear to be an excellent method, since it enables the elector to express his choice unmistakably. In all the other countries under consideration, it is the practice to use voting papers. As a rule, they bear the name of the candidates or of the list of candidates, sometimes the political party to which they belong and even their addresses.

Where the electorate includes a large number of illiterate persons, that procedure is obviously inadequate to ensure that the ballot is fair, since it assumes that all the voters are able to read and write. The remedy is to place a mark or symbol on the voting slips so as to identify the competing candidates unmistakably. This method is used, for example, in Ceylon, Egypt, India, the Sudan, Turkey and the Republic of Vietnam. In the United States, the elephant and the donkey shown on the voting papers, as symbols of the Republican and Democratic parties respectively, are explained by American tradition and political usage, as well as by the predilection for advertising techniques there.

In Israel and Iceland, instead of a symbol we find one or two letters of the alphabet assigned to each list. In Laos, candidates draw by lot a number traced by dots on a rectangular board, like a domino; the board is hung up in the polling booth under the photograph of the candidate; while in Egypt, the Sudan and Turkey, the use of different colours helps to distinguish the various candidates.

These procedures are the result of the genuine anxiety to make the electoral operations fool-proof, so that any voter, whatever his mental ability, can cast his vote for the candidate or list he wishes to see elected.

(b) Collection and Count

This is the operation by which the ballot papers are collected and the votes counted. It culminates in the announcement of the results, or declaration. The way in which this is done depends on the method used, which means that it varies considerably from one country to another, so that it is impossible to go into the details of the various methods used. However, in all instances we find a series of measures designed to safeguard the validity of the election. They consist mainly of efforts to keep proper order at the polling stations, supervision of the polling operation, the actual counting of the votes and announcement of the results.

Generally, each polling station is placed under the authority of a body, as a rule of the electoral college type, which we may call collectively the returning officers. Four main systems are found, each in its own way designed to secure impartiality. The most widespread is that by which a number of electors work jointly with the local authorities. This is the system applied, for example, in France, Laos, Monaco and Yugoslavia. In the countries where there has been British influence, the returning officers are civil servants. In addition to the United Kingdom itself, this system is found in Australia, Burma, Ceylon, India, Ireland, Japan, Pakistan and the Philippines. In Norway, Switzerland and Egypt, the practice is for representatives of the various parties to sit at the same table, where they can keep a mutual check on one another. In the USSR and the People's Democracies, electoral committees are composed of delegates from the social organizations and workers', employees', peasants' and military personnel organizations whose nomination must be confirmed by the People's Councils. In Czechoslovakia the electoral committees include representatives of the various political parties and the various organizations associated within the National Front.

Whatever the composition and designation of the body, the returning officers constitute a real administrative authority; they are responsible for the maintenance of order at the premises where the balloting takes place and for seeing that the often complex rules governing the procedure for casting votes are observed. In particular there must be no suggestion of partisanship likely to interfere with the results of the election. The police can only intervene as a rule at the express request of the administrative authorities, who are in sole charge of the polling stations.

However, in countries where the impartiality of the administration can presumably be regarded as beyond reproach, since it is in charge of the whole poll, the police assume direct reponsibility for the maintenance of good order. This is the practice in the United Kingdom, Ceylon, the Sudan and also in Indonesia, Israel and Norway.

Actually, incidents are rare, since the polling operation is also under the watchful eye not only of the electors taking part, but also of the representatives of the candidates themselves who have the right to be in the polling station throughout the proceedings. Most systems allow representatives of the candidates to be present in this way as an additional safeguard of fairness in the elections.

The counting and checking of the votes are carried out as a rule under one and the same control, and the announcement of the results is a mere formality. According to the polling procedure used, this is the responsibility either of the local authorities in charge of the count, or of a central State body which collects the returns sent in by the polling officers for the different polling stations. This is the practice in Brazil, Burma, Denmark, the Federal Republic of Germany, Indonesia, Israel, the Netherlands, Norway, Poland and Syria. In many countries, including Czechoslovakia, representatives of the Press may be present at the count. In the USSR the election results are established by the electoral commission of each constituency which then hands a certificate to the candidate elected.

In brief, polling is conducted according to a considerable number of very different systems, the only feature they have in common being the concern to ensure that the count is completely free and fair. This is the intention behind the public nature of the electoral operations and the control exercised in their different ways by the voter himself, the candidate and the political parties, not to mention Press, radio and television.

(c) Fraud at Elections

The complexity of the electoral operations and the physical difficulties involved would appear to favour dishonesty at the polls and, in actual fact, different devices have been used to this end, such as substitution of ballot boxes, personation of voters and tampering with the returns.

But nowadays the amount of electoral fraud has been greatly reduced, as a result of a number of measures which are embodied in the electoral laws of virtually all countries:

(a) The organization of a more effective check on the identity of the voter which rules out any dishonesty short of complicity by the authorities responsible for the vote; the elaborate system of safeguards laid down in countries like Burma is evidence of their intention to achieve this end.

(b) The public nature of the election—the ballot box and the counting of the votes being under the supervision of the citizens themselves. In Denmark, Sweden and Australia, the fact that the elections are under public supervision is regarded as sufficient of itself to frustrate any attempt at fraud; in the USSR representatives of the social organizations and of the Press may be present when the votes are counted.

(c) The fact that representatives of the candidates are on hand with the specific task of supervising the conduct of the polls. In some countries, for example in Ireland, they have more or less official status and functions as 'personating agents'.

(d) The severity of the penalties inflicted on persons found guilty of fraudulent practices, for which most electoral law prescribes harsh penalties, generally imprisonment. The sentences may be up to two years, as in Finland and the USSR, or as much as five years in Rumania. The penalties may also carry loss of civic rights for a specified period, as is the case in the Federal Republic of Germany and Austria.

Thus we see that most countries are on the way towards total elimination of fraud at the polls, and it is rare nowadays to find countries like Ceylon which still regard this as a major problem.

(d) Disputed Returns

Except in the case of Turkey, the announcement of the results is never final. It is always possible to have a check made to verify that the election has been carried out in a completely regular manner by appealing either to Parliament itself or to a judicial body.

Traditionally, this checking is done by Parliament itself, which thus becomes the tribunal to settle its own election. The wisdom of this may appear debatable. The arguments put forward to justify it are: (i) the independence of Parliament *vis-à-vis* the other two powers, the executive and the judiciary, and (ii) the sovereignty of Parliament. Parliament comes first in the hierarchy; hence it is superior to any other body in the State and therefore it would hardly be proper for a mere judge to scrutinize its election.

These two arguments are accepted more or less unanimously in Europe, where the normal practice is for the verification of credentials to be done by the House itself on the report of a credentials committee. This is the practice in the USSR and the People's Democracies of Albania, Bulgaria, Czechoslovakia, Poland and Rumania, and in such Western European countries as Belgium, Denmark, France, Italy, Luxembourg, the Netherlands, Sweden and Switzerland. Norway also defers to the sovereignty of Parliament, but in a rather unusual way—the validity of the elections is verified in turn by two credentials committees, one set up by the outgoing Parliament and the other by the newly elected Parliament. With regard to countries outside Europe, the United States of America and Laos leave it entirely to their assemblies to satisfy themselves that the credentials of their own members are in order.

The dangers inherent in this system are of course obvious. While entrusting the power of decision to Parliament rules out any government interference in the admission of members on their election, it does not offer them any protection against lack of impartiality on the part of their political opponents.

Hence, since the problem is the settlement of disputes, which is the function of judges, a tendency has been growing up recently in favour of handing over the power of decision to strictly judicial bodies. In Spain and Monaco, it is entrusted to the ordinary courts; but more often than not the responsibility is given to a higher court—the High Court or Constitutional Court, as in Australia, Burma, Ceylon, Ireland, Japan, Pakistan, the Sudan and Syria.

In India there are special tribunals responsible for settling electoral disputes placed before them by petition.

Some constitutions partly follow both these theories, bearing in mind both the political aspect of the election and also the necessity for an authority which will be bound by constitutional and statutory rules; and these have instituted a mixed system.

In the Philippines, for example, the body which validates the elections is an electoral tribunal which, although appointed on a political basis—its members being chosen from the House itself— has judicial status; its decisions are final. In Egypt, disputes are settled by the Court of Appeal, subject to ratification by a two-thirds majority in the National Assembly, within two months after the documents have been referred to it. In Finland and Brazil, the division of the power to decide election cases follows a complex set of rules: but, generally speaking, Parliament is required to intervene in only a small number of cases, like a court of appeal. In the Federal Republic of Germany, on the other hand, the Bundestag decides in the first instance as to the validity of elections, but its decisions may be challenged by appeal to the Federal Constitutional Court. In the United Kingdom, electoral disputes are settled in the courts, but other disputes relating to the functions of qualification and disqualification for membership come under the jurisdiction of the House.

The range of procedures for the verification of credentials is thus very wide, but on the whole it is governed by the conception of the sovereignty of Parliament. Occasionally there is a definite miscarriage of justice, where political passions prevail over strictly judicial considerations, but fortunately such cases are few and far between.

VII

The Candidates Elected

Qualification—Incompatibility of Occupation—Candidature and Political Party—Election Campaigns—Parliamentary Mandate

The opportunity for a citizen to become a Member of Parliament is limited by legal rules arising out of the principles of qualification and incompatibility of occupation as well as by practical difficulties, particularly in regard to candidature and the electoral campaign.

1. QUALIFICATION

Qualification is the personal suitability of the candidate to be chosen by the electors to sit in Parliament. In countries which have parliamentary government, qualification, like the franchise, should aim at universal application. Any limitations should not be such as to strike at the free choice of the elector, but should be dictated by practical considerations, devoid of any political motive.

In theory, there are three possible systems: (i) qualification coinciding with the franchise, so that every voter is qualified; (ii) narrower in scope, in which case the mere fact of being an elector does not confer qualifications; (iii) broader than the franchise, so that a person can be qualified without being an elector. This last system is somewhat illogical and is rarely found. The first of the three would appear to be the most normal for democratic countries; yet few countries actually apply it, the argument being that if the purpose of an election is to select a body representing the best elements of the population and capable of looking after the affairs of the nation, we are surely entitled to ask of that body qualifications which hardly seem necessary for the ordinary elector. Hence in most countries the conditions for qualification for membership of Parliament are more stringent than those required for the right to vote. The difference applies mainly to age, nationally and conduct.

The criterion of mental ability for candidature is primarily the age of the candidate. In thirteen out of the forty-one countries, the age requirement for the prospective members of Parliament is the same as for electors—Albania 18, Australia 21, Bulgaria 18, Ceylon 21, Denmark, 23, Finland 21, the United Kingdom 21, Ireland 21, the Netherlands 23, Norway 21, Spain 21, Switzerland 20, and Yugoslavia 18. Everywhere else, and in particular in Czechoslovakia, Poland, Rumania and the USSR, a certain experience of life is felt to be indispensable. However, the law is not very exacting as to the extent of such experience since, with the exception of Belgium where a candidate for the Senate must be forty years old, the required age nowhere exceeds thirty. This is the figure chosen by Egypt, Laos, the Netherlands, the Sudan, Syria and Turkey, which thus demand most in regard to age. The usual minimum age limit is 25 years, as in Belgium, the Federal Republic of Germany, India, Indonesia, Italy, Japan, Luxembourg, Monaco, Pakistan, the Philippines, the United States and the Republic of Vietnam. Austria stands apart, with 26 years.

The countries which go furthest in subordinating the notion of competence on the part of Members of Parliament, as measured by

36

age, to the idea of universal qualification, are France (for the National Assembly), Rumania, Sweden and the USSR, where 23 is the lower age-limit, and still more Burma, Brazil, Ceylon, Czechoslovakia, Israel, Poland and the United Kingdom where elected members must have reached 21 years of age.

The demands in respect of mental ability are more severe in Egypt, Laos, Syria, the Sudan and Turkey, where illiterate persons are debarred from election—no doubt because they still represent a fairly high proportion of the population—while Laos disqualifies persons suffering from contagious and incurable diseases, as well as opium addicts.

In view of their future responsibilities, prospective Members of Parliament must show that they really belong to the country whose destiny will be in their hands. For this reason, many states make the conditions of nationality and residence applied to candidates for Parliament stricter than those applied to mere electors. In the Philippines, for example, only citizens by birth are qualified. In Syria and France, the requirement is ten years' citizenship, in the United States seven, in the Republic of Vietnam five, and in the Federal Republic of Germany one year. This measure of self-protection against the possibility of recently naturalized aliens entering Parliament cannot be regarded as a serious encroachment upon the principle of democracy; it is a question of degree.

The nationality qualification is frequently supplemented by a residence condition, e.g. three years in Australia, one year in the Philippines. In some cases, in France, for example, candidates are not qualified until they have completed their military service. In addition to other qualifications candidates must be morally beyond reproach, or at any rate a higher degree of rectitude is required of them than of electors in such matters as electoral corruption (Australia, France, India, Ireland, Laos, the Sudan, the United Kingdom and the Republic of Vietnam), or insolvency or bankruptcy (Australia, France, Ireland, the Sudan, Sweden, Turkey, the United Kingdom and the Republic of Vietnam. In Denmark, persons convicted of an offence which would be regarded by public opinion as unworthy of a member of the Folketing are declared disqualified. It need hardly be said that in Syria, Monaco, the Sudan and Switzerland, women are disqualified, since they do not have the vote.

In a general way, these are the conditions governing qualification. For the most part, they are based on unexceptionable arguments which do not in any way jeopardize the principle of universal qualification. Mention should be made, however, of two instances where the underlying intention would appear to be entirely

37

political, however justified they may be by a determination to protect democracy against its enemies—certain former Nazis are barred in Austria, and Fascists in Bulgaria. There do not appear to be any such restrictions or any other specific regulations limiting qualification in Albania, Poland, Rumania and Yugoslavia, where there is no exception to the principle of universal qualification. In Czechoslovakia only citizens sentenced to loss of civic rights are disqualified.

On the other hand, the system adopted in Laos reverses this principle—disqualification is the rule and qualification the exception. The only persons who can become members of the National Assembly are those holding certain degrees or diplomas, and some classes of leading citizens. To a lesser degree, a somewhat similar principle holds good in regard to the Belgian Senate and the Irish Seanad.

The type of disqualification on the grounds discussed above might be described as 'absolute' in the sense that it is a bar to election throughout the countries concerned. Side by side with this type of disqualification we find a 'relative' disqualification, where the candidate is debarred from election only in certain specific constituencies. This curious system is applied in France and, to a lesser degree, in the United Kingdom. Whereas absolute ineligibility is related to certain requirements of mentality and conduct the idea behind 'relative' disqualification is to safeguard the freedom of the vote by preventing people from taking advantage of the influence they have acquired through their official position in particular constituencies.

As a general rule, officials in positions of high authority come into this category. In France, *préfets* and *sous-préfets* are 'relatively' disqualified, as are also certain judicial officers and army generals in command of home forces. The individual concerned is debarred only in respect of the constituency in which he is serving and the bar does not apply beyond a certain period after he has given up his post. In the Republic of Vietnam, this principle is applied even more widely, and in Syria it affects all officials whose emoluments come out of the Treasury. The special treatment of certain types of public officials is even more strictly defined when we come to the question of incompatability of occupation, though here the end in view is entirely different.

2. INCOMPATABILITY OF OCCUPATION

Incompatability of occupation is the rule by which a Member of Parliament is debarred from following certain occupations during his term of office. Theoretically, this is quite distinct from disqualification, which constitutes a complete legal bar to membership. Incompatibility of occupation, on the other hand, does not affect the validity of the election; all it does is require the Member of Parliament, once elected, to choose between his former occupation and his new office. In practice, the distinction is extremely subtle. Certain legislatures regard the two ideas as identical and consider only their effects, ignoring the question whether the obligation to choose comes before or after the election which would appear to be the main theoretical difference. At all events, this obligation expresses perfectly well the essential purpose, namely, to ensure that Members of Parliament are independent of the executive and, to a very much lesser extent, of private interests.

The chief types of incompatibility of occupation, as of 'relative' disqualification, are connected with public office. But here, what matters is not the freedom of the elector; the aim is to safeguard the freedom of the elected candidate and to guarantee the separation of the arms of the State. Parliament cannot afford to have its members serving itself and the Government at the same time, or parliamentary control would cease to exist. The result, as a general rule, is that a person cannot be both a civil servant and a Member of Parliament. However, in the USSR, Albania, Bulgaria, Poland, Rumania and Czechoslovakia, such an incompatibility of occupation does not exist, except in respect of the President of the Republic of Czechoslovakia. This is also the case in Spain, where the separation of powers is not recognized.

In the Western-type democracies—except for Denmark, Finland, Iceland and Sweden—the law forbids plurality of office in the case of:

(a) Anyone whose salary is paid out of public funds; this is the case in Australia, Belgium, Ceylon, France, the Federal Republic of Germany, India, Ireland, Israel, Laos, the Netherlands, Norway, the Sudan, Switzerland, Syria and the United Kingdom, with Yugoslavia following the same pattern.
(b) Civil servants who occupy high public office; this is the rule in Brazil, Indonesia, Luxembourg and Monaco.

In most countries to be mayor or a local authority officer is incompatible with a seat in Parliament.

With regard to judicial officers, the rule of incompatibility of occupation applies most widely in Belgium, Brazil, Ceylon, Egypt, France, India, Ireland, Israel, Luxembourg, Monaco, Switzerland, the United Kingdom and Yugoslavia. In the Netherlands and Finland, it applies only to members of the Supreme Court. In Italy and Norway, judicial officers may sit in Parliament; so may members of the armed forces on active service in Yugoslavia and Norway, though this is ruled out for all members of the armed forces in Belgium, Finland, France, Indonesia, India, Ireland, Israel, Laos, Luxembourg, the Netherlands, Syria and Turkey, and for chiefs of staff in Brazil, and officers and non-commissioned officers in Egypt.

In some countries, a problem arises in regard to priests and ministers of religion, whether or not their stipend is paid by the State. In India, Israel, Luxembourg, Switzerland, Turkey and the United Kingdom they may not sit in Parliament.

As a general rule, incompatibility of occupation does not affect university professors, on the grounds of the independence which their standing and character normally give them; but in Australia, Ceylon, France and India, persons whose income is derived from State funds come under the same heading as civil servants.

In principle, the incompatibility of public office with membership of Parliament means that civil servants have to resign from their posts, sometimes even before standing for Parliament. But in a number of countries this has been felt to be unduly harsh; and so, in France, Israel, Laos and the Netherlands, a civil servant who is elected retains his status as a civil servant. He is merely required to cease working and he is placed in a special category as 'on leave' or 'seconded', so that he is able to keep most of his rights, especially in regard to promotion and superannuation. The practice of seconding exists also in the Federal Republic of Germany: re-entry into the civil service is possible on vacation of the seat in Parliament, and all pension rights are kept.

This relaxation of the rules of incompatibility of occupation is tending to become more widespread in respect of civil servants. At the same time, the concern to ensure the independence of Members of Parliament in the face of financial, economic or social pressure has become more marked. In actual practice, however, this has no very noticeable effect, since the difficulty of finding a criterion to determine whether a given individual is subject to too much influence is almost insurmountable, and there is a danger of disqualifying extremely able persons who might render valuable service to the country.

Whether this is so or not, in France, Belgium, Ireland, Italy and the United Kingdom, the management or administration of undertakings which enjoy special advantages from the State or in which the State has an interest is regarded as incompatible with the duties of a Member of Parliament. In Syria, India, Israel and Turkey, notaries and ministerial officials cannot be Members of Parliament.

In some quarters it is felt that the rules of incompatibility of occupation, as applied to private employment, are not sufficiently strict. However, the hope of eliminating influence exerted by economic and financial circles over Members of Parliament merely by the stricter application of the incompatibility principle is illusory. All that would happen is that the rights of the electors would be curtailed without making the members any more independent.

In some countries incompatibility of occupation is based on plurality of political office. For example, a person should not at one and the same time be a member of both Houses. On the other hand, a member is seldom barred from holding elective office in local government along with his seat in Parliament.

The question of plurality of office—parliamentary and ministerial —goes beyond the problem of incompatibility of occupation; it belongs rather to the realm of constitutional theory. In other words, it depends on the very structure of the State—whether it is founded on the strict separation of powers or on a more flexible principle, as applied in countries of the 'cabinet government' type, or on any other system.

There is incompatibility between ministerial and parliamentary office in all countries which apply the separation of powers. This is the aspect, moreover, which has most impressed public opinion. It is strictly applied in presidential systems, such as those of the United States of America, Brazil, the Philippines, and the Republic of Vietnam. Likewise, members of the Government cannot, at the same time, be Members of Parliament in Indonesia, Monaco and Switzerland. In Laos, the office of Minister is incompatible only with that of King's Councillor.

On the other hand, the rule of incompatibility is inconsistent with the spirit of parliamentary government, where it is desired that most ministers be Members of Parliament so that close contact may be established between the Parliament and the Government. It will be remembered that, for a long period in Britain, members who had been named ministers had immediately to stand for re-election in order to have their seats confirmed. But this requirement, which was abolished in 1926, had a very different reason: it aimed at having M.P.'s accession to government office ratified by the electors and not at establishing a rigid barrier between Parliament and the Government. Besides, it could not, by definition, be considered as contrary to the principle of a ban on plurality of office.

Certain countries have gone even further in their search for closer links between the Parliament and Government by requiring ministers to be Members of Parliament. This is the case, more particularly, in Ceylon, Ireland and Pakistan. In Spain, ministers are members of the Cortes *ex officio*. In Burma, a non-member who has been appointed to ministerial office cannot stay in office for longer than six months unless he becomes a Member of Parliament. In Australia, the Constitution provides for a three-month time-limit.

Such severe measures are, however, the exception, even under the parliamentary system of government. As a general rule, although combined government and parliamentary office is allowed, it is not obligatory. It is moreover possible to mention at least three countries in which the functioning of the parliamentary system is accompanied by a prohibition on plurality of office: Luxembourg, the Netherlands and Norway. In Luxembourg, a seat in Parliament is incompatible with being a member of the Government. In the Netherlands, a Member of Parliament who becomes a minister loses his seat. The candidate on the combined list who came closest to him at the election takes his place in Parliament. Conversely, if a minister is elected, he must, within a period of three months, decide between his seat and his office of minister. In Norway, any Member of Parliament who becomes a minister is replaced, in the Assembly, by a substitute. But he can, upon resigning from office, resume his seat in Parliament.

The peculiar habits, fears and prejudices of each country, which have produced so many variations on the theme of incompatibility of occupation, make it difficult to reach a conclusion of general application. The only common feature which can be isolated is the ultimate goal sought by all countries, a guarantee of the independence of Members of Parliament.

3. CANDIDATURE AND POLITICAL PARTY

Qualification and incompatibility of occupation do constitute limitations on the freedom of candidature in a legal and formal sense, but they are not very wide in their application; the practical limitations are far more important. In principle, any citizen who complies with the legal obligations is qualified. But if he is to stand any chance of being elected he must, at any rate within his own constituency, have the backing of an organization which will enable him not only to bring his views to the notice of public opinion, but to put up a fight against the opposing political forces. Generally speaking, to meet these two conditions together is beyond the resources of a candidate who stands for Parliament as an independent; but the task is greatly simplified for a candidate who enjoys the support of one or other of the political parties. These are associations of citizens who share the same views on certain issues and policies which they endeavour to promote by getting candidates of their own elected to Parliament. According to the theory maintained in the Socialist states, a party is to be defined as a political organization which expresses the interests of its class and gives direction to the political struggle waged by that class.

However, while the close link between the candidate and his party is an unalterable fact, it is not necessarily sanctioned by the law; on the contrary, in many countries, standing for Parliament is regarded as an individual act, which bears no reference to the political context in which it is undertaken. One might even say that in most democracies individual candidature is theoretically the ordinary legal procedure—individual freedom must not be interfered with. At the same time, so that the election can have its full meaning, some countries have felt the need for an official structure on the principle that the candidate should represent a definite current of opinion and not simply obey a personal impulse which may be frivolous or extravagant.

In the countries which have been influenced by Great Britain, as well as in certain Northern European countries, this realistic outlook is reflected in the stipulation that the candidate must be backed by a certain number of citizens—ranging from ten in the United Kingdom and Ireland, twelve in Iceland, twenty-five in the Netherlands and Denmark, and thirty in Finland, to fifty or a hundred in Norway, two hundred in Indonesia, and three hundred, four hundred or five hundred in Belgium. But, according to the national groups which took part in the Inquiry, this guarantee is furnished by the political parties themselves whose role is thus quite obvious to all. The support they give to the candidates is, therefore, given an official character, which is recognized by the electoral laws of the countries concerned.

Some countries draw legal conclusions from this *de facto* state of affairs and do not recognize individual candidature, only the political parties having the right to put forward candidates. This is the situation in the Federal Republic of Germany, at any rate in regard to the national lists, which must have the sanction of the national executive committees of the parties. In Austria, in the same way, only the party lists or 'proposals for election' are valid. The practice is similar in Brazil; while in Sweden, although strictly speaking there is nothing to prevent an individual from standing for

43

Parliament, no list of candidates is acceptable unless it bears the name of a political party.

Whether the candidate stands for Parliament on his own account or is backed by a group of electors or a political organization, it is hard to conceive of an election without the intervention of parties. They are essential to the functioning of the democratic system, since they express in public life the various political views of the electorate.

If the electoral contest is to be fully effective, this diversity of opinion must be reflected in the existence of several parties. Where their existence is subject to authorization, as in Turkey or Brazil, or where certain parties are outlawed, e.g. the Communist Party in the Federal Republic of Germany, Burma and Brazil, and the National Party in Syria, the electoral campaign is affected thereby. In Egypt, the only grouping allowed at present is the National Union; its purpose is not to put forward candidates, but merely to oppose some of the other candidatures. This unusual method of selection does nevertheless amount to the exclusion from politics of those who oppose the régime.

In the People's Democracies where party antagonism is unknown (even though several parties may exist, as in Bulgaria, Czechoslovakia, Poland and Yugoslavia), all the social organizations, following broad public discussion, come to an agreement with the party or parties on the best candidates whose names, in a single list, are then submitted as a whole to the electorate by the organizations concerned. Past experience has shown that they are assured of the mass support of the people.

In the USSR, the right to present candidates belongs to the Party and to the social and workers' organizations. This right is exercised by their central and local headquarters and by the general meetings of workers, or employees in institutions and various undertakings, of military personnel within their individual units, of peasants in the *kolkhoses* and villages, and of workers and employees in the *sovkhoses*.

Whether the system is individual candidature or single list, the importance of the Party—acting officially or unofficially—is always in evidence. Hence the electors exercise their choice only within limits laid down by the parties. They make their choice from among the different candidates, if there are more than one, but they do not actually choose the candidates. In most instances, this is done by political bodies. Different systems are applied in this connexion:

(*a*) Candidates may be nominated by the party executive or 'caucus'. The choice is left to a few leading figures or politicians and is made in secret, without consulting the electors, or even the party members. This is the oldest method and may be open to criticism; nevertheless, it is the method most commonly used.

(b) In Belgium, the Federal Republic of Germany, the Netherlands and Sweden, party members nominate candidates, either directly by the party convention or through the appointment of delegates at regional congresses. This is a more democratic system than the preceding one, but its effect is to foist on those who vote for the parties' candidates the candidates chosen by the party members only.

(c) In certain states of the United States the system of 'primaries' is found. Here the electors themselves hold a preliminary ballot at which they choose one of several candidates to run for office on behalf of the party at the actual elections. The difficulty lies in the actual organization of this ballot and in the fact that it is impossible to determine precisely which electors shall take part. Moreover, all it does is shelve the problem, since eventually it is more often than not the party executive which nominates the 'candidates for candidature'.

(d) In the Soviet Union and the People's Democracies, on the other hand, the nomination of candidates is done by the electors grouped together in the manner already referred to. All these bodies finally settle on a single list. The pre-election thus is more important than the election proper, but even here the party plays a decisive role.

In the Western-type of democracy and in the People's Democracies alike, the whole point of the system whereby candidates stand for election is that candidates have to have party backing. What the wording of the Constitution in many cases suggests is actually the expression of a fundamental political reality which is found in every country and which it is the object of every Parliament to develop.

4. ELECTION CAMPAIGNS

The period between the nomination of the candidates and the date of the actual elections is taken up with the election campaign, designed to make known the personalities of the candidates and the opinions they hold so that the electors can vote in full awareness of the issues at stake. Thus it constitutes an indispensable phase of the electoral

45

procedure, though it is frequently ignored in works on constitutional theory.

However, it does raise one difficult problem, how to make sure that the various candidates all have the same means at their disposal in attempting to gain the support of the electors. For a long time this was the candidate's own affair, and in some countries it still is. But the publicity required today for an effective campaign is a costly item and can create real inequalities which are incompatible with the democratic principle that everyone should be given a fair chance and that elections should be kept free from the power of money. For this reason, in many countries nowadays a good deal of legislation is devoted to the election campaign, with a view to ensuring real fairness for all candidates.

This concern for fairness for all candidates or among lists of candidates applies only to countries where rival candidates or lists are competing. In countries where a single list is presented to the electorate, the campaign no longer consists of a competition between various candidates; its purpose is to ensure full-scale attendance at the polls. Its effectiveness is inversely proportional to the number of abstentions and, as we have seen, this proportion is for the most part negligible. This publicity is a joint effort by all the organizations, whether party, syndical economic, social or cultural, which at an earlier stage have collaborated to choose the best candidates and to draw up the single list put before the electors.

In the Western-type of democracy, however, the problem of fairness among the candidates is of vital significance. Some states have come to the conclusion that the best way of solving the problem is still to pretend that it does not exist. Thus, for example, in the Scandinavian countries and most of the democracies of Western Europe, there are no regulations governing election campaigns. In Finland, Norway, Sweden, Denmark and Iceland, as well as in Austria, Belgium, the Federal Republic of Germany, Luxembourg, the Netherlands and Switzerland, the freedom of action of the candidates is limited only by the ordinary rules of law, especially those relating to the maintenance of public order.

This non-interference on the part of the authorities in regard to elections is explained partly by the desire to show strict neutrality towards all the candidates and partly by the fact that the organization of the parties involved is stable, powerful and well-balanced; for in these countries the election campaign is a party rather than an individual matter and to this extent any disparity in the resources and facilities employed is appreciably reduced. The difference would be more keenly felt in countries which lack this equilibrium if they did not take steps to cope with it by laying down cut-and-dried regulations circumscribing election campaign publicity and making its dissemination possible for all candidates alike.

In those countries where there has been British influence, this is done by setting a limit on the amount a candidate is allowed to spend on his election campaign. In the United Kingdom, Ireland, Australia, Burma, India, Ceylon and the Sudan, as well as in the Philippines and Japan, the law fixes a ceiling for election expenses. Sometimes it is a definite sum—in Australia £250 for members and £500 for senators, in Burma 15,000 kyats; in other countries it is worked out on the basis of a complex calculation, as in Japan and Ceylon. For the system to be effective, the accounts have to be carefully audited and in many cases this is by no means easy. And quite apart from any limit on expenses, there may have to be audited accounts as a check on the activities of the parties during this hectic period, as in the United States and Brazil. In Israel, the only item considered is the cost of hiring halls for holding meetings.

These various regulations governing election expenses, while actually designed to ensure fairness among the candidates, do at the same time help to prevent attempts at corruption more effectively than the measures taken in countries where there are no such regulations. The penalities for electoral corruptions are severe in countries like Burma, the United Kingdom, Ireland and Australia. Two aspects of electoral corruption have caused much concern to the legislatures in Ceylon, the Philippines and Brazil—the problem of free transport to the polling station and that of free food and drink to the electors. The Japanese practice in this respect is interesting, as refreshments may be served provided they are restricted to tea and cakes.

Another way of curtailing election campaign publicity is by setting a limit to the material means which candidates may employ. In the United Kingdom and in Japan, there is a strict limit on the number of vehicles which may be used for election purposes. In Burma, public meetings are prohibited; only person-to-person publicity methods may be used. In Japan, the use of loud-speakers is restricted by law.

As regards the use of posters, an essential proviso is that it must be possible to ascertain where they originated and who is responsible for them. In France, Monaco and Brazil, the authorities provide special placcs where they can be displayed, and they are not allowed to be put anywhere else. In Australia and Israel, posters may not be above a certain size.

Apart from these detailed regulations governing the use of publicity media, facilities are as a rule granted to all candidates to enable the less well-off to bring their opinions to the notice of the electors so that they all face the polls on equal terms. In France and in Sweden, radio and television services allow each party an equal amount of time to present its case.

In most countries, candidates enjoy various monetary concessions, which are substantial inasmuch as they spare the candidate considerable expense, e.g. free postage for their election pamphlets, free printing of a certain number of posters and circulars, exemption from taxes on publications, etc. Brazil has even gone so far as to give priority to candidates in the installation of telephones. In France, the principle of fairness is carried still further, to the point of allowing a candidate travelling expenses, varying in amount according to the size of the constituency. In the USSR, all expenses arising out of the election campaign are covered by the State.

In spite of all efforts, more often than not fairness is only partially ensured. The rules designed to put a stop to specially favourable treatment for certain candidates on the part of the authorities to prevent the wealthy candidate from obtaining an advantage over his poorer competitor and to ensure that everybody has his say in complete freedom are extremely intricate, and infringements are difficult to penalize. Few countries have set up special machinery for dealing with disputes arising out of the election campaign. As a rule, this problem is dealt with as part of the control exercised over the elections themselves, in which case it is the responsibility either of Parliament, in countries where Parliament itself verifies the credentials of its members, or of the courts. The courts are, of course impartial, but they may be disinclined to give such details the attention they deserve.

The *de jure* equality of the candidates must therefore be put against a *de facto* inequality; but most states have at least managed to ensure that all candidates have a reasonably fair chance. In the older democracies, this is all that is required, since the pressure on the electorate is now dependent not merely on the weight of the propaganda brought to bear, but on the strength of the case it is designed to support.

5. PARLIAMENTARY MANDATE

This is the name frequently given to the representative function of Members of Parliament. It is not a very satisfactory term, since in most instances the relationship between the member and the elector cannot be described as a real 'mandate'. In most states the elected members are the representatives of the nation as a whole and not specifically of those who elected them. The Parliaments of those countries have at all times striven to shake off their bonds in regards to the electors. They have not always succeeded in doing so, but in the Western-type of democracy there is evidence of their intention in the fact that the imperative mandate has no validity and that there is no machinery by which a member can be unseated by his constituents or the party which put him up for election.

In many other countries, notably in the Socialist states, the member is bound to carry out the mandate given him by the electorate. That is why his mandate is called 'imperative'. If the member loses the confidence of the electors, he may be unseated. In the USSR a member may be unseated at any time following a decision by a majority of the electors of a constituency, if he has failed to justify the faith put in him or if his behaviour proves unworthy of a member. This also applies in Albania, Czechoslovakia, Rumania and Yugoslavia, where the law required members to give a regular account to their constituents of how they have fulfilled their mandate. However the power to unseat Members of Parliament is very rarely used.

In countries where the imperative mandate and the power to unseat are not recognized, there is no constraint of this kind on Members of Parliament; this does not mean, however, that there is no link between the elected member and his constituents. In fact, close contact is invariably maintained, not because it is required by law, but because of the members' desire to keep the electorate properly informed. The penalty which the member risks by not keeping in close touch with his constituency is not being unseated, but simply not being re-elected. The only difference is how soon the penalty has to be paid, and this depends on the length of the period for which the member is elected. Democratic theory calls for short Parliaments and frequent appeals to the electorate, but long Parliaments promote stable government.

Parliamentary experience and practice, irrespective of differences of constitution, have succeeded in reconciling this contradiction and have found a solution which would appear to suit the requirements of most countries; they have made the parliamentary term four years, which has been long enough for carrying out major schemes without losing contact with the electorate. Notable exceptions are the United States, with a two-year term, and Czechoslovakia with six years; three years is the term fixed by Australia, Spain, the Sudan and the Republic of Vietnam, while Parliament holds power for five years in Ceylon, Egypt, France, India, Ireland, Italy, Laos, Luxembourg, Pakistan and the United Kingdom.

In Turkey, the Grand National Assembly can, if it sees fit, decide to extend its powers for a further year. The same applies to the Chamber of Deputies in Burma; in case of emergency, it can prolong its term of office from year to year, subject to agreement by two thirds of its members. But it should be noted that, except in Burma, Iceland and the Sudan, the upper Chambers of bicameral Parliaments are renewed less frequently than the lower Chambers, for reasons already explained.

A whole Parliament can be prematurely ended by statutory or governmental dissolution of Parliament, the latter method being directly bound up with the relationship between Government and Parliament, which will be discussed later, and individual seats can be vacated by resignation or explusion or, of course, by death.

With the exception of Norway, all countries give the members of their Parliaments the option of resigning. In Finland, France, Italy, Japan, Monaco and Sweden, a resignation to be effective must be accepted by Parliament itself or by its Bureau or its President; it may be useful to be able to go into the reasons why the member is resigning and, if necessary, to refuse to accept his resignation if the reasons are of an improper nature. Resgination may also come about automatically, where it is occasioned by incompatibility of occupation. A Member of Parliament who undertakes duties incompatible with membership of Parliament is presumed to be tacitly resigning his seat. All the Assembly does is take due note of the fact.

A distinction must be drawn between expulsion and resignation. The former is based not on the principle of incompatibility of occupation, but that on disqualification. (This, at any rate, is the classic interpretation). Parliament may not expel a member except on the basis of judicial decisions or documents establishing beyond question the incapacity or the bar on grounds of misconduct which has been incurred by the member while he has been in Parliament. Its power to do so must be limited by the law defining qualification. The reason for this narrow interpretation is to prevent expulsion from turning into a disciplinary action, or indeed a political action, which in the hands of an unscrupulous majority might become a dangerous weapon to be used against the minority. A number of countries have decided that the risk was worth taking, pinning their faith on the political acumen of their statesmen; thus, in the United Kingdom, Denmark, Australia, Japan and Spain, 'improper conduct' is a sufficient motive for expulsion. In Burma, Finland, the Sudan, Ceylon and Australia, absenteeism may be penalized in this way. At times, expulsion may be in the nature of a political measure, e.g. in the Federal Republic of Germany, in the case of Members of

Parliament who are found to have misused their rights in order to try to upset the liberal, democratic constitutional order, or who belong to an unconstitutional party. Admittedly, the Bundestag, the Bundesrat or the Federal Government merely lodges the petition. The actual sentence of expulsion is pronounced by the Federal Constitutional Court. In Egypt, the Assembly itself takes the decision, but the support of two thirds of the members is required, so that members who lose the confidence and respect of their colleagues can be expelled. In such circumstances, there is of course danger of political revenge being a motive. Expulsion is unknown in Iceland, Indonesia, Ireland, Israel, the Netherlands and Norway. Elsewhere, in so far as it arises out of the rules of qualification for membership, it is hardly open to criticism. In Parliaments where it is used as a disciplinary measure, it is an exceptional procedure.

In this field, as in many others, practice has to reconcile points of view which theoretically are poles apart. Doctrinaire principles invariably lose something of their stiffness when they come into contact with reality. Parliament benefits from this tendency for, if the institution is to develop and thrive, it needs rules that are definite yet flexible, and not a set of rigid precepts.

ORGANIZATION OF PARLIAMENT

I

The Legal Position of the Member of Parliament

Immunities—Parliamentary Remuneration

Once his fellow-citizens have expressed their confidence in him by sending him to Parliament, the member is faced with heavy responsibilities which will make claims upon his time and give him much to think about. If he is to carry out his responsibilities conscientiously, and do his duty properly, he must have complete independence. In principle this is ensured by his legal position, which is governed by provisions of two main types—his immunities, which safeguard his independence of conduct, and his emoluments, which make him financially independent. Without considering their purpose, public opinion often looks askance at these privileges, perquisites or prerogatives, and they make an easy target for the demagogue, even in countries which take pride in their parliamentary institutions.

1. IMMUNITIES

Parliamentary immunities protect members against the possibility of legal actions being brought against them by the Government or by private individuals. They constitute derogations from the principle of the equality of citizens before law and justice.

Originally their purpose was to secure the precarious situation of elective assemblies in the face of powerful Governments which could bring influence to bear upon the courts. With Parliament at the level of development it has reached today, they are less obviously justifiable. Nevertheless, they still keep their essential *raison d'être*, since they are not simply favours granted to members in their private capacity, but rather rules of general import designed to ensure the smooth running and complete independence of Parliament.

For this reason immunities are related primarily to the exercise of parliamentary duties. Here the independence of the elected member is guaranteed by his legal 'non-accountability', which is generally admitted by most constitutions, those of Monaco and Sudan being exceptions. 'Non-accountability' applies to anything spoken or written or any act committed by a member of a parliamentary assembly in the ordinary course of his official duties: speeches delivered in the House or in committee, interventions from the floor, introduction of Bills and motions, including any explanation of the reasons for them, reports, oral or written questions, in short any act which presupposes that the person performing it is acting in the course of his parliamentary duties—which in fact anyone not a member could not perform. Immunity applies to these specific acts only, but within this narrow field it is quite categorical: the protection afforded is absolute and life-long. The member cannot have any criminal charge or civil action brought against him for these acts, even after he has ceased to be a member.

There is almost complete unanimity concerning these various features of 'non-accountability' although in British law the actual term 'parliamentary non-accountability' is unknown. The principle exists, nevertheless, in the form of 'parliamentary privilege', and its effects are the same as those produced by law in other European countries. Some constitutions, however, provide that any abuse of 'non-accountability' should be liable to legal action; under the Constitution of the Federal Republic of Germany, for example, immunity does not cover defamation of character and insult, even when committed in the course of parliamentary duties. Similarly, in Denmark and Iceland members may be held accountable for their actions, subject to the authorization of the assembly to which they belong. In Finland and Sweden the authority to prosecute requires five sixths of the votes cast to be in favour.

These are the few exceptions to the principle of 'non-accountability' which does not, of course, release Members of Parliament from obedience to the orders of the House governing the conduct of debates or from their moral responsibility to the public. This is a matter for the voters to assess and, if need be, breaches can be checked by not re-electing the offender. In the final analysis this democratic check on parliamentary activity is what gives immunity its proper significance in the political field; and, this check apart, Members of Parliament must be granted the utmost freedom and independence.

'Inviolability' or protection from legal process ensures that Members of Parliament are protected against legal actions brought against them for acts committed outside the orbit of their office, in other words, acts which the ordinary citizen might commit. On the face of it, this seems too great a privilege, less obviously justifiable than 'non-accountability'; hence it does not meet with the same unanimous approval in all constitutions. For example, the Netherlands does not consider inviolability essential for the protection of their Members of Parliament against unwarranted prosecution. In Sweden a member of the Riksdag may be arrested and held in custody provided that a judge on the basis of a preliminary examination deems it necessary. In Great Britain the idea has never been entertained that 'inviolability' could interfere with the workings of penal law. It applies only in civil matters and its only effect is to prevent the arrest of Members of Parliament during sessions and for forty days before and after the session. Since imprisonment for debt was abolished in 1869, for practical purposes members come under the ordinary law, subject to the ruling of the Speaker, whose authority is regarded as constituting an adequate safeguard against threats from outside. Moreover, the complete independence of British judges from the executive provides a further substantial guarantee. This system, evolved in the House of Commons, has been adopted by countries like Australia, India and Pakistan, which thus do not grant any real privileges to the members of their Parliaments. In Burma freedom from arrest (in the case of civil actions only) applies only for the duration of the session or, when both Houses meet in joint session, for fourteen days before and after the meeting. In most other countries, fear of encroachment by the executive upon the liberty of Members of Parliament is much more manifest: since arrest for civil offences has been abolished in the majority of legal systems, attempts to ensure the protection of Members of Parliament against possible action by their Governments have been made mostly in the field of criminal law. The problem has been solved in two ways, one dictated by practical considerations and the other based on more strictly legal principles.

Some countries consider that the all-important consideration is to see to it that Members of Parliament are able to participate in the work of the Chamber in spite of any opposition from the Government. Their answer is to prohibit the arrest of members while they are travelling to and from Parliament or while they are attending Parliament. This is roughly the course adopted by the Constitutions of the United States, the Philippines, Indonesia, the Republic of Vietnam, Ireland, Norway, Ceylon and the Sudan; and incidentally, in the first five countries 'inviolability' does not cover what are regarded as the major offences—treason, felony, and sedition—nor does it apply to offenders *in flagrante delicto*. A feature common to all these Governments is the absence of parliamentary interference in the proceedings which are taken, so long as the constitutional and legal rules are observed.

In the other countries where the principle of immunity from arrest in criminal cases is recognized, the procedure is much more complicated, reflecting both the desire to safeguard the liberty of members against any improper attack, and the fear of establishing an excess of privilege which might be open to criticism. It originated on the continent of Europe, and has spread to such countries as Brazil, Egypt, Iceland, Japan, Laos and Turkey. In general, 'inviolability' in these countries has three regular features: authority to prosecute is granted by the Assembly; offenders *in flagrante delicto* form an exception; and 'inviolability' is limited to the duration of the session. In these countries, a Member of Parliament who has committed a crime or offence may not be prosecuted, arrested, or detained, unless authorization is given by Parliament, after it has considered whether there is a *prima facie* case. The task of determining whether the action is based on political persecution is in principle entrusted to a committee which has to report to the House; it may be either the committee of justice, the legislative affairs committee, or the standing orders committee. In Belgium it is a special *ad hoc* committee, and in France and Italy a special permanent committee.

Since immunity is instituted in the interests of Parliament and not for the personal benefit of its members, it has a public character which precludes a member from waiving it if Parliament considers that it should not be waived. Personal waiving of immunity is permitted only in Switzerland.

Prior authorization by Parliament is not required in the case of offenders *in flagrante delicto*; the immediate arrest and prosecution of the member against whom the charge is made is therefore possible without recourse to any other form of proceedings. The essential feature of *flagrante delicto* as laid down by the code of criminal procedure in each country, is that they enable the person committing the offence to be identified unequivocally, ruling out any risk of mistaken identity or tendentious interpretation of the facts.

One of the most awkward problems raised by the principle of 'inviolability' is the question of duration. Actually, the term 'inviolability' is rather a misnomer since normally constitutions limit it to the duration of the particular session. This does not by any means imply that when the House is not sitting the member reverts to the rule of ordinary law. Parliaments are always kept informed of any prosecution of a member when the House is not sitting and it is the business of Parliament to call for the suspension of the prosecution as soon as the session begins. In certain cases they may take such a step during recesses, through the Bureau, as in France, through the Council of State, as in Poland, or through the Presidium, as in Bulgaria, Rumania and the USSR. In the last-named country immunity is of particularly wide scope. The consent of the Supreme Soviet is necessary before a member can be brought to court or arrested; during recesses the consent of the Presidium is required.

Needless to say, in countries which do not have the sessional system, 'inviolability' covers the entire term of office; this is the case in Austria, Brazil, Denmark, the Federal Republic of Germany and Turkey.

Immunities are not the only privileges granted to Members of Parliament. To ensure that their time is not taken up with tasks which do not come within the scope of their duties, the principle of the equality of citizens in regard to public obligations is waived in certain instances. For example, in Australia, France, the United Kingdom and Burma, Members of Parliament are exempt from jury service, and in Israel they are exempt from compulsory military service. Furthermore, certain constitutions have limited the obligation upon Members of Parliament to give evidence in a court of law. In Israel members are not allowed to give evidence. In the Federal Republic of Germany, members need only give evidence if they so choose. In Italy, the United Kingdom and Turkey authorization has to be obtained from Parliament. In the other countries which apply the system of 'inviolability' in criminal matters the prosecution of a member for refusing to give evidence also requires the authorization of Parliament.

In view of the number of constitutions which make provision for parliamentary immunities, they would appear to be necessary. Nevertheless when they apply to infringements of the ordinary law they constitute a definite derogation from the principle of equality before the law. Parliaments must avoid the natural tendency of all institutions to place a broad interpretation upon the provisions from which they benefit and extend their privileges beyond the limits laid down by law, thus transforming them into personal prerogatives. The prestige of the Parliament would be the first to suffer as a result of this course.

Offences against Parliament

Among the privileges enjoyed by the House of Commons protection against being brought into ridicule or contempt figures prominently. To ensure this protection there is an intricate procedure by which the House itself acts virtually as a court of law. When a formal accusation is made before it by one of its members the grievance is referred for investigation and advice to the Committee of Privileges set up at the beginning of each session. Upon receiving the report of the committee, the House of Commons decides upon the punishment to be imposed on the offender; penalties range from admonition by the Speaker to reprimand or even imprisonment. This curious procedure, in which the distinction between judge and plaintiff is blurred, is practised also in Australia, India, Pakistan and the Sudan. In Ceylon the judicial authority is the Supreme Court, except for minor offences which are dealt with by a reprimand from the Speaker. In the Philippines the ordinary courts share with Parliament the right to prosecute offenders for criminal offences.

Several countries have not regarded it as necessary for Parliament itself to judge offences. These are referred to the judicial authorities, generally at the request of the President of the Assembly. This is the procedure followed in Austria, Belgium, Denmark, Egypt, the Federal Republic of Germany, Iceland, Spain, Sweden, the United States of America, and Yugoslavia.

Whatever the practice followed, the essential problem is to determine the gravity of the offence. It is difficult enough to discuss the principle underlying the action to be taken on, say, physical violence or assault and battery against a member; but to decide what in Great Britain is termed 'contempt to any member of the House or to the House collectively' must indeed be puzzling. Since in practice it is usually the newspapers that are guilty of such contempt, it raises the whole problem of the freedom of the Press, and hence of freedom of speech, which hardly comes within the scope of this study. But to keep to concrete facts, the main point at issue is where the right to criticize ends, and where defamation begins. In the opinion of an Australian Speaker 'newspaper criticism is not a breach of privilege unless something is done to coerce or impede members, or bring Parliament into contempt'. It is unfortunate that 'Contempt of Parliament' is not a legal concept, for there is no doubt that the existence and cohesion of a society implies a respect for certain collective values which in democratic countries include Parliament.

On the other hand, criticism is as much both the prerequisite and the machinery of democracy as it is of scientific progress. The application of harsh laws may well jeopardize the rights of the minority. A liberal outlook would suggest not considering offences against Parliament as a special type of offence. Thus in Albania, Burma, Poland and Rumania, there is no special category for offences against Parliament, which are placed on the same footing as

C*

offences committed against the State authorities. Parliament is not protected for its own sake but because it is part of the Government. The ordinary rule of law is applied in Finland, Luxembourg, the Netherlands, Norway, Sweden and the Republic of Vietnam, which means that the offence is not punishable unless it would be punishable if committeed against any individual or any other organization.

Then there are countries like France, Indonesia, Israel, Laos, Monaco and Switzerland which do not regard a wrong done to Parliament as an offence against the law, and it is therefore not liable to any penalty. This extreme point of view, the outcome of a desire to avoid any encroachment upon freedom of speech, hardly helps to ensure the protection of Parliament and is open to abuse and might give rein to irresponsible anti-parliamentary activity. In this respect, few countries enjoy such a calm and peaceful state of affairs as that suggested in the reply by the Czechoslovak Government: 'The people hold their National Assembly in too high a regard for charges ever to arise'.

2. PARLIAMENTARY REMUNERATION

A seat in Parliament is everywhere rightly considered as a vocation and not a livelihood, though paradoxically, the principle of unpaid service, which would seem to be the logical corollary, has been abandoned everywhere. This being so, the old controversy as to whether Members of Parliament should be paid is merely academic. But instead, we get the knotty problem of members' emoluments, one of the questions most apt to arouse indignation in public opinion—which more often than not is ill-informed on the subject.

'No pay means that the poor have no say'. Aphorisms of this kind, based as they are on democratic principles, explain why the remuneration of Members of Parliament is an essential feature of their legal position—the elector must have full liberty to choose the man in whom he places his confidence, and such a man may not necessarily be rich. A seat in Parliament involves considerable expense inherent in the members' duties (travelling and hotel expenses, secretarial services, etc.); moreover the member cannot continue to look after his own affairs in the normal way.

When Parliaments hold only short and infrequent sessions, it is of course possible to limit the remuneration to the duration of the session, and to fix it at a relatively low figure. In actual fact, only three countries employ this system—Iceland, Switzerland and the Netherlands (First Chamber). Everywhere else the growing claims of parliamentary life on the members' time and the increasing frequency and duration of sessions have made it necessary to introduce emoluments on an annual basis, designed to provide Members of Parliament with the means of livelihood which they can no longer earn from their former occupation. Consequently, the nature of parliamentary remuneration has gradually changed; instead of being a mere reimbursement of expenses, as it used to be, it has become, to some extent at least, a salary. Apart from the consequences this may involve in regard to taxation, the change implies the principle that Members of Parliament are 'paid' for the services they render, and increases the temptation to consider a seat in Parliament as just another 'job'. This alteration in the character of the payment made to members can be noted in countries like Austria, Finland, France, Laos and Japan, which have not hesitated to link parliamentary remuneration directly with the salaries of certain grades of civil servants. This has, of course, the virture of avoiding the possibility of playing to the gallery when circumstances make salary increases necessary.

In certain countries, fixed annual emoluments, which tend to be criticized by people who do not realize just how the expenses which a seat entails mount up—secretarial work, car, two establishments, subscriptions and contributions of all kinds—are supplemented by a daily subsistence allowance, the principle advantage of which is that it stresses the special nature of membership. It also has the further advantages:

(a) Of discouraging absenteeism, about which public opinion is particularly sensitive, by relating the member's remuneration in part to actual attendance.

(b) Of reducing the fixed emoluments by making the purpose simply the reimbursement of expenses incurred in the course of parliamentary duties.

Generally speaking, this system is seen in action in the United Kingdom and in those countries where the influence of British institutions is still considerable: Burma, India, Israel, Pakistan, Brazil, Indonesia and Japan have likewise adopted it. In Japan, Members of Parliament receive, over and above their regular salary and a daily allowance, special allowances as reimbursement of expenses incurred in the performance of their work, and an 'end of sitting' payment made twice a year.

In Western Europe the daily allowance is not popular. In Norway it is based on the distance which the member must travel. In the Federal Republic of Germany the method of remuneration is complicated by the fact that there are three types of allowances—

cost-of-living allowance, a lump sum refund of out-of-pocket expenses, and mileage and daily subsistence allowances. The calculation of these is governed by extraordinarily complicated rules. The same complicated system is found in Italy; there is a lump sum payment for attendance for the session, but this is reduced in proportion to the number of absences, the amount of the reduction varying according to whether the member lives in Rome or the provinces, whether sittings take place in the morning or afternoon, and during the summer vacation or during the rest of the year. The blanket system adopted in Luxembourg has the advantage of reducing the remuneration to a single type of payment which includes both reimbursement of expenses and remuneration for participation in the work of Parliament; there is a fixed yearly maximum which may be reduced according to the number of meetings which the member has failed to attend.

In this connexion the practical difficulties involved in checking the attendance of members may be mentioned. Many different methods of doing this are employed. The most common is the keeping of a register. In Brazil, presence is recorded by the use of attendance tokens. In India, a member travelling from the provinces is only required to prove that he is in town to qualify for the payment. Among the countries which pay members a daily allowance are the USSR, Albania, Bulgaria and Rumania. In Poland, members in Warsaw for the session of Parliament are housed in an hotel placed at their disposal. In Albania and the USSR, members living in the capital cannot claim the daily allowance, which is thus tantamount to a travel allowance. A similar system obtains in Finland and Spain.

In all the other countries, the remuneration of members is payable whether or not they attend the sittings. Nevertheless, though it is a single payment, it consists of two parts—salary, and reimbursement of out-of-pocket expenses—and it is difficult to determine the relative size of each. However, the way in which the remuneration is regarded for tax purposes throws some light on the question. In general, compensation for out-of-pocket expenses is not taxable; in those countries where the whole of the amount payable is thus regarded no tax is payable. Where it consists in part of salary this is subject to tax, after the deduction of professional expenses. In Australia, the United Kingdom and the Netherlands, proof of these expenses may be furnished by the member himself. In many cases, the amount is estimated as a fixed figure: 45 per cent of the remuneration in France, half in Belgium, and two thirds in Norway.

The variety and complexity of the methods used in calculating parliamentary emoluments makes generalization very difficult. The actual rate of pay cannot be taken as a valid criterion because of the differences in the economic situation of the various countries and the varying obligations which parliamentary duties entail. Furthermore, within each country, differences in the situation of members are found, even though they all receive the same remuneration; it may be affected by the distance which they have to travel. This inequality is taken into account in Australia, Bulgaria, Denmark, the Netherlands and Sweden. In most cases the inequality arises from legal or practical incompatability of occupation, which may make it impossible for some Members of Parliament to engage in any gainful occupation outside their parliamentary duties, whereas others may be able to carry on their profession or enjoy their private means. In the USSR and the Peoples' Democracies real equality among Members of Parliament is ensured more satisfactorily, since they all continue in their profession or trade. In addition, Soviet members receive monthly compensation for out-of-pocket expenses.

All this explains why it is imperative to ensure, whatever the circumstances, that Members of Parliament are able to live in a manner in keeping with the dignity of their high position. It may also justify the award of retirement pensions, particularly to those who have had to relinquish all other sources of income—the idea behind the Polish and British systems. Elsewhere no such restriction arises and any Member of Parliament who has sat for a certain number of years, varying from eight to ten, and has reached an age varying from forty-five to sixty-five, is entitled to a pension. This is the practice in Australia, Belgium, Finland, France, Iceland, Norway and Sweden. In the Netherlands all former members of the Second Chamber of the States-General enjoy the right to a pension, proportionate to the length of time for which they were members, after the age of sixty-five or, should they still be members at that age, on vacation of their seats. In Laos and Syria only those who were formerly civil servants have a right to a pension. Burma, Ceylon, Egypt, Iceland, India, Ireland, Israel, Italy, Japan, Luxembourg, the Philippines, Spain, Switzerland and the United States of America do not consider it necessary to grant retirement pensions to the members of their Parliaments.

Besides emoluments and pensions, there are various advantages attached to a seat in Parliament which are designed to help the member to perform his duties efficiently. It is a general practice to grant Members of Parliament transport facilities. These take various forms, from reduced fares exclusively for journeys between a member's constituency and Parliament to free travel anywhere. In Iceland, travelling expenses are refunded upon submission of a claim.

In Japan, the Netherlands, the Philippines and the United States a lump sum travel allowance is paid. French and Syrian Members of Parliament have the right to free travel on the State railways.

Some rather unusual practices are worth noting. In Laos, a member's servant enjoys the same privileges as his employer; in Ceylon the same applies to a member's secretary, though he is only allowed third-class railway travel. In Australia, members' wives are allowed four free journeys to Canberra a year. An Indonesian member is allowed one trip a year, all expenses paid, to any part of the country.

The high cost of correspondence has led the authorities in the majority of countries to allow Members of Parliament free postage, at any rate for the part of their correspondence directly connected with their parliamentary duties. However, in Burma, Denmark, India, Ireland, Italy, Laos, Luxembourg, the Netherlands, Spain, Sweden and Syria, this type of expense must be met by the member himself, since he is assumed to be able to meet it out of his emoluments. The same assumption is made almost everywhere in respect of private secretaries and office premises. Few countries can emulate Australia and Japan in providing each member with a secretary and an office.

The impressive list of the perquisites enjoyed by Members of Parliament may be misleading. Actually their economic position is not always an enviable one. It is difficult to assess the full extent of their obligations, but in all countries these are heavy enough to necessitate regulations designed to make it possible for any person, whatever his social position, to hold a seat in Parliament, and to keep him free from the influence of political, or financial groups, which would inevitably be brought to bear were inadequate official remuneration provided. It is difficult to find the golden mean owing to the danger of turning parliamentary office into a profitable trade and thus robbing it of much of its honour and prestige.

II

The Officers of Parliament

The Directing Authority of Parliament—The Administrative Services of Parliament

Parliament is not merely a convenient term for use in propounding theoretical points of constitutional law; it is also something much more concrete. Beneath the constitutional edifice a substructure, frequently a complex one, develops, and in actual practice this has tended to follow a more or less uniform pattern. To ensure that its work runs smoothly, Parliament appoints a leader, sets up an administration, and has an independent organization, the nature and individual features of which reflect a common purpose, however different the systems.

1. THE DIRECTING AUTHORITY OF PARLIAMENT

In spite of the special nature of the recruitment and the legal position of its members, Parliament 'is, after all, only an assembly of men, which, like any other body, must be directed by some authority'. This authority can be traced back as far as 1377, i.e. to the very origin of Parliament. In those days, members of the House of Commons had felt the need to designate one of their number to 'take the Chair of this House as Speaker'; hence the origin of the office of Speaker. Over the centuries, the duties of this high dignitary have gradually evolved, after many vicissitudes, until today the office of Speaker is one of high prestige, a model admired and copied, but when all is said and done—inimitable. For a long time it was the Crown's nomination that mattered in the election of a Speaker; but nowadays it is the election that matters. This victory for democracy, subsequently won by the majority of the world's Parliaments, has not extended from the House of Commons to the House of Lords next door, which is still presided over by a member of the executive, the Lord Chancellor; but his role is extremely limited, since it consists in no more than putting questions to the vote; he does not intervene to regulate the conduct of debates. Fortunate indeed is a House that can successfully impose its own rules of discipline.

The other exceptions are the Spanish Cortes, whose President is nominated by decree of the Head of State, and the two Chambers in the Netherlands. Actually, here the Crown appoints the President of the First Chamber from among its members; for the Second Chamber it merely approves the choice of the members; three names are presented as a list, and the first is automatically appointed. The constitutions of certain federal states provide that the Vice-President of the Union is President of the upper House *ex officio*. This is the case in Brazil, India and the United States of America, though in India the President is elected by the two Houses in joint session.

The principle of an elected President is recognized in all other Parliaments; in many cases an absolute majority is required, at least at the first count, since this establishes the presidential authority on a wider basis. The ballot is also secret in most instances—an essential feature in view of the impartiality demanded by the office. The successful candidate is presumed not to know who has voted for him, so that in principle he will not be under any obligation towards them. The election is therefore technical and personal rather than political in character.

The prestige which has come to be attached to the office of Speaker of the House of Commons absolves the House from this requirement. The election is usually made unanimously after an understanding has been reached between the Government and the Opposition, and is moved by two members. It is traditional to re-elect the retiring Speaker, and we have to go back to 1835 to find an instance where this custom was not observed. This is the pledge of his impartiality, the essential characteristic of his office. From the day of his election, the Speaker severs all links with his own party, even going so far as to avoid personal contacts, which might give grounds for suspicion of partiality. He has an official residence, a high salary, and upon retirement he is raised to the peerage and enjoys a pension. The pomp and ceremony connected with his position help to create around him the aura of a judge. Inside Parliament, he actually does enjoy this power and he wields it with sovereign authority; 'The Speaker like the Pope, is infalliable', were the words of Mr Speaker Lowther on one occasion. He regulates the conduct of debate at his own discretion and there is no appeal from his decisions. He tries to ensure that parliamentary business is despatched rapidly according to the will of the majority, while respecting the rights of the minority. He formulates new rules for parliamentary procedure in accordance with custom, subject, naturally, to the consent of Parliament. As Jennings says: 'The Speaker's authority is greater than his power'. To the world he represents the unity of the House of Commons and within the House he ensures that debate is productive and dignified.

Apart from his numerous duties in taking the Chair, the Speaker is responsible for administrative matters within the House, a task which, though not inspiring, is not less arduous. He must be both judge and administrator. He is assisted by his two deputies—the Chairman of Ways and Means, and the Deputy Chairman, who take the chair when the House sits as a Committee of the Whole House. There are several committees set up to deal with purely administrative questions; they advise the Speaker without encroaching upon his authority or his prestige.

This office, patiently moulded by centuries of experience, has naturally been both admired and copied. In all the countries which have been influenced by Great Britain there is a Speaker, at least in the lower House. As in Great Britain, he holds office for the whole Parliament; he represents Parliament in its relations with the outside world and he wields authority both in regard to procedure and in regard to the administration of Parliament.

In Australia certain departments are administered jointly by the Speaker of the House of Representatives and the President of the Senate—the library, official reporting of debates and administration common to both Houses. Special committees assist them in this task.

Burma, Ceylon, India, Pakistan and the Sudan have also followed the example of Great Britain but with varying success, for it is difficult to create overnight an institution like this, which has taken centuries to evolve.

The fact that the Speaker of the House of Representatives in the United States, like the Speaker of the Commons, has the casting vote, does not mean that he fulfils the same functions. The resemblance ends with his title and the principle of placing control of debate in the hands of one man, and does not cover those facets of the post which in practice go to give it its richness in the United Kingdom. Since he is elected by one party, and not by the unanimous vote of all the representatives, it is hard for him to play the part of impartial judge. Hence, his authority suffers thereby, since he has to share it with the Committee on Rules, the Chairman of the Ways and Means Committee, and the floor leaders and party policy committees.

The Presidents of the Irish Dail and Seanad, though they do not have the title of Speaker, emulate his position as far as possible, even in their exercise of the casting vote in the event of a tie: they preside over sittings, represent their House in its external relations and are responsible for its administration. They are at the same time Presidents of the Procedure and Privileges Committee. They also have important constitutional prerogatives, such as membership of the Council of State, and of the committee which may be set up under certain circumstances to replace the Head of State.

The Speaker of the Knesset in Israel must also act as Head of State in the event of the President's indisposition or absence. Within the House the authority he wields throughout the legislature is backed up as regards the procedure and administration of the House by that of the eight deputy speakers, who thus form with him the nucleus of a college, called the Presidium, which is found elsewhere in the form of a Bureau. In Japan the administrative Sub-Committee Council assists the President of each House in his administrative duties.

But as in the House of Commons, the common characteristics of these different Houses of Parliament is the establishment of an individual authority covering all aspects of parliamentary activity, usually with a term of office for the whole life of the Parliament. In the Icelandic Althing, however, the President's term of office lasts only one session.

It is not the duration of the Speaker's term of office which distinguishes the British system from that of other countries, for there are many Parliaments which elect their President for the duration of the Parliament—Albania, Austria, Bulgaria, the Federal Republic of Germany, Indonesia, Italy, Poland, Rumania and the USSR. (The others elect their Presidents annually or by the session). The essential feature in Britain is the concentration of power in the hands of a single individual. For unlike the British system, in many Parliaments the President is surrounded by a body of the 'college' type which, under various names, has partial or complete responsibility for the working of Parliament. This college is always elected, except in Spain. It may be very small—in Denmark, Norway and the USSR it consists only of the President and the Vice-Presidents. On the other hand, the number of its members may be considerable, as in the French Assembly, where the Bureau comprises, in addition to the President, six Vice-Presidents, fourteen Clerks and three Quaestors. The fact that they are so many is explained partly by the extent and variety of duties to be performed, and partly also by the desire to associate representatives of all political groups in its major decisions as a guarantee of their regularity. But not all countries have adopted so systematic a procedure combining the President and the members of the Bureau in a close network of collaborative effort. The Bureau or its equivalent is often regarded merely as a consultative body designed solely to assist the President in his difficult task and not to act as a check on his work or even to take decisions in his stead. This is precisely the role of the Council of Elders in the Federal Republic of Germany and Poland, elected in the former by proportional representation from among the political groups and, in the latter composed of the chairmen of the permanent committees and the parliamentary groups, as well as the members of the Presidium.* Similarly, in the USSR, the Council of Doyens, made up of representatives of the Republics, territories and regions, is also an advisory body. It may submit for examination by the

* Except in Poland, where it operates as a Bureau in the accepted sense of the term, the Presidium in some People's Democracies—Albania, Bulgaria, Rumania and the USSR—is a collegiate body elected by Parliament and assuming in particular the role of Head of State.

Supreme Soviet proposals for the order of business and to candidatures for membership of such bodies as are elected by the Supreme Soviet. The functions of the Council of Doyens, of the President of the Chambers and their assistants must not be confused with those of the Presidium of the Supreme Soviet of the USSR, of the Presidium of the Bulgarian National Assembly, of the Presidium of the Albanian National Assembly and of similar bodies existing in the other People's Democracies.

The role of the Bureau is generally confined to administrative and financial questions, as in Australia, Belgium, the Federal Republic of Germany, Italy, Monaco, Spain and Switzerland. The Laotian and Turkish Parliaments have a similar authority, under the aegis of the President, to deal with the same questions. The Bureau is, however, seen at its most important in Brazil, Egypt, France, Indonesia, Luxembourg, Rumania, Syria and the Republic of Vietnam, where constitutionally it has the duty as a body of directing the work of Parliament. It should be noted that in Finland it is sub-divided into the Presidential Council (comprising the President, the two Vice-Presidents and the chairman of committees) which handles procedural matters, and the Chancellory Committee, in which the President, the Vice-Presidents and four elected members deal with administrative questions.

Apart from administrative and financial management, the Bureau as a body has only a restricted number of duties, rarely of a political character. In Czechoslovakia, however, the Bureau has an unusually important role; it interprets the laws; assesses their constitutional validity and the legality of other decrees; is responsible for placing before Parliament an indictment against the President of the Republic or a member of the Government; appoints the non-elective committees of the House; and enacts emergency legislation when the Parliament is not sitting, subject to ratification in due course. In France and Switzerland too the role of the Bureau extends beyond the administrative sphere, since it may be called upon to interpret the standing orders and see that they are observed; while in Belgium, Bulgaria, France, Laos and Luxembourg, it may have to represent Parliament in official ceremonies. In practice, the work of the Bureau is mainly carried out by its individual members, the President, Vice-Presidents, Secretaries and Quaestors.

Like the Speaker in Great Britain, the President has in all countries first and foremost the responsibility of conducting the actual debates with the maximum of impartiality. This office is all-important since calling members to speak is the very life-blood of parliamentary activity. Hence has has to see to it that the standing orders or rules of procedure are carried out, to maintain order in the House, and to impose measures to enforce his rulings. Impartiality demands that he should not participate in the debates or, in certain countries, in the voting, even if he has the right to do so. For the same reason, he is the last to vote in the Netherlands, in order to preclude the possibility of influencing his colleagues. In some cases, he is empowered to convene Parliament; his signature validates legislative enactments; he may even have a direct hand in the promulgation of laws, as in Brazil, or, if necessary, he may take over when the Government cannot carry on, as in France.

These are duties bound up with the work of Parliament, and they do not prevent the President from assuming direct responsibility for the administrative services, as he does in Austria, Egypt, the Federal Republic of Germany, Japan, Laos, Monaco, Syria and Turkey, or even controlling expenditure, as in Austria, Rumania, Syria, the Republic of Vietnam and Yugoslavia.

There are few countries where the President has an important role to play outside Parliament. We have already mentioned Ireland and Israel. In France the constitutional prerogatives of the President of the National Assembly makes him the second ranking figure in the State. He takes the place of the President of the Republic in his absence, is consulted as to the dissolution of Parliament, takes over as President of the Council and Minister of the Interior if dissolution is preceded by the passing of a motion of censure; and is a member of the Constitutional Committee and President of the Council of the Republic.

The Vice-Presidents' only function as a rule is to take the chair in the event of the President's absence. In Belgium, the Vice-Presidents preside over the permanent committees; in Spain they are responsible for the servicing of meetings (minutes, documentation, voting, etc.), and in Czechoslovakia they assist the President. They vary in number from country to country according to the number of meetings held and sometimes to the number of political groups which must be represented. This explains why there is only one Vice-President in Switzerland, but six in the French National Assembly. As a general rule there are two (Brazil, Egypt, Luxembourg, Poland, Rumania, Sweden, Syria and the Republic of Vietnam; and in the Second Chamber in the Netherlands); there are three in Bulgaria and Turkey, and four in the Federal Republic of Germany, in the French Council of the Republic, Italy and the USSR.

The Bureau may also include officers whose main function is to assist the President either in the servicing of meetings, as in Belgium, the Federal Republic of Germany, Luxembourg and Turkey, or simply in the counting of votes, as in France, Monaco, Switzerland and Syria, or in the preparation of the official reports of debates, as in Egypt. In Norway, the officers write the reports themselves, as they do also in Syria and Turkey for secret sessions. The scope of their duties is broader in Albania and Yugoslavia, where they supervise the work of the Secretariat, i.e. the general administration of the House. They have a similar task in Brazil, but in addition they are empowered to authorize expenditure up to a certain figure (50,000 cruzeiros).

The French National Assembly is again unusual in the impressive number of its officers (fourteen), though the Federal German Bundestag has even more—twenty-one. There are ten in the Polish Parliament; eight in Egypt, Italy, France (Council of the Republic) and Brazil; six in Bulgaria and Turkey, and two in Laos, Luxembourg, Monaco and Norway.

Quaestors are a less common institution. In Europe they are found only in Belgium (where they are not part of the Bureau of the House of Representatives), in France, Italy and Turkey; outside Europe, in Laos, Syria and the Republic of Vietnam. They are always few in number—usually three, but only two in the Republic of Vietnam and one in Laos. They deal mainly with the financial aspects of parliamentary problems; in France, Laos and Turkey, the terms of employment and promotion of officials come under their jurisdiction, while in Belgium, Italy and Turkey, they are concerned with problems of protocol and the organization of ceremonies. Generally speaking, practical material matters are their special province. Their responsibilities often entitle them to privileges such as official quarters or special allowances.

In every country various factors—the power of tradition, the interests of efficiency, the prestige of office, the concern for objectivity, the political situation, respect for the letter of the law— have helped in varying degrees to fashion an authority which is responsible for the smooth running of Parliaments. These examples of some of the systems existing in various countries have shown the great importance of the role played by the President. His is the dominant personality; towards him all eyes are turned; it is usually to him that members address their speeches. The present tendency is to make his position more and more important. He must possess a large measure of personal authority, objectivity and flexibility, and the ability to make prompt judgments—qualities which are seldom all found in one man. For this reason Parliament itself must always have the last word, even though smooth running demands that the President should be given the utmost latitude; for he is at the helm as the servant of Parliament and not as its master. All assemblies depend for their usefulness upon the men at their head.

2. THE ADMINISTRATIVE SERVICES OF PARLIAMENT

Once its directing authority has been set up, Parliament must have a whole series of resources, intellectual and material, at its disposal to enable it to carry out its work and to exercise its power in the country. It is the function of the administrative services of Parliament to provide these resources, under a director who is responsible to the President or to the Bureau.

(a) The Secretary-General

Whatever his title happens to be—Secretary-General, Clerk, Greffier, Director—this senior official is responsible for a series of tasks the mere enumeration of which reveals their importance; first of all, he is a technical adviser to the President, who draws continually upon his experience and thorough knowledge of all the problems of parliamentary practice, particularly during sittings of the House, when tricky questions of interpretation of rules of procedure often crop up; he is in charge of the work of the Secretariat and the operation of the administrative services—personnel, supplies, accommodation, accounts—unless, as sometimes happens, this is made the responsibility of a second high official, the Secretary-General of the Quaesture or the Serjeant-at-Arms. In other words, the task of the Secretary-General is to see that all members, without discrimination, have at their disposal every possible facility to help them to carry out their parliamentary duties. The abilities required for the performance of this task render it essential to be particularly careful in making an appointment to this post.

Few countries have retained the system of appointment of the Secretary-General by the executive. However, it is still practised in Ceylon, Ireland, Monaco, and even in the United Kingdom, where Parliament is notoriously jealous of its privileges. In Ceylon, though the Governor-General appoints the Clerk of the House, the House itself may demand that his services be terminated. In Ireland it is the Prime Minister who nominates him, but only on the recommendation of the President of the House and of the Minister for Finance. In the United Kingdom the Clerk of the House of Commons and his opposite number in the House of Lords—Clerk of the Parliaments—are appointed for life by the Crown; thus they have an independence which such a method of appointment would hardly seem likely to give. In Indonesia appointment by the Government is only a formality; actually it follows election by Parliament. The practice of allowing Parliament to choose its own Secretary-General would seem more compatible with the nature of the office. Nevertheless the system of election, although based on a democratic outlook, carries with it the risk of transforming a technical office into a political office subject to the vagaries of successive majorities, even though the ballot is secret. In the United States the election of the Clerk at the opening of each Congress has the effect of making him dependent on the parties. In Luxembourg, the official is elected for three years. Certain provisions may reduce the effect of this drawback; in Norway, candidates are proposed by the President of the Storting and in Finland by the Chancellery Committee. In the Sudan a resolution to appoint a Clerk must receive two thirds of the votes, and in Belgium, the Greffier is elected for life. In Sweden, the secretary is elected annually, although in practice he is automatically re-elected each year. In Japan, although in theory he has to be elected, in actual fact the President nominates the Secretary-General by agreement with Parliament.

It is logical for the Secretary-General to be designated by whomsoever is best fitted to appreciate the requirements of Parliament and to make a choice based essentially upon technical competence. This is what happens in most Parliaments where the authority responsible for its functioning—President, Presidium, or Bureau—has the task of choosing the director from among the qualified officials in the parliamentary administration.

(b) Parliamentary Offices or Departments

As these officials constitute an independent body, the department to which they belong should, of course, be sufficiently large to allow the director to be selected from it. This is not always the case. The number of parliamentary officials varies considerably from country to country, according to the amount of work to be done by each Parliament and the place it occupies among the public authorities of the nation. The number may vary from a mere handful of employees, as in the Sudan or Switzerland, to several hundreds as in the Federal Republic of Germany or Japan. But a detailed study carried out by the Association of Secretaries-General of Parliaments shows that there is something approaching a fixed ratio between the number of Members of Parliament and its total staff—one or two officials per member. This is not, however, always the case; in the Netherlands the ratio is roughly one official for every two members. At any rate, certain duties are regularly to be found in the list of parliamentary offices, whether they are directly connected with the day-to-day routine of Parliament or have to do with the administrative and financial arrangements.

Unquestionably, the hub of parliamentary activity is the debate in the House; in order to make the proceedings available to the public an official records department is organized in every Parliament. In some countries—Belgium, Ceylon, France, Indonesia, Luxembourg, Rumania, Switzerland and the United States the records are of two kinds:

(a) Summary reports for rapid distribution, especially to the Press, giving the gist of the proceedings.

(b) A verbatim report which records exactly what was said at each sitting.

Finland, Laos, Spain, the Sudan and Turkey appear to use only the first system. In Sweden, on the other hand, there are no summary reports but only a verbatim report which appears in two successive editions, only the second of which is regarded as official. In Parliaments where two or more languages are used—Belgium and Finland for example—a special branch deals with the simultaneous interpretation and the translation. As the USSR is a multi-national state, the reports of the Supreme Soviet are translated from the language of each speaker into fourteen other languages and published in fifteen.

Sittings are of course never arranged casually. They must be prepared down to the last detail, along lines set forth in the standing orders, by the officers of the House. Members are supplied with the documentary material they need by the library, the home and foreign documentation services, and the committee clerks. Other offices take charge of the publication and distribution of parliamentary papers and the keeping of the archives.

All these tasks—and the list does not pretend to be complete— have to be carried out for the benefit of all the members, on the basis of strict neutrality and without any outside interference with the proceedings. This can only be achieved in so far as the administrative services of Parliament are provided by an independent organization operating exclusively for the benefit of the House.

III

The Independence of Parliament

Administrative Independence—Appeals against the Decisions of the Bureau or Directing Authority of the House—Financial Independence—Procedural Independence—Political Groups —Committees

The independence normally enjoyed by Parliaments is a natural phenomenon; it derives from the power of self-organization inherent in all official meetings. But it also stems from the political evolution of any country, and it is bound up with the historical development of parliamentary prerogative; and is a manifestation of the pre-eminence of Parliament among the authorities of state. Parliament, as the product of the sovereignty of the people, from which all power emanates, must not be subject to any other authority in any field of its activity. Under some constitutions the independence of Parliament is the corollary of the principle of separation of powers, which keeps the legislative distinct from the executive.

In practice this independence is not always as firmly guaranteed as the strength of the case for independence might suggest it should be. Depending upon the form of government, it is encroached upon to a greater or less degree; nevertheless such is the strength of the principle that in practice it is possible to find evidence of it in most branches of parliamentary activity. We have already seen that it dictates the character of the administrative services. It also affects the question of appeals against decisions made by parliamentary bodies; but its consequences are particularly noticeable in settling the grants of funds to be made to cover expenditure on Parliament and in the rules of procedure or standing orders to which that is subject.

1. ADMINISTRATIVE INDEPENDENCE

To say that the administrative services of Parliament are independent means in the first place that they come exclusively under the authority of Parliament's directing body. The particular nature of parliamentary work explains why this condition is usually met. Countries like Rumania and Monaco, where the officials come under the executive, are exceptional and the Federal Republic of Germany is another exception, since the administration of Parliament forms an integral part of the Federal administration, except that the power

73

of appointment is vested in the Presidents of the Bundestag and the Bundesrat and not in the Federal President. In Ireland only the Clerk and Clerk-Assistant, the Superintendent of the Houses, and the Librarian and Assistant Librarian are regarded as officers of the two Houses—the other members of the staff are civil servants.

Absolute independence would mean that the staff would not only be completely independent of government authority; it would also have to be free of all control by the civil service—in regard to recruitment, salary scales, promotion and discipline. It would have to have special terms of employment worked out on the basis of the peculiar requirements of parliamentary work. Actually there are, many Parliaments—Albania, Brazil, Bulgaria, Burma, Egypt Indonesia, Laos, Norway, Pakistan, the Philippines, Poland, Sweden, Switzerland, Turkey, the USSR and Yugoslavia—in which this logical conclusion is not drawn and the staff is recruited from the civil service and is subject to all the relevant regulations. The position of Czechoslovakia is noteworthy in that it is the only one of the Peoples' Democracies that grants parliamentary officers special terms of employment.

Where special terms exist, they are worked out by Parliament or by some delegate body—as a rule the Bureau—and incorporated into the standing orders. This is the case in Australia, Belgium, Czechoslovakia, Luxembourg, Spain and the Republic of Vietnam. Sometimes a special resolution has to be passed—as in Denmark, and the Sudan or legislation may be necessary, as in Ceylon, India, Israel and Japan.

It should be stressed that special terms of employment does not mean privileged employment; generally speaking, the rules governing employment are practically identical with the civil service regulations. This explains why, apart from distinctions of form, there is a kind of compounding of the parliamentary staff and the civil service, which is reflected, if not in interchangeability staff, at least in similarity of terms of employment. In short, the only special feature of the administrative offices of Parliament is the nature of their work and the particular obligations inherent in exclusive service to the House.

2. APPEALS AGAINST THE DECISIONS OF THE BUREAU OR DIRECTING AUTHORITY OF THE HOUSE

The fact that the decisions of Parliaments' directing authorities cannot or may not be challenged in a court of law raises the problem of the independence of Parliament in relation to the judiciary. This particular aspect of the principle of independence usually passes unnoticed, since it is rarely embodied in law, and thus is seldom tested. It is not at all a matter of legislative action which could ultimately be supported by reference to constitutional powers but exclusively a matter of administrative acts which by their nature do not differ in any way from acts done under the ordinary law except that they are taken by Parliament itself. But should the fact that these acts are done by a sovereign body render them unassailable? Most countries would reply in the affirmative, on the grounds that the sovereignty of Parliament extends to all acts performed in its name or on its behalf. In Great Britain, for example, to challenge a ruling of the Speaker would certainly constitute a breach of privilege and hence would be punishable, and this notion is generally recognized.

The problem hardly ever seems to have been considered as a whole because very few concrete cases have arisen, and the cases that have arisen have involved only two kinds of action—that taken in regard to parliamentary officials, with due reference to their terms of employment, and administrative action affecting the interests of persons not connected with Parliament. The result is that few countries have taken the trouble to define the scope of such action carefully and to devise a procedure for appeal against it.

In several countries the application of the ordinary law is apparently sufficient to cope with this kind of dispute. Indonesia, Ireland, Norway, the Philippines and Sweden would appear to come into this category. In the Federal Republic of Germany the situation is clearer: anyone may challenge the decision of the Presidents of both Houses in their capacity as heads of the administration before the ordinary civil, administrative, industrial or disciplinary courts. In Brazil and Egypt this kind of case is brought before the highest legal authority—the supreme federal Court of Justice and the Council of State respectively. In Belgium, Burma, Ceylon and Luxembourg, while the possibility of such appeals is recognized, it is felt that it has still to be decided which is the proper court to hear such cases. In India and the Netherlands third parties have no right of appeal; that right is granted only to members of the parliamentary staff who feel that they have been damnified by a decision affecting their careers.

The decided vagueness which surrounds this particular aspect of the independence of Parliament is largely due to the lack of case-law on the matter. It may therefore be said that there is no appeal rather because of the practical impossibility of making an appeal than because of concrete established principles.

3. FINANCIAL INDEPENDENCE

The financial independence of Parliament—one of the more important corollaries of the sovereignty of Parliament—raises few problems. If Parliament is to be completely independent it must have at its disposal means adequate to ensure its freedom of action. The old saying: 'He who pays the piper calls the tune' applies very much to the provision of funds to meet the expenditure on Parliament. But to keep to the subject of procedure, the principle of independence is seen in operation at two stages—in the preparation of the estimates and in control over expenditure.

As a general rule, Parliament itself decides upon its own expenditure in accordance with estimates drawn up by one of its delegate bodies—the Bureau or a select committee—on the basis of figures prepared by the administrative services. Hence the only problem is how far the executive is to have a hand in the allotment of funds, since at one stage or another these must be shown in the national estimates.

The system in force in Belgium, Denmark, Egypt, France and Italy allows the assembly the maximum degree of independence; after separate discussions without interference from the Government, the latter is informed of the total sums required, the figure then being entered as a matter of form in the national estimates without awaiting approval—in fact the Government is not even consulted. In Australia, Austria, the United Kingdom, Luxembourg, Norway, Pakistan, the Sudan and Switzerland the estimate for Parliament goes through the same channels as the estimates for any ministerial department, i.e. in principle, before it can form part of the national estimates, it must have the approval of the Treasury, the Minister of Finance or some other equivalent part of the executive, which in practice does not make many modifications even when it is in theory at liberty to do so, as in the Netherlands. Here Sweden has adopted an unusual practice: it is for the Commissioners of the National Office for Public Debt to draw up the estimate for the Riksdag; they submit their proposals to the Government for inclusion in the general estimates. This practice is in conformity with the principle of the financial independence of Parliament, for the commissioners are elected by and are solely responsible to the Riksdag itself.

The executive takes a more positive hand in Monaco, where the Royal Government must approve the estimates drawn up by the National Council; in Ireland, where the ceiling is fixed by the Minister for Finance; and in Ceylon, where the estimate for each

House is examined by the Speaker and his Advisory Committee which includes the leaders of the political parties and the Minister of Finance or his deputy. In the Federal Republic of Germany, the estimates for Parliament must be submitted to the Cabinet, which may withhold its approval. If it does so, it must put forward amendments which in the last resort will be accepted or rejected by Parliament. Japan goes a step further: the task of drawing up the estimates for Parliament is the responsibility of the Government following consultations with the Presidents of both Houses. In the event of a dispute, the decision rests with the Diet. The practice of including parliamentary expenditure in the national estimate is found in all countries. It enables the figures to be debated in Parliament in the same way as the expenditure of a ministerial department. Actually this seldom happens, since the estimates will have been drawn up by a parliamentary body where any objections will have already been made.

Thus, it is clear that Parliaments with few exceptions enjoy real and demonstrable independence in drawing up the estimates for expenditure in themselves; but control over the spending is rather different. Parliament should not be afraid of having its account audited. Just as it is reasonable that Parliament should be allowed to decide, without let or hindrance, what expenditure will be necessary, so it is to be expected that like any other funds, those allocated to Parliament will be audited to ensure that they have been used for their proper purpose and administered wisely and efficiently. This at least is the theory in a number of countries, which draw the logical conclusions that parliamentary expenditure should follow the ordinary rules, and that therefore the spending must be scrutinized not only by a special parliamentary committee but also by some body, with experience in financial matters, which is both unconnected with Parliament and independent of the executive. In Great Britain the authority is the Comptroller and Auditor General, who is appointed by the Crown. A similar officer is found in Burma, Ceylon, India, Ireland and Norway—here he is elected by the Storting. In Austria, Japan and the Netherlands the Court or Board of Audit may legally intervene; in the Federal Republic of Germany the Federal Audit Office has a similar right; in Egypt and Syria the accounts are by tradition audited annually by a member of the Audit Office acting in an advisory capacity. In Sweden this is done by the National Debt Office.

However, in other countries, the sovereignty of Parliament is more vigorously upheld, and no other authority is permitted to interfere in its financial affairs even *ex post facto*. This does not by any means imply complete lack of control; but such control is exercised by a qualified body within Parliament itself. Systems are very varied and range from *ad hoc* committees in Rumania and Turkey to the Chairman of the House in the USSR. In Belgium, Egypt and France the auditing of accounts is carried out by the Accounts Committee, in Pakistan by the Finance Committee, and in Yugoslavia by the Administration Committee. In Syria it is the task of the Quaestors, and in Finland of the Chancellery Committee; in Ceylon it is the task of the Advisory Committee, assisted by the Clerk, and in Bulgaria of the President of the Presidium himself. In actual fact the scope of this procedure is often substantially reduced because of the time lag between the expenditure of the grant and the auditing of the accounts. (The same applies of course to the national expenditure.)

4. PROCEDURAL INDEPENDENCE

The principle of the procedural independence is found in all democratic countries; it allows Parliament, within the framework of its constitutional functions, to exercise complete control over its own activities. Parliament decides its own method of working, and the standing orders it adopts not only fulfil the technical function of ensuring smooth running; they also have great importance in the Government of the country, for their provisions can give an unexpected twist to the Constitution, if by any chance there is a point in its application that has not been explicitly covered. They constitute a kind of 'manual of parliamentary practice' which gives life to the Constitution enabling Parliament to show its true nature and making for a majority which can be effective without infringing the rights of the minority.

The standing orders of most Parliaments aim at achieving this objective. They do, at any rate in their nature, their drafting, and their validity, have certain features in common:

(a) In the first place, every standing order consists of a resolution or a series of resolutions adopted by the House itself without any government interference. In this way it differs from a statute which, as we shall see later, is most often the product of a combination of the powers of the State. There are certain exceptions, however; the standing orders of the Spanish Cortes are laid down by law, in agreement with the Government, while those of the National Council of Monaco are approved by the Prince. Occasionally, there are standing orders which emanate from a variety of sources—constitutional, legal and internal. In Japan for example the main provisions are embodied in the Constitution and in a 'Diet Law'. In Iceland, in Austria and in Czechoslovakia, they are part and parcel of the ordinary body of legislation. In Sweden, the scope of the standing orders is the joint-product of the Constitution and the law on the Riksdag, of the Riksdag's rules of procedure concerning matters of common interest to both Houses and adopted jointly by them, and of the house rules of each House, which relate only to secondary matters.

Once again, Great Britain is the country where the diversity of origin of parliamentary procedure is at its most fascinating. To begin with the least important, there is the Parliament Act of 1911 which laid down the respective powers of the two Houses, and the Statutory Orders (Special Procedure) Act of 1945; when there are the hundred or so standing orders which fit into the classic category of rules of procedure; lastly there is the vast body of tradition and precedent, accumulated over several centuries, scattered through the 'Journal of the House', in part brought together in certain special collections, but kept alive through regular application by members and officials of Parliament. Except for the Australian Senate, where since 1903 precedents have been systematically incorporated into a code of permanent standing orders, they nowhere have codified authority. The reason for this is that in most countries the preparation of the standing orders is a matter of detailed study conducted by specialist bodies which endeavour to foresee and settle all procedural problems. The task is undertaken by various bodies—in Finland, by the Speaker's Council; in the Netherlands by a committee consisting of the leaders of the main political groups, assisted by the Clerk; and in the USSR by the Council of Doyens. In most cases Parliament instructs one of its committees—Constitutional Committee, Standing Orders Committee, Committee on Procedure, House Management or Administration Committee—to present a report to be debated, amended and accepted by the House. Israel is an exception, since the rules of procedure need not be passed by the Knesset before they can come into force; they merely have to be laid on the table of the Knesset by the House Committee.

(b) Although the standing orders are drawn up for its exclusive use, the House is nevertheless bound to observe them as long as they remain in force. We have seen that it is one of the duties

79

of the President, sometimes with the assistance of the Bureau, to ensure with the utmost impartiality that they are followed. In the Federal Republic of Germany, however, there is a specific provision whereby in exceptional circumstances the Bundestag, if it sees fit, may depart from its standing orders in certain respects, subject to the approval of two thirds of the members present. This procedure is not common; generally speaking when certain rules no longer answer their purpose, the members must move amendments to the rules by a procedure similar to that by which the rules originally were made. Draft amendments are studied by a committee and then placed before the House, which makes the final decision to accept or reject them.

In some countries, motions to amend the standing orders are regarded as a sufficiently serious matter to warrant additional safeguards. In this connexion it is interesting to note that in Britain and Ireland there is a device whereby changes in standing orders are given a trial period during which they are provisionally applied to allow their merits or demerits to become apparent. The Brazilian system too demands a long period of reflection; several days' notice must be given of motions to amend the standing orders before they can be passed, four in the Chamber and three in the Senate.

In Austria laws relating to standing orders can be enacted only if at least half the members are present and if two thirds of them vote in favour, while in Japan, although motions for alternation are drafted by an *ad hoc* sub-committee of the House Management Committee, they are not submitted to the House until they are accepted by representatives of all parties, so that the final decision is unanimous.

(c) The standing orders are permanent, that is to say, in the majority of countries at least they go on from one Parliament to the next. There are few countries which like Norway and some of the People's Democracies—Albania, Bulgaria and Poland—restrict their duration of that of one Parliament. As a matter of fact too much importance should not be attached to such departures from the rule, for in practice a newly elected Parliament simply takes over the existing orders which have stood the test in time. This practice is thus yet another manifestation of the sovereignty of Parliament, since it establishes its right to define its own working rules. The right is, of course, implicit in the power of each House to revise the standing orders if it so desires.

If we consider that no court of law is competent to look into the application or violation of standing orders, it is quite clear that the independence of Parliament is more than an empty phrase. It is the duty of each House to define its own prerogatives; the only safeguard lies in the profound knowledge which members have of parliamentary practice, of constitutional propriety and, in the last analysis, in the continuous watch kept by public opinion.

5. POLITICAL GROUPS

Under representative forms of government, parties have become the instruments for the expression of the people's will. In the liberal democracies their essential purpose and the most easily observable aspect of their activity is that they send as many representatives as they can to Parliament. This is what gives an election its meaning, and the contest continues to be carried on inside Parliament through political groupings which bring together members belonging to the same party or holding the same views, to make so many units to be thrown into the battle for political supremacy.

For a long time official recognition of the powers of political parties and parliamentary groups—which reflect the parties fairly accurately—lagged considerably behind the important part actually played in public affairs by these organizations, and in many countries this is still the case. According to certain theorists, the representative system in its ideal form would have no room for political groups, since each member would represent the whole nation, his function being to contribute to the expression of the nation's will by his speeches or his vote, both of which must square with his conscience.

In actual fact, even though they have continued to be ignored by constitutions, laws, and even by parliamentary standing orders, political groups have gradually become part and parcel of modern parliamentary practice. The idea of the group derives in the first instance from man's natural tendency to consort with those who hold the same views as himself; it has gained ground for historical reasons, since political groups have played a major part in all the movements which have brought about constitutional changes and the emergence of new states; and it has developed for theoretical reasons which have led many countries to adopt proportional representation, a system favourable to the formation and growth of political groups. Finally it reflects a psychological feature of modern

D   81

life, namely the sense of discipline and the predilection for collective activity. These reasons explain why the position of political groups within Parliament, which is bound up with the nature and evolution of every form of government, is marked by great diversity.

At the one extreme, there are countries where political groups have no *raison d'être*, e.g. those where only one party is recognized. In the Soviet Union, members who are also members of the Communist Party form a single group and this is also the case in Yugoslavia. In Bulgaria, the National Assembly comprises groups made up of the Communist Party and the National Agrarian Union. The Czechoslovak National Assembly is made up of groups of all the political parties represented in that Assembly. Similarly, groups of the United Workers Party, the United Peasants Party, etc., figure in the Polish Diet; the various parties however unite in a National Front. In addition, the Parliaments of certain Socialist states comprise regional groups who have a hand in the establishment of steering committees in fixing the order of business, etc. As well as the People's Democracies, there are other forms of government which militate against political splintering. For example, there are no political groups in the Spanish Cortes, or the Monacan National Council. In Egypt, the idea of National Union for the realization of the aims of the Revolution rules out the formation of separate groups.

Yet the phenomenon of the political group is closely bound up with the development and functioning of parliamentary democracy. It provides the backbone of parliamentary activities, or at any rate those which are most in the public eye. Paradoxically, the majority of long-established European democracies such as Belgium, Finland, Iceland, Luxembourg, the Netherlands and Norway, fight shy of official recognition of political groups. In most cases allusion to their existence is made only indirectly, and only in so far as they figure in the composition of certain parliamentary bodies. In the same way the British Parliament does not recognize them as such. They are swallowed up in the more practical and realistic system of majority and minority, or Government and Opposition, which lends great flexibility to parliamentary government. This system further promotes the concentration of political parties, which at its best leads to the two-party principle found in Great Britain. Following the British example, Australia, Burma, Ceylon, Ireland, the Philippines and the Republic of Vietnam have adopted the same system. More often than not it is found along with the single ballot and the individual vote, which reduces differences of opinion to a blunt 'for' or 'against'. Thus the Opposition achieves official standing in Parliament, one of the indications being the payment of a salary to its leader as potential head of the Government.

In most countries the Government v. Opposition system conceals a wide range of political groups, and the fluid nature of these groups can have serious repercussions on the stability of government—as it has in France. Because of this, an attempt has been made to cut down the number of such groups by stipulating a minimum size of membership. In the French National Assembly a political group must have at least fourteen members, and in the Council of the Republic eleven, before it can officially participate in the activity of Parliament. In the Federal Republic of Germany groups of less than fifteen members do not enjoy the privileges granted to recognized groups, and the consent of the Bundestag is required for the formation of groups consisting of members who do not belong to the same party. In the Swiss National Council a group must have at least five members. In Israel and Turkey three are sufficient to form a group in the Knesset and in the Grand National Assembly respectively. This minimum, which is almost self-evident from the very definition of the word group, guards against the kind of fantastic situation found in the Australian Senate, where a single senator has been deemed to constitute a separate party and it has been ruled that two could take upon themselves the titles of Leader and Deputy Leader of the party. The Parliaments of Albania and the USSR demand the same minimum of three members; but the groups in question have, of course, no political significance; they are set up in connexion with certain rules of procedure dealing with the conduct of parliamentary business.

The question of remuneration of the leaders of the Opposition may have a direct bearing on this matter. In Australia no payment is made to leaders unless their group consists of at least ten members, and in the Irish Dail, seven. The question of the size of political groups is bound up with that of their internal organization. The bigger the group the more powerful it will be; but its power demands a considerable degree of discipline. Once more it is the British House of Commons that provides the most striking example. In Great Britain parliamentary group and political party merge into one another; the members direct the party but are themselves directed by the leaders, and their 'Whips' are Members of Parliament. The Whips of the majority hold official posts either in the Treasury or the Royal Household, but their main function is the marshalling of party forces. At the time when the office was created, in the first half of the nineteenth century, the task was made easier by the profusion of posts, titles, decorations and patronage handed out. Today

83

the Chief Whip, with his assistants, under the direction of the Cabinet, draws up plans for the parliamentary session in consultation with the Whips of the other parties, prepares a timetable, forecasts possible Opposition tactics and allots tasks within his own party. He also has the task of smoothing out differences between the leaders of the various shades of opinion within the party. Most important of all, he has to marshal his troops so that in the event of a division there will at all times be a sufficient number present to ensure a majority. In short, he plays the part of an energetic and tactful liaison officer between the Government and the back-benchers, explaining points of procedure, passing on instructions, and at the same time keeping an ear cocked to gauge the trend of public opinion. The Opposition Whip has similar duties to perform, but he is more concerned with his extra-parliamentary activities, i.e. preparing for victory at the next elections. The office of Whip is a purely British institution; it is found in Ceylon and Ireland and as far as one can see in all Commonwealth countries which have based their Parliaments on those of the United Kingdom.

In the United States the power of the Whips is very much more restricted. All that is expected of them is to see to it that members are present when their party needs them. In other words, the Whips perform duties which in other Parliaments devolve upon the party officers, generally a chairman and a number of secretaries. These officers are responsible for calling meetings and for promoting consistency in the political and legislative activity of the party members. The latter may also have an administrative secretariat which with very few exceptions (Ceylon, the Netherlands, Norway and Turkey) is independent of the parliamentary staff, owing to the principle of neutrality that governs the official employee. Generally speaking, Parliament provides political groups with the necessary material facilities only—places for their meetings and office accommodation.

On the whole it may be said that the internal organization of political groups is extremely flexible, reflecting the nature of the function they perform. This function cannot be defined exactly; it is difficult to describe with precision a type of activity which is mainly political and consists of the assessment of measures necessary to the carrying on of responsible government, and playing a vital role in moments of crisis. As far as parliamentary procedure is concerned, political parties are rarely mentioned, though in actual fact their activity is considerable. They keep an eye on important issues; study parliamentary Bills before they come up for debate in committee or in the House, and decide which of their members shall speak on behalf of the whole group when a particular Bill comes up for debate. Sometimes this decision gives the group representatives the right to speak first in the debate, as for example in the Federal Republic of Germany, and Turkey. Other members may, of course, express their personal views and record their disagreement by voting contrary to the line taken by the group. Few groups are so well integrated that their discipline is perfect. This is only achieved where the members are entirely under the control of the party; and while it may not be consonant with the principle of national representation, it nevertheless indicates the present-day trend in parliamentary practice.

Parliamentary standing orders sometimes recognize the existence of political groups, if only to ensure that they are fairly represented in the most important parliamentary bodies: (i) the Bureau in France and the Federal Republic of Germany; (ii) the body responsible for drawing up the order of business: the Chairmen's Conference in France, the Steering Committee in Indonesia, the House Management Committee in Japan, the Council of Elders in Poland, and the Order of Business Board in the Republic of Vietnam (in Pakistan, Switzerland and the United States, there is direct consultation between the President and the political groups); and (iii) Committees—in the great majority of Parliaments the composition of committees is based on the principle of proportional representation, and all political groupings are represented in proportion to their numbers. It may be noted that in the organization of debates in Ceylon, France, Israel, Japan and the Netherlands, the speaking-time allotted to each group also depends upon its size.

The time would seem to have passed when political groups were in theory not recognized. The combined importance in politics of the groups in Parliament and the parties in the country as a whole is such that today it is impossible to leave them out of account. Furthermore since in large Parliaments it is easier to discuss the many day-to-day problems with the representatives of groups rather than with each individual member, there is a growing tendency towards cohesion and consolidation of the groups. Whether this is in itself a good thing or not will depend upon what the purpose of a seat in Parliament is considered to be—individual action involving individual conscience only, or organized, disciplined, collective action. In any case, individual initiative is no longer a workable policy today, in the political field or anywhere else. And in an era of mass opinion, political groups have a fundamental task to perform, by acting within Parliament as a permanent link between the Government and public opinion.

6. COMMITTEES

Unlike political groups, committees are provided for by the standing orders of all Parliaments. They meet a practical need: the House as a whole is an unwieldy body, too cumbersome to deliberate efficiently on all the problems put before it, unless these have already been given preliminary consideration. But the division of labour, the principle underlying specialization, must not be used by the committee as a pretext for taking to itself powers which properly belong to the House itself, and thereby substituting itself for Parliament, even in a small way.

However, pressure of circumstances, which has become more and more marked as the necessity to remedy abuses or to confer new benefits has required more and more parliamentary interference, has led to the steady development of parliamentary committees until today it is the backbone of parliamentary work. The British House of Commons for a long time did not follow the general trend, for it resorted to the device of laying aside the more stringent rules of debate and sitting as a 'Committee of the Whole House'. This committee is simply and solely a working body, comprising all the members of the House who wish to take part, under the chairmanship of the 'Chairman of Ways and Means'. The Speaker is not present (a vestige of the days when his duty was to the Crown and his taking the chair might be awkward if delicate questions were being discussed by the Commons). In spite of the growth of standing committees, which were found necessary towards the end of the nineteenth century owing to the increased amount, complex character and more and more technical nature of the legislation to be enacted, the Committee of the Whole House is today an essential part of British parliamentary practice. This committee regularly examines major issues, in particular those relating to expenditure and taxation, and in other matters lays down the main financial conditions by which the individual committees set up to consider matters of detail are bound. The Committee of the Whole House has, however, no final power of decision and the House itself remains the sole authority. Because of this machinery, any piece of business has to follow a complex procedure involving a large number of successive stages originally designed to obviate hasty decisions advocated by the Government. Today, though it is an anachronism, since the House has become the sole authority for disposing of its agenda, the system continues to give satisfactory results expecially in allowing every Member of Parliament to participate in the discussion of problems of a general nature which it would not seem right to hand over for study to a few members.

The fact that this system works satisfactorily has caused it to be adopted in its general lines by a number of countries such as Ireland, Ceylon and Pakistan. It is also found in the Parliaments of Denmark and Iceland, though it is seldom used. In principle, it still reflects the notion that committees are subsidiaries of the Chamber itself, and that both their powers and their terms of reference must be circumscribed.

This same notion is inherent in the so-called 'section' system, whereby the House as a whole remains the only deliberative body, but for convenience of debate it is divided into a number of sections, sometimes drawn by lot, which study one particular problem simultaneously. Thus all Members of Parliament theoretically take part in the debates on the same topics, which makes the system very similar to that of the Committee of the Whole House. In theory this system applies in Belgium, where the Chamber can be divided into five sections; but in fact it is very rarely used. The only countries where it still has some practical application are Luxembourg and the Netherlands, especially in the First Chamber. There incidentally it gives rise to a somewhat complex procedure—each of the five sections appoints rapporteurs, and these form a body known as the Committee of Rapporteurs, which alone is entitled to submit conclusions to the House. Occasionally large-scale Bills are also handed over for further study to a 'preparatory committee', which makes a conspectus of the discussions which have taken place in its own meetings and in the various sections.

Because of its ponderousness, this procedure is tending to fall into disuse. It makes almost impossible demands on Members of Parliament, who are expected to have a hand in everything that is going on. Moreover, the method of drawing the names by lot for the setting-up of the sections has the effect of giving them more often than not a different political balance from that of the House as a whole, which is bound to impair the value of the section as a deliberative body. Hence there has been a growing tendency away from the purely arithmetical division and in favour of a division of labour based on the special qualifications, knowledge, and even the likes and dislikes of individual members. It is after all on the face of it more reasonable, and certainly better policy, to leave nothing to chance and to employ each Member of Parliament where his services can be most useful, at the same time making due allowance for the relative strength of the various shades of political opinion, and thus improving the legislative output, which will be in the hands of the majority, but with the minority acting as a check.

These are the various considerations that have led to the

committee system, as found nowadays in all Parliaments, even those which still operate on the principle of the Committee of the Whole House or use the section device. It has become the rule that no issue should be submitted to the House which has not been previously discussed in committee, i.e. by a body small enough to enable the work to be dispatched rapidly and more thoroughly.

An essential distinction must be made however between temporary or *ad hoc* committees and permanent committees. *Ad hoc* committees are set up to deal with a particular Bill and are wound up as soon as their deliberations are completed. There is for practical purposes no Parliament which applies this system exclusively. However, it is the regular method of drafting legislation in Denmark where, apart from certain special committees specified in the standing orders, all committees are *ad hoc*, and are dissolved as soon as the question referred to them for examination has been dealt with by the House as a whole. The same would appear to be the case in Burma, Ceylon, Iceland, and India, where most Bills are referred to committees set up specially, unless circumstances require that they should be considered in the Committee of the Whole House.

The so-called standing committees of the House of Commons are half-way between being permanent committees and *ad hoc* committees. They approximate to the permanent committee inasmuch as they are not restricted to the consideration of a single Bill. But with the exception of the 'Scottish standing committee', their terms of reference are not specialized; they consider any Bill allocated to them by the Speaker. Since they have no exclusive fields to work in, they are simply designated by the letters of the alphabet—A, B, C, D, and so on. At the same time, they recall the *ad hoc* type of committee by reason of the procedure governing their composition. They consist of a more or less permanent nucleus of twenty members, a further number up to thirty being added on the strength of special qualifications. This involves so much changing that it is difficult to give the word 'standing' anything like the sense of 'permanent'. In Ceylon, the number of members attached to a standing committee on a temporary basis may not be more than seven.

While keeping the name 'standing committees', several countries which have copied the British type of Parliament use a system of committees which is unlike their original model in that they are quite specific in their terms of reference. Thus in India we find 'standing committees' on Rules and Petitions, and in Ceylon a 'standing' House Committee, 'standing committees' of Standing Orders, Public Petitions, and Public Accounts; in Burma there are the Panel Chairmen, the Privileges Committee, and the Public

Accounts Committee. In all these cases, it would appear that the terms of reference of these 'standing committees' are restricted to two fields: the internal business of the House and Finance. In Great Britain, these duties come within the orbit of the 'select' committees, which are 'special' committees inasmuch as they deal with particular matters, though their practically automatic renewal at the beginning of each session gives them a quasi-permanence and makes them approximate to the Continental type.

To say the least, there is a certain amount of confusion in this matter, arising mainly from the fact that all these types of committee have evolved slowly as the practical need has arisen. When such bodies have been set up by the Parliaments of emergent states in imitation of British parliamentary practice, their complexity has often caused them to lose their original character.

The position is much more straightforward in countries where the system of permanent committees with specific terms of reference is used—which is incidentally the majority of countries. Committees are called permanent in so far as their members are appointed once and for all, irrespective of the work they have to do, for the duration of the session or of the Parliament. In most Parliaments the life of such committees is the length of the session but some Parliaments depart from this rule and make the life of the committee the same as that of Parliament. This is the case, for example, in the Federal German Bundestag, the Swiss Federal Assembly, the Austrian Nationalrat, the Belgian Parliament, the Israeli Knesset and the Japanese Diet. The long lifetime of the committee gives its members a chance to acquire real knowledge of their subject, but at the same time there is the danger of increasing its powers unduly, to the detriment of those of the House itself. In practice, there is little or no difference between lasting for the session and lasting for the Parliament, since the statutory renewal at the beginning of each session usually involves very few changes in the composition of committees. All it means is that changes of membership can be made, which may not be possible in the course of the session.

Committees are called 'special' where they are concerned with one particular branch of activity (finance, foreign affairs, social affairs, education, etc.) and are entrusted with the study of all Bills or other matters relating to that particular field. The degree of specialization differs according to the country. The most convenient system as far as the work of Parliament is concerned is where the terms of reference of the committees correspond with the responsibility of the various ministerial departments. This is roughly the position in the French National Assembly, with its nineteen

D* 89

major committees, and in the Japanese Diet and the Spanish Cortes, with sixteen each. In Norway there are thirteen, in the Italian Chamber eleven, and ten in Indonesia. The link between ministries and committees is not regarded as desirable either in the Federal German Bundestag, which has no less than thirty-eight permanent committees, in the United States, where the number varies with each Congress, but is regularly more than thirty, in Sweden where there are ten, or in Israel where there are nine. In the Egyptian Parliament there are twenty-five committees. In Finland there are five 'statutory' committees (constitutional law, laws, foreign affairs, finance, and banking) as well as so-called 'extraordinary committees' set up regularly to deal with economic, social and cultural affairs, and questions of communications and defence.

In the USSR and other Socialist states permanent committees are also to be found. In the Supreme Soviet of the USSR we find the following permanent committees: the Mandates Committee, the Legislative Proposals Committee, the Budget Committee and the Foreign Affairs Committee. In addition, an Economic Committee exists within the Soviet of Nationalities. These committees are elected by both Houses during the first session of each legislature. They are empowered to request ministers, commissions institutes and civil servants to supply documents and other material, together with reports on matters relevent to the committees' activities. Their right to hear such reports at their meetings is widely exercised by these committees, and this enables the Supreme Soviet to supervise the work of the bodies falling within its province. Members of the Supreme Soviet who are not committee members have the right to participate in the meetings but may not vote. The committees are responsible in their work to the House that elected them; when the House is not sitting they submit reports on their work to Presidents of their respective Houses. In the Rumanian Grand National Assembly and the Yugoslav Parliament however, the number of committees roughly corresponds to the number of major fields of public administration.

The Austrian National Council, which makes liberal use of the permanent committee system, gives special importance to one of them, the so-called Main Committee, whose function is not merely to deal with matters referred to it, but also to co-operate directly with the executive in the drafting of some Bills. It also elects a standing sub-committee whose practical function is to act as substitute for the National Council in its relations with the Government in the event of dissolution, or when the National Council is unable to meet. The powers of committees of this kind go far beyond the scope of legal drafting and are more akin to that of government control. A comparison between this procedure and that found in Italy, where committees have genuine legislative powers, and in France, where the committee tends to be transformed into a critic of government action, illustrates very clearly the naturaly tendency of permanent committees of the specialized kind to encroach upon the functions both of the House and of the executive.

There is no such danger in the 'standing committee' system as applied in Great Britain, owing to the fact that their centres of interest are widely dispersed, their powers are limited and their composition is fluid. They may be regarded simply as sections of the entire House, organized exclusively to relieve Parliament of part of its burden and to speed up work on legislation. That is the difference between the British system and the other committee systems. It is universally recognized that the British standing committees, even though their powers are limited, do a sound job; and they are certainly less open to criticism than permanent committees of the specialized kind. They might usefully be taken as a basis for any reforms, in cases where the need is felt most keenly. Actually, the way in which this kind of system works is hard to envisage outside the framework in which it was fashioned and brought to maturity, for the peculiar spirit underlying it, the political atmosphere in which it thrives, and above all the special nature of the relationship between legislative and executive, are not commonly found.

However, theoretically some flexibility can be given to the Continental type of permanent committee by the power to set up *ad hoc* committees which Parliaments have. Actually, in most cases this procedure is seldom used, since the area not covered by the permanent committees is very small. The second Federal German Diet appointed only two such committees, and the 84th American Congress five, and this would appear to be the maximum number ever reached in forms of government where the permanent committee is the rule. In the Netherlands, however, Bills presented by several ministers are remitted to *ad hoc* committees, with the result that such committees are resorted to fairly frequently.

The committee of inquiry is a special type of *ad hoc* committee. Its peculiar feature is the power of investigation granted to it in virtue of the resolution of the House which sets it up. Exceptional powers of this kind, which sometimes make the committee virtually a court of law, especially in its capacity to summon witnesses, explain both why such committees are temporary and, when all is said and done, uncommon, even though there is provision for them in most Parliaments, except in the Sudan, Sweden and Switzerland. An

91

inquiry does not always necessitate setting up a 'special committee', for powers of investigation may be given to existing committees. For example, in the Federal German Bundestag, while a committee of inquiry can be set up on a motion supported by one quarter of its members, the Constitution has vested permanent powers of investigation in the committee set up to watch over the rights of the Bundestag *vis-à-vis* the Federal Government and in the Defence Committee. In France, the United States and Japan, any committee can obtain such powers from Parliament without difficulty.

A further means of giving flexibility to the permanent committee system is the power in certain circumstances to meet jointly for the study of particular problems affecting two or more of them. But the application of this procedure is in actual fact very limited, first because the committee mainly concerned can always ask for an opinion from the other committees concerned, at any rate in Belgium, Egypt, Finland, France and Rumania, for example. Secondly, the system of referring complex problems to *ad hoc* or special committees, especially in countries where this is the usual practice, constitutes an excellent means of avoiding complicating the procedure, since committees sitting jointly are not generally empowered to take decisions. The only exceptions are Great Britain, Turkey (where however the express authorization of the Assembly is required), the United States Congress, and the National Council of Monaco.

Subject to what has been said above, there would not appear to be any major obstacle to joint meetings. Nevertheless, in Austria, Finland, Pakistan and Switzerland they are prohibited, if not formally, at any rate by established practice. In most Parliaments, there is nothing to prevent them taking place, but the need does not appear to have been felt. They have never been used in Burma, India, Spain or the Sudan, and they are quite exceptional in France, the Federal Republic of Germany, Laos, the Netherlands and Norway. Their usefulness is recognized in parliamentary practice only in a small number of countries—Indonesia, Israel, Luxembourg, the Philippines, Syria and the Republic of Vietnam; the only countries where they appear to be generally used are Albania, Bulgaria, Czechoslovakia and Poland. The list shows how exceptional is recourse to joint meetings of committees of the same House; Indeed, in so far as they constitute nothing more than fact-finding meetings, the question arises as to whether they serve any really useful purpose.

Bicameral Parliaments may need to set up joint committees of both Houses in order to function properly. Their characteristics will depend essentially on the terms of reference given to them. In

Parliaments which are bicameral in name only, joint committees, are inherent in the very nature of that form of government. Hence the thirteen committees of the Norwegian Storting are permanent joint committees, with the exception of the Protocol Committee, which comes under the Odelsting. The same applies to the Icelandic Althing, which regularly appoints three joint committees, and empowers the other eight committees of each House to sit jointly if they so desire. In Australia and Sweden, although the two Houses are more definitely separated, joint committees are the rule.

The usefulness of establishing permanent joint committees may be seen in certain Parliaments where they are used for the study of common problems of a purely parliamentary kind. This is regular practice in the Netherlands for the running of such services as are common to both Houses; it is also found in India and Japan for questions of parliamentary remuneration. In Ireland it applies to matters of catering, the library, and standing orders (private matters); in the Sudan to immunities and the library; and in Australia to standing orders, the library and printing.

In actual fact, the joint committee system is particularly valuable for the drafting of legislation. Its function in this case is to provide suitable machinery for making joint decisions in regard to legislation which has to be passed by both Houses. If there is disagreement between them, the appropriate committees meet and examine jointly the matters in dispute. This procedure is found in Great Britain, Burma, Ceylon and Japan. In India, joint committees can draw up a single report on certain types of Bill. In Ireland, the committees of the two Houses meet jointly to consider financial and private Bills; in the USSR, their terms of reference and their powers are fixed by the Supreme Soviet.

The problem of relations between the two Houses is dealt with in an unusual fashion in the Federal German Parliament. The Bundestag and the Bundesrat set up a 'permanent arbitration committee' consisting of eleven members of each House, its task being to prepare a compromise solution in the event of any dispute. A similar committee functions in the Austrian Parliament, but only for financial matters and cases where the Federal Government opposes a Bill approved by the Diet.

No such body is to be found anywhere else except in Brazil and Laos, and in the Philippines for constitutional reform. On the other hand, there are many bicameral Parliaments where, as in France, the only way in which committees can settle their disputes is by negotiations of an unofficial character conducted by some of their members, and in particular by their rapporteurs.

Joint committees may be set up for other matters as well as legislation, as they frequently are in the United Kingdom. There are also some in Italy, for example, to examine the working of the state issuing bank, the administration of public debt, the savings banks and provident funds, radio and television, customs, etc. In Switzerland there are two such committees, the 'Finance Committee' and the 'Alcohol Committee', and these are in fact permanent in character. Since the war, the French Parliament has had only one, which dealt with the simplification of regulations governing entry to the country.

Such is the very diverse nature of parliamentary committees. The vital role they play in parliamentary work makes the question of how their members are chosen a matter of particular importance. It should be pointed out in the first place that the law and standing orders seldom make it obligatory for Members of Parliament to take part in the work of committees. As a rule members are free to join, or to decline to join, bodies which may be regarded as mere working groups; but there are countries (Belgium, Egypt, Japan, Monaco, the Netherlands and Norway), where participation in the work of the committees is not a privilege but a duty. In Spain and Sweden this is not a formal obligation, but Members of Parliament are more or less required by established practice to undertake committee duties. In the Parliaments of Australia, Burma, Iceland, and Poland, the standing orders specify that members may not evade their committee duties once they have been nominated to serve on the committees. In practice, Members of Parliament attach such importance to committee membership that the real problem is not so much to make participation in committee work obligatory but rather, in the interests of a division of labour, to limit the number of committees to which anyone may belong. It is surely not a very wise policy to make demands on the interest and the ability of an individual member over too many different fields, or to establish definite privileges for the more influential, let alone to fail to take advantage of the contribution which each member could make. Moreover, the fact that the meetings of committees are frequently held simultaneously may make it physically impossible to take part in all of them. In most Parliaments, members may sit on several committees. There is a rule to the contrary in the House of Representatives of the United States and in the Burmese, Indonesian and Norwegian Parliaments; while in Egypt, Israel, France, Rumania, Turkey and Yugoslavia, and in the American Senate, members may not sit on more than two committees, or three in Syria and the Republic of Vietnam.

94

Bearing in mind what has been said above, there are three methods of nominating members to serve on committees:

(*a*) By the President or the Speaker.
(*b*) By a committee specially set up for the purpose.
(*c*) By the House itself.

However, these three methods actually amount to one only, its main feature being the part played by the political parties or groups, where they exist, except in the Spanish Cortes, where appointment is the responsibility of the President alone, and in Brazil, Burma (except for the Public Accounts Committee and the Special Committees), India and Japan, and partly in the Philippines as well, though the President or Speaker makes his choice in the light of the particulars furnished in advance by the party leaders. In the Netherlands, the Second Chamber has made a practice of leaving its President to deal with appointments. The President endeavours to fulfil this task with the utmost impartiality, taking into account the relative size and importance of the various groups and the special knowledge of particular members.

In a number of Parliaments, the appointment of committee members falls to one particular committee set up specially for the purpose. In the House of Commons, the Committee of Selection, which is itself a select committee, chooses the members of the standing committees, after consulting the party Whips. The same practice is followed in Ireland, Israel, the Sudan and Ceylon. In the Norwegian Storting, an election committee consisting of thirty-seven members fulfils the same function, as do the forty-five 'electors' in the Finnish Parliament. The procedure by which the members of committees are appointed by the Bureau is confined to Switzerland.

Generally speaking, appointments are made by the House itself, which as a rule does no more than ratify the choice made by the political groups. The composition of committees follows the same principle everywhere, namely proportional representation of party political views. Whatever the procedure used, this rule, sometimes embodied in standing orders and always respected in actual practice, makes the committees Parliaments in miniature, which are more suitable than the House itself for studying particular matters fully, and are able to reflect the preponderant weight of the majority and the check exercised by the minority. In the USSR and the People's Democracies the House takes into consideration the qualities and interests of members when nominating its committees. Similar regard is paid in other countries.

The concept of the committee as a faithful reproduction of the House itself may be upset in the event of some of its members being absent. To cope with this drawback, some Parliaments have instituted the 'alternate' system by which a number of alternates are chosen along with the titular members and sit on the committees in the event of the members proper being absent or unable to attend. The system would appear to be chiefly characteristic of the countries of Western Europe, since with the exception of Brazil it is not found anywhere except in Austria, Belgium, Finland, France, the Federal Republic of Germany, Luxembourg, the Netherlands and Sweden. It should further be noted that it is sometimes restricted to the more important committees or those which require a quorum in order to function, as for example in the Luxembourg Chamber and the French National Assembly. Nor is the number of alternates always the same as that of the titular members. In Finland it is only one third, in Belgium and in the Council of the Republic of France, half the number plus one. Mention must be made finally of the system in force in some Parliaments, by which a member of a committee is at liberty to ask one of his fellow-members to substitute for him at a particular meeting, without any official procedure being involved.

With the exception of these few devices enabling committees to keep their original complexion at crucial moments, the replacement of members of committees can only take place by the ordinary process of nomination, in spite of any delay this may cause. It may be considered desirable for committee members to take part in the actual work of committees, not only by voting when the occasion arises, but by following all the items through from beginning to end and making their personal contribution to the decisions reached.

This continuity of effort is always desirable and, at times, especially in conjunction with seniority, it can be grounds for nomination to the different committees. Privileges in regard to committee membership are never laid down officially, but they do arise naturally in practice, since political parties are bound when making up their nominations to committees to take into consideration the experience acquired by the senior members in certain specific fields. In fact this has become virtually the rule in the United States and the Philippines, as well as in Ceylon for the Committee of Selection and the Standing Orders Committee. In Great Britain, Members of Parliament of longer standing are given preference over others as members of committees. Seniority also plays an important role in Sweden, but here again, this is a natural development rather than the outcome of definite rules.

The question arises whether meeting in public, which is inherent in the functioning of representative government, should extend to the work of committees. It is a moot point. Those who are in favour of meeting in public argue that no aspect of parliamentary activity should be withheld from public knowledge; hence in the USSR, Albania, Bulgaria, and Yugoslavia, persons other than members are admitted to meetings of committees. The same is true in Brazil, Japan, the Philippines and the Sudan. In the United States Congress meetings are public more often than not, but committees may decide to hold them in private, especially in the case of confidential hearings of witnesses or when votes are to be taken. In the House of Commons, the practice of meeting in public of the Committee of the Whole House extends to the standing committees which are simply an outcrop of it. On the other hand, select committees are at liberty to decide not to hold their meetings in public, and they frequently exercise the right.

Those who are against meeting in public point out that the work of committees is provisional in character, and should not commit any of the members taking part. It is for the House as a whole to take the final decisions, and to do so publicly. Moreover, the way in which an individual behaves in private is not the same as it is in public. Frankness and mutual trust are affected by the presence of an audience, and there is no doubt that off-the-record discussions tend to prevent playing to the gallery, encourage a spirit of compromise, and make for quicker and more satisfactory results.

These arguments would appear to have been given weight in most Parliaments, and strangers are not allowed to attend the meetings of committees. This does not mean that the work is necessarily kept secret. In fact, as a general rule a certain amount of publicity is given in the form of short Press releases. The fact that certain standing orders authorize the members of a Parliament to attend the meetings of committees to which they do not belong does not imply that their debates are made matters of public knowledge. The right to attend meetings but not to participate in the debates exists in a large number of Parliaments—in Austria, Egypt, the Federal Republic of Germany, the United Kingdom, India, the Philippines, Syria and the Republic of Vietnam, as well as in the Italian and Belgian Senates. In Finland it is restricted to the meetings of the 'Grand Committee'. In the Netherlands, however, the members of the Second Chamber may not only attend but also take an active part in the meetings of committees to which they do not belong when those meetings are being held to examine a Bill. This is not so in the case of meetings devoted to other work, such as the hearing of ministers, etc. In any event, only committee members have the right to vote in their respective committees.

In the People's Democracies and the USSR, any Member of Parliament has the right to take part in committee discussions in an advisory capacity. The position is the same in Brazil, Japan, Laos, Monaco, Turkey and the United States. In the Parliaments of other countries—France, the Federal Republic of Germany, Israel, Luxembourg, Norway and Spain for example, as well as in the Belgian House of Representatives—Members of Parliament who are not members of a particular committee may attend its meetings only as listeners or in an advisory capacity when Bills are being discussed. In Ireland, the permission or express request of the committee is necessary before any non-member of the committee may attend its deliberations, irrespective of whether he wishes to proffer advice or merely wishes to hear what is said.

Like the assembly to which they belong, committees are subject to a directing authority in the conduct of their work. The officers of a committee comprise first of all a chairman, usually assisted by the vice-chairman, and sometimes secretaries. In some Parliaments, this directing body also includes a permanent rapporteur, as in Turkey, Syria and Egypt, who acts as a kind of mouthpiece for the committee in regard to all legislative matters. In the French Parliament, the general rapporteurs of the Finance Committees perform a somewhat similar function. But apart from the Polish committees, which are headed by a Presidium, the main figure is as a rule the chairman of the committee, though the standing orders usually have nothing to say on the question of the extent of his powers. It is safe to say, however, that they are more or less the same in all Parliaments, i.e. as far as the handling of the debates is concerned, they correspond, *mutatis mutandis*, to those of the President in the House. The chairmen of committees have no disciplinary powers, except in the case of Committees of the Whole House in the British Parliament or those modelled on it; but they nevertheless perform an important political function, first by their work on the committee, and secondly because they frequently take part in the work of certain parliamentary bodies such as the Speaker's Council in Finland, or the Conference of Presidents in France, designed chiefly for the drafting of the order of business.

By virtue of the democratic rule, it would seem reasonable that only the chairmen of committees, like the President of the House, should be elected to office, and this is in fact what usually happens. Election may be the privilege of the Chamber itself, as in the USSR, Albania, Bulgaria, Laos and the Republic of Vietnam. The same rule is followed in Pakistan and the Sudan (for select committees) and there is a similar provision in Ireland and Japan, although in Japan the President himself makes the appointment.

The United States Congress in electing chairmen takes particular account of seniority, and for practical purposes this is the decisive qualification. But the general rule is that the committee elects its own chairman. This is true of most Parliaments including those of Czechoslovakia Rumania and Yugoslavia, as well as those of Australia and Ireland, although these countries belong to a family which tends to fight shy of the election procedure in favour of other systems which put greater stress on technical ability than on purely political considerations, on the principle that committees are technical bodies set up for the convenience of the House, and that political strife and personal rivalry are out of place there.

This principle is found regularly in Parliaments of the British type, which find it preferable to give the Speaker a fairly free hand in the nomination of persons to direct the work of committees. He has the exclusive responsibility in India and the Sudan. But the complexity of the British committee system is evident here too. We find, for example, a curious institution known as the Chairmen's Panel, consisting of a list of names from which the Speaker chooses chairmen as they are needed. This system ordinarily applies to the standing committees, and is followed in Burma, Ceylon and the United Kingdom. In the House of Commons, the Committee of Selection plays a similar part in regard to the chairmanship of committees on opposed private Bills. A parallel to this is found in the Bureau of the Swiss Federal Assembly, except for the Finance Committee which selects its chairman itself.

The *ex officio* chairmanship of committees is another peculiarity of the parliamentary system based on the British model. As we have already seen, in the House of Commons, the Committee of the Whole House is presided over by the Chairman of Ways and Means, who is also in charge of the work of the Standing Orders Committee and the procedure on Private Bills. In India, if the Deputy Speaker is a member of a committee, he always takes the chair. The same applies to the President of the Senate in Australia, and he also presides *ex officio* over the three committees of the House, which deal with its internal matters.

The *ex officio* chairmanship of committees is the general rule in the Belgian Parliament. The President of the House, or a Vice-President delegated by him, directs the business of the permanent committees and has no right to speak or vote. The idea behind this is to keep the actual direction of all parliamentary work in the hands of the Bureau of the House and to make quite certain that committees do not enjoy too great a measure of independence especially in the matter of control of the executive.

The various procedures which take away from the committees the right to choose their chairmen themselves have the effect of preventing the majority party from automatically monopolizing all the chairmanships of committees. The preponderance given to the majority groups by the proportional rule would inevitably lead to a monopoly if some curb were not put upon it, either by a simple unofficial agreement between the political groups, as happens in Finland, France, the Netherlands and Sweden, or the recommendation of a superior body like the Knesset Committee in Israel, or the application of cut-and-dried rules, as in the Federal Republic of Germany, where prior to the election of committee chairmen the Council of Elders lays down the strict proportions to which the committees must conform. There is a similar system in the Polish Parliament, although party opposition in this case does not have the same importance as in the Western-type of democracy. Furthermore, the allocation of chairmanships between majority and minority obviously does not apply in Parliaments where the concept of majority and minority has no meaning—in the USSR and the People's Democracies, Egypt, and Monaco. It is also true of Spain. Conversely, where this concept constitutes the very basis of the way in which the system functions, the logical conclusion is for the majority to hold the reins in all committees. The most striking examples of this are the United States Congress together with the Parliament of the Philippines. The situation is similar in most of the Western democracies, subject to the modifications already referred to, deriving from institutions like the Chairmen's Panel in the British type of Parliament, which ensure that the Opposition is fairly represented. In the Japanese Diet, likewise, the President endeavours to bear the rights of the Opposition in mind. There are also traditional exceptions, like the Public Accounts Committee in the House of Commons, where the chairmanship is invariably given to a member of the Opposition.

Apart from these few cases, the allocation of chairmanships among the various parliamentary groups certainly does not appear to follow definite rules. The powers of a chairman are too important for the majority party to be readily prepared to hand over any chairmanships to the Opposition. But in the final analysis, parliamentary systems still rest on certain conventions tacitly accepted by all, and the concessions made to the Opposition constitute one such convention. As regards the composition of committees, the convention is applied almost one hundred per cent but the same cannot be said of the chairmanships. Nevertheless, it would be fair to say that the majority and the minority, or Government and Opposition, which taken together constitute the nation, often find it possible to work together to promote the better working of Parliament.

Once they are set up, with a chairman at their head, committees operate according to a variety of methods which obviously cannot be examined in detail in a work like this. What would make the task unusually difficult is the fact that the rules of procedure of individual committees are seldom laid down precisely. Generally speaking, in practically all Parliaments these rules are based on the corresponding rules governing debates in the House itself, though they are less formal, since, if committee work is to be fruitful, it must be sufficiently flexible to allow of constant interplay between the various points of view—a flexibility its limited membership is designed to give. Disputes are rare, and are generally settled by common agreement. There are, however, a few special rules concerning such matters as the order of speakers or the quorum required for meetings and especially for voting; but these rules constitute mere exceptions, or departures from the general provisions governing debates in the House. The parallel between procedure in committee and procedure in the House is not impaired by the fact that in some Parliaments, those of Belgium, Israel, Spain, Switzerland and Syria, for example, there are special orders governing procedure in committee, or by the fact that in most countries committees are the sole authorities for the organization of their own business. In law and in practice, the procedure copies that of the House under both systems.

Thus in the French Parliament or wherever committees are organized on similar principles, debate is divided into general consideration followed by consideration paragraph by paragraph of the report drafted by the rapporteurs. In the committees of the House of Commons, on the other hand, there is no general debate on the principles of Bills; these are laid down by the House itself, and the task of the committee is to examine the clauses within the principles already established.

Whatever the system, all the deliberations at the committee stage logically culminate in the preparation of a report designed to bring to the notice of the House the opinions and findings of the committee. In French-influenced Parliaments, a report on each item is drawn up by a member chosen by the committee from among the majority for or against the Bill under discussion—not necessarily the same as the government majority. In some Parliaments the rapporteur is one of the officers of the committee, and is appointed once and for all as mouthpiece for the committee's views. This is the case in Egypt, Syria, Turkey, and in the Finance Committee in the French National Assembly.

Questions which are agreed in committee are invariably introduced in the House by means of a report; but some Parliaments (India, Pakistan, Ireland, and the Australian Senate) do not appoint a rapporteur; instead they follow in this matter the current practice of the House of Commons, where the chairman of each committee submits a draft report which is generally accepted as a basis for the committee's report. In the Knesset in Israel, we again find the chairman of the committee in principle responsible for drawing up the report, except where he belongs to the minority party, in which case a member of the majority party may replace him as rapporteur. Similarly, in the American Congress, it is the chairman who presents the report to the House. In the Netherlands, however, the report is drawn up by the Clerk or one of his assistants under supervision by the committee which must approve each item before it is submitted to the Chamber.

There is one final question concerning the conduct of business in committee—whether committees are bound by the rules applying to sittings of Parliament as a whole. As a general rule they are not, since the flexibility characteristic of working methods of committees extends to their timetable. However, some Parliaments which believe strongly in the notion of restricting the powers of committees and keeping a tight rein on them, do not allow them to sit when the House is not sitting. This is true, for example, of Belgium, Burma, Ceylon, the United Kingdom, Indonesia, Iceland, Luxembourg and Syria. But even in these countries, there are ways round the prohibition. In Burma, for example, it applies only to Bill committees and not to the Public Accounts Committee and select committees. In Iceland a similar system holds good. In Great Britain, committees may meet with the authorization of the House, in Norway subject to that of the Presidency, and in Israel at the request of the Government or of one third of the members of the committee.

There is no doubt that since committees are designed to prepare legislation, it may be better to allow them to sit whenever they like, if necessary notwithstanding the adjournment of the House. The advantage of this is that it spreads the work demanded of committee members over a longer period and gets rid of items cluttering up the sessional programmes, at the same time making it possible to give problems a more thorough study in an atmosphere free from the haste which short sessions are likely to entail. On the other hand, the system has the inherent danger, already pointed out, that the committees may take advantage of the free hand given them and gradually usurp the powers of the House.

The committee system has two essential characteristics: in the first place, it fulfils a vital need, which has made itself felt everywhere owing to the increase in the amount of parliamentary business; and secondly, it is governed by flexible rules in keeping with its purpose, which is to render services of a technical rather than a political kind. But the need for committees and the latitude given to them must be duly circumscribed. The sovereignty of Parliament is indivisible. It forms a complete entity upon which committees must not seek to encroach. The organizational freedom which they now enjoy must not develop into independent action. The function of the committee, important and effective though it is, must be exercised with sufficient discretion to ensure that it does not embark on activities which are really the prerogative of Parliament itself.

IV

Sittings of Parliament

The Chamber—The Parliamentary Timetable

In spite of a certain similarity in organization and structure, all Parliaments, whatever the form of government of the country, have their own individuality, and the peculiarities of each are seen most clearly in their sittings. This suggests two questions, and the answers to them may be very helpful in determining the essential features of any given Parliament: where does Parliament sit, and when does it sit?

1. THE CHAMBER

The connexion between the shape and arrangement of the Chamber of the House and the form of government of a country may seem very slight. After all, the architecture of the Chamber is frequently a matter of historical circumstance, and it may be pure chance that has made it the home of a Parliament. But it is not always a mere legacy from the past. It may also reflect a state of mind, a particular outlook, or an unusual political situation. The most important question is how the seating is arranged within the Chamber, since this may not necessarily correspond to the shape of the Chamber itself. For

103

example, in the Federal Republic of Germany, Monaco, Ireland (Seanad) and Switzerland (States Council) the Chamber is rectangular but the seats are arranged in a semi-circle.

The seating arrangement most commonly found is semi-circular. The members' seats are spread out fan-wise, facing the President or Speaker. This allows the space allocated for seating to be split up into any number of segments which can expand or contract with the growth of the various political groupings. This arrangement is especially appropriate to multi-party systems, since it can show the political strength of the parties at any given moment, however fluid the groupings and relative numbers.

Apart from this, it has such practical advantages in the way of visibility and acoustics that it has been adopted by most Parliaments including those of Poland, Rumania and Yugoslavia. In the Parliaments of the other People's Democracies—Albania, Bulgaria and Czechoslovakia, and in the USSR, where political distinctions between the various groups have not the same importance as in the Western-type of parliamentary democracy, the seating arrangement is altogether different: the Chamber is rectangular and the seats are arranged in parallel rows facing the President and the rostrum. A similar arrangement is found in the Philippines, in Turkey and the Republic of Vietnam.

The Chamber where the British House of Commons sits is also rectangular, but it is divided down the middle, so that the two series of parallel benches face each other, on either side of the Speaker. This arrangement is admirably suited to the two-party system—or at any rate to a strict observance of the 'Government and Opposition' principle which can be applied even in the event of a number of 'splinter' parties arising. The example of the House of Commons has been followed in the Parliaments of Burma, Ceylon and the Sudan, and it is also found in Indonesia, and the Second Chamber of the States General in the Netherlands.

The natural tendency of members to form into groups according to their political leanings is reflected in the allocation of seats within the Chamber. But, in a number of countries, the seats are allocated on a different system—alphabetically, as in the Spanish Cortes, or by electoral constituency, the arrangement favoured in Czechoslovakia, Rumania and the USSR. In the Soviet Union the deputies sit by delegations, according to the particular Republic, Territory or Region they represent. Another system is to allow the members to choose their own places. This makes for a certain grouping by outlook or sympathies if not by political views. Albania, Bulgaria and Yugoslavia follow this practice.

Where there is a two-party system or a Government and Opposition, the practice is simply to divide the Chamber in two. In the House of Commons, the members of the Government party and the Opposition party face each other. No member has an individual seat assigned to him for the very good reason that there are only enough seats for about half the number of members but the arrangement is clear and straightforward, especially as the first two benches on either side are reserved for the leaders of either party, and the rest are for the back-benchers; those who sit in the rows below the 'gangway' are sometimes regarded as sitting there because of a difference in some political view from those of the majority of the party. Every Parliament has of course its traditions of this kind which in some cases give it its particular character.

Where the Chamber is semi-circular, the division between Government and Opposition does not raise appreciably more difficulties. It is noteworthy, incidentally, that as a general rule, except in Ireland, the Government parties sit to the right of the President and the Opposition to his left. But this idea of 'right' and 'left' has a very different meaning in Parliaments which carry on the tradition established by the first Constituent Assembly in France. The degree of 'progressiveness' of political ideas, as opposed to conservatism which occupied the right, was indicated by moving along the benches towards the left away from the President. This tradition has become so strong that it has taken on a symbolic meaning, so that the terms 'right' and 'left' are used today even in countries where the seating arrangement is not the same as in the French Parliament. Awkward problems arise at times when the seats are allotted after a general election, especially if most of the political groups insist on being regarded as more progessive than everyone else, and hence on sitting on the left.

This veering towards the left, of course, adds yet another to the many factors tending to keep political groups apart and illustrates how the identification of political thought and relative position in a semi-circular Chamber may entail the risk of excessive compartmentalism. An attempt has been made in some countries to offset the effects of this either by breaking up the political groupings or by not permitting any physical manifestation of the idea of 'right' and 'left' in the Chamber. In the First Chamber of the Netherlands Parliament, the members are seated in alphabetical order. In Laos, Norway and Sweden, there is also a splitting up of political groups: members sit in the alphabetical order of their constituencies. In the Philippines, places are drawn by lot. The Japanese Diet and the Knesset in Israel have adopted systems of their own based on the number of members in each group. In the Knesset, the political groupings are placed in descending order of size, from left to right. In Japan, the largest party occupies the centre of the Chamber, and the other parties are located on either side in order of size. In the Netherlands Second Chamber, the terms 'left' and 'right' have a very special meaning. The members continue to arrange themselves according to their political affiliations, but the parties based on religious principles (the Catholic and Protestant Parties) sit on the President's right and all the rest (Labour, Liberal, Communist) on his left. In the Swiss National Council, the language question plays a part in the allocation of seats. As a general rule, the French and Italian-speaking members sit on the left, and the German-speakers on the right.

The few examples show clearly how far the outward appearance of a House may depend on the way in which the members are seated; indeed, the seating arrangement may be a factor in accentuating or weakening the crystallization of various political groupings. But the outward appearance of the House is affected to an even greater degree by the length of time for which it sits.

2. THE PARLIAMENTARY TIMETABLE

Should the independence of Parliament as determined above give it the option of deciding for itself how and when sittings should take place and how long it should continue in session? Or should the authorization to sit be laid down by some other authority? The question is pertinent, since the answer to it largely determines the function of Parliament and its influence on the government of the country.

It is important first and foremost in discussing the meetings of Parliament to define carefully the terms used: the sitting is the actual coming together of the representatives on a given day for discussion; the session is the period during the year (there may be more than one and the length may vary) when Parliament has the legal right to meet and to transact its business. Thus the sitting takes place within the session. In most cases, Parliament itself is responsible for arranging its sittings within the period of the parliamentary session. Hence the only problem is the session, that is to say, the legal principles on which it is based, and its duration.

The way in which this problem is tackled derives from one or other of two contradictory constitutional traditions: the so-called 'monarchist' or authoritarian tendency to curb the action of

Parliament by making the frequency and length of the sessions a matter for the Government to decide; and the democratic or republican tendency to vindicate the sovereignty of Parliament, jealously guarding their independence and giving them a free hand to choose the time for holding their meetings.

This is what is sometimes called the 'permanent assembly' system. It would be more appropriate to describe it as the permanent session system, since it implies not so much uninterrupted sitting as the uninterrupted power to sit. In actual fact, legally speaking, there are no sessions of either House of Parliament; there are only sessions of Parliament. Thus throughout the existence of any legislature, its Houses are at liberty to sit and transact business as and when they see fit. Theoretically it is in session all the time. This is the system in force in the Federal German Bundestag which, except for the recess it allows itself in summer and a few public holidays, is in permanent session in a three-week cycle—two weeks of sittings and one week with no sitting.

The permanent assembly system, which strictly speaking does not recognize the existence of sessions, may nevertheless find them convenient, provided they open on a specified date and their closing date is determined simply and solely by the opening of the following year's session. In Denmark, under constitutional law the Folketing convenes each year on the first Tuesday of October, the first day of the parliamentary year. Officially it remains in session throughout the entire year, even though ordinarily it does not meet at all during most of the summer. In Norway, Parliament begins its annual session on the first week-day after 10 January and may continue to sit, if it so desires, until the end of December. In the Netherlands, the session lasts in practice from the third Tuesday in September till the Saturday preceding the third Tuesday in September of the following year. Each House decides of its own accord on what days it will sit during that period. Neither House appears to take unfair advantage of its permanent character—the First Chamber sits on an average forty-five days a year, and the Second Chamber ninety days.

Thus, provided there is no likelihood of abusing the system, the practice of permanent session enables Parliament to devote as much time as it chooses to the effective performance of its duties, and ensures that its work remains independent of the executive. But a danger arises when it puts no limit on its sittings. A Parliament which sits permanently is likely to be muddle-headed and over-excited, and party bickering is rife. Permanence fans the flames of artificial feuds which do not necessarily reflect the country's real feelings; antagonisms are aggravated and embittered: what is still worse in a

107

parliamentary system, it almost inevitably succeeds in hamstringing the Government by a constant series of motions of censure on trivial matters which leave no time for administration. Government action gives way to political tourneys, with unfortunate consequences for ministerial stability, unless precautions are taken, as in the Federal Republic of Germany, to prevent constant resignations of the Government.

At the other end of the scale from the permanent session we get the system whereby the sessions are fixed by the executive. This system is monarchical in origin, and the underlying principle is that the assemblies need not be summoned on a permanent basis in order to transact their legislative business and that it might do more harm than good to prolong their term beyond the time needed. Where this system is applied in its pure and unadulterated form, the King, or in a general way the executive, summons Parliament and brings the session to an end. This idea is hardly compatible with the parliamentary principle whereby Parliament is supposed to control the Government and must be free to do so without the Government's permission. Nevertheless, theoretically this is the system in force in Britain. The summoning and dissolution of Parliament are sovereign acts pertaining to the Crown. The only condition laid down in any act of Parliament is that a new Parliament must be summoned within three years of the dissolution of the previous one.

In practice, the necessity for voting the estimates for renewing each year the authorization to maintain a standing army and to prolong each year the Army Act—the statute ensuring the discipline of military personnel—very early placed the sessions of the British Parliament on a regular footing. But just as there is no written stipulation as to holding sessions, so there is none regulating their maximum length. For example, the session which began on 11 November 1914 lasted until 27 January 1916. It might be said that the British system, in theory of a very cut-and-dried type, is complerely devoid of rules and regulations. For all that, the British Parliament does normally hold a session each year from October or November to the end of July.

Between the permanent session at the one end of the scale and the session fixed by the executive at the other, there is room for any number of systems which attempt to strike a balance between completely contradictory ideas; the principle of the sovereignty of Parliament and the exigencies of practical government, parliamentary control and the freedom of the executive. One method is to lay down, irrespective of any action by either the executive or Parliament itself, certain periods when Parliament can sit and transact its business.

In many countries the Constitution specifies the date of the opening of the session and its length. Thus in the United States, Belgium, Brazil, Egypt, France, the Philippines and Sweden, Parliament meets by law on a fixed date. Prorogation may be either on a date laid down by law (in Sweden the spring session must end by 31 May, in the United States by 31 July, and in the Philippines the session may not last more than a hundred days); or again it may come about by executive decree, after a specific lapse of time, e.g. seven months in France, forty days in Belgium, etc. In Finland, the Diet Act provides that Parliament must meet each year on the first week-day of February and end its session 120 days later. The Dutch Constitution provides for the opening of Parliament by the Queen on the third Tuesday of September. Bulgaria has an interesting feature—if the President does not summon Parliament on the stipulated dates (1 November and 1 February), it can meet on its own initiative.

The difference between this system and the preceding one is that Parliament has not the right to sit continually, but it has the right to meet automatically for a minimum term. This safeguard is not so reliable where the meetings, though laid down in the Constitution or by law, are not convened automatically, but where Parliament is summoned, as a rule by the Crown or the executive. This is the system applied in most of the countries which at one time or another have been under British influence. Apart from the United Kingdom, where nothing is written down, the constitutions of these countries require the sovereign or the Government to summon Parliament at least once a year. The virtue of this system is its flexibility as compared with the rigid system of sessions convened automatically—which may coincide with 'slack periods'. It allows for adaptation of the arrangement of the sessions to fit in with the requirements of parliamentary business. But where the executive, though responsible for fixing a date for opening the sessions, is not subject to any penalty for failure to do so, the proper working of the Parliament may be jeopardized.

Neither sessions fixed by law nor imposed sessions, as we have seen, cover an entire year, so that there are long periods while Parliament is in recess, during which events may occur of sufficient gravity to warrant recalling Parliament. To cater for this eventuality, most constitutions allow for the possibility of emergency sittings. These may be summoned by the executive—the most frequent procedure, and the most rational, since the Government is in the best position to judge whether an emergency sitting is needed. It cannot be refused this right, since it is indissolubly bound up with the efficient functioning of Parliament. But the real problem is how far Parliament itself should be at liberty to call for an emergency sitting without incurring the drawbacks of the permanent assembly system. Many constitutions have a saving clause of this kind, with fairly strict conditions, e.g. a request by at least half the members as in Egypt, Finland, France, Laos, Norway, Poland, Sweden and the Republic of Vietnam. Some countries are less exacting, and the executive is under constant threat from a third of the Members of Parliament in Bulgaria, the Federal Republic of Germany and Rumania, a quarter in Austria, Japan and Syria, a fifth in Turkey, or at the will of twenty-five members in Israel. The Supreme Soviet of the USSR can be convened for an emergency meeting by the Praesidium, acting on its own initiative, or at the request of a single Republic of the Union. In practice Parliament seldom takes the initiative in regard to the session, particularly as where it can do so, it usually holds fairly long sessions anyway.

While the regulations governing parliamentary sessions are definitely important, the length of the sessions themselves is a good deal more important. It is easily the most revealing indication of the relative importance of Parliament in any country. There is often a wide discrepancy between the letter of the law and what actually happens, as in Great Britain, where we saw that Parliament sits for a lengthy period each year, though there is no written statute requiring it to do so.

The various systems can be divided into three categories according to the length of their parliamentary sessions. Generally speaking, in the older European democracies, Parliament is in session for at least half the year—which means roughly, if we allow for the long summer recess and public holidays, that Parliament is more or less permanently in session. This is true of Austria, Belgium, France, Ireland, the Netherlands, Sweden and the United Kingdom. Outside Europe the practice is much the same in Australia, Brazil, Egypt, Iceland, Israel, and the United States, while Parliament in Japan, Laos and the Republic of Vietnam has five to six-month sessions. The sessions are distinctly shorter in small countries such as Switzerland, as also in former British Dominions like Burma, India and the Sudan, where the session is about three months. Finland and the Philippines have much the same system. The third category covers the USSR and the countries of Eastern Europe, where the sessions of Parliament are very short. But the technical work devolving upon these Parliaments is done in the main by their committees, which sit more frequently.

This aspect of parliamentary practice shows how far such activities can vary according to the nature of the session. In most Parliaments these activities are performed in three main directions: legislation, Budget, and Government control, each of which will be discussed in the three succeeding sections.

Part Two

THE LEGISLATIVE FUNCTION
OF PARLIAMENT

E

THE LEGISLATIVE FUNCTION
OF PARLIAMENT

The essential function of Parliament is to make laws. This generalization arises from a confused notion of what the democratic tradition ought to be and from an academic approach, rather than a practical one; for in practice, the boundary lines defining the spheres of action of the different state bodies are not always clearly drawn.

Since the seventeenth century, writers on the subject have attempted, one after another, to delimit precisely the field of action of the various bodies by drawing up a classification of the functions of the State. Thus a theory has been evolved—the so-called 'separation of powers' which takes the delimitation of functions as the starting point for establishing the constitutional structure of democracies. No theory has been more readily accepted than that of the division of the sum total of a state's authority into three spheres—legislative, executive and judicial. Even today this division serves as a framework for many constitutions and treatises on law.

Of the three spheres, the legislative is without question the most important, since it consists in promulgating general, impersonal rules of law. It lays down basic principles which the executive has to apply and the judiciary has to use as its frame of reference. The legislative body thus takes precedence over the other two, since it defines the framework by which their action is circumscribed. In a democratic system, this legislative body is Parliament. It represents the sovereign people, and therefore it alone is competent to express the will of the people in the form of law.

Unfortunately, those who frame constitutions have seldom taken the trouble to analyse those components of the notion of 'law' which would help to pinpoint accurately the real object of legislative functions, and thus give a clear concept of the function of Parliament as opposed to, say, executive functions, which are the province of the Government.

In other words, the stubborn facts will not be bound by the rigid framework of a classification which is purely verbal, and the terminology only adds to the confusion, the terms 'legislative' or 'legislature', 'executive' and 'judicial' or 'judiciary' being applied indiscriminately to both the functions and the bodies which exercise the functions. Thus there is a temptation to regard the three bodies as each specializing in the exercise of one specific function—which is rarely the case. Legal decisions

115

have made it clear that one particular function can be shared by more than one of the three.

Occasionally, the three bodies are by-passed and the sovereign people finds itself entrusted with the task of making laws—or at any rate helping to make them—thus whittling away the monopoly enjoyed by Parliament in legislative matters. Examples of such methods of direct democratic rule, which are not easy to reconcile with the principles of representative systems, were common enough after the First World War, but are rare today. It is a well-known fact that this type of democratic rule is still found in Switzerland, particularly in respect of constitutional issues; but fewer people are aware that provision for the referendum procedure in such matters exists also in a number of other countries: Australia, Denmark, Egypt, France, Ireland, Italy, Japan, Spain and USSR.

Side by side with the constitutional referendum there is the legislative referendum, still more restricted in its use. For that reason, the criteria for recourse to the referendum are fairly stringent. In Switzerland, where it is resorted to more frequently than anywhere else, it requires a petition by 30,000 electors or eight cantonal governments. In Italy, it is used for the partial or complete repeal of an Act of Parliament where this is sought by 500,000 electors or five Regional Councils. In Denmark, it can only be instituted by the members of the Folketing. It can be moved for by one-third of the members and it constitutes the final appeal against an Act that has once been passed.

As a legislative procedure, the referendum has been decidedly on the decline in most Western democracies; but it has swung back into favour elsewhere. In Spain, the Head of State can decide that legislation shall be put to the popular vote on the grounds of its 'constitutional importance' or its 'public importance'. Several of the Socialist states also make provision for the use of the referendum in legislative matters. This is the case in Yugoslavia; and in the USSR, for example, popular consultation or referendum is possible on the initiative of the Presidium of the Supreme Soviet or at the request of a Union Republic. Similarly in Bulgaria, the Praesidium of the National Assembly can initiate this procedure. In Albania, a referendum may be held by resolution of the People's Assembly or at the Government's instigation. But though there is ample provision for it, the referendum is seldom used; there are no circumstances in which it is mandatory. Before the people can be called upon to express an opinion, the consent of some authority is invariably required, whether it is the Presidium, Parliament or the Government though the responsibility of that authority for general legislation may vary considerably. The law thus remains essentially the work of duly constituted authority. In general, it is Parliament that has the monopoly; in other words, a parliamentary decision is both necessary and sufficient for the final enactment of a law.

In the republican type of democracy, there is no question of this—the legislative operation is completed once Parliament has done its work. In Presidential systems of the United States type, however, the Head

116

of State has the power to veto legislative measures adopted by Congress, the idea being first of all to put a curb on any tendency to rashness on the part of Parliament and secondly to make the equality of powers effective. Congress still has the final say, since the veto is not absolute, and can be overridden by two thirds of the members of both Houses. In Finland too the President enjoys a right of veto similar to that of the President of the United States but with the difference that a general election must supervene, and the new Parliament must confirm its original vote with a simple majority in order to override the opposition by the Head of State. Somewhat analogous to this right of veto—though its effects are distinctly less marked and the motivation in principle purely formal—is the request for a second deliberation, whereby the Head of State requests Parliament to reconsider a Bill before it finally comes into effect. This procedure is used in France and the Republic of Vietnam particularly.

In democracies of the monarchy type, especially those of Northern Europe—Belgium, Denmark, Norway, the Netherlands and Sweden—the Sovereign theoretically participates along with Parliament in the act of legislating. In actual fact, though the Constitution may state that the function is exercised jointly by the King or Queen and Parliament, nowadays the part played by the Sovereign—Royal Assent—is in general a pure formality, even where it is stipulated that the assent must be given before a Bill can be regarded as on the Statute Book. In the Japanese and Laotian Constitutions there is no mention of the Emperor and the King respectively, in regard to legislative functions.

In the United Kingdom and the Commonwealth countries, legislation is exclusively the function of Parliament and is not shared with any of the other powers of the State. However, in accordance with a basic maxim of the English legal system, a law is not passed until the Royal Assent has been given. The apparent contradiction is not really a contradiction for, in virtue of an equally basic principle, the Sovereign is regarded as a constituent part of Parliament, as defined by Lord Coke in the seventeenth century:

> 'Parliament is the highest, the most honourable and the final Court of Justice in England. It is made up of the King, the Lords Temporal and Spiritual and "the Commons".'

The consent of the Crown is thus as necessary for the enactment of a law as the consent of Parliament. Hence in theory the Sovereign could stand in the way of a Bill becoming law. In practice, the evolution of the parliamentary system has made personal resistance on the part of the Monarch inconceivable.

In Spain we find a more significant part played by the Head of State. His powers in legislative matters combine with those of the Cortes. In the first place, he possesses the constitutional power to legislate on all matters not coming within the jurisdiction of the Cortes; but this power is extremely limited, since there are very few such matters. Secondly, laws passed by the Cortes only acquire binding force when assented to by the Head of State. This right of approbation—which is real and not a mere formality—is what marks most clearly the legislative power of the Head of State.

In the Socialist states, on the other hand, constitutional theory and practice deny the executive all right of veto, legislation being regarded as solely a matter for Parliament, and subject to these few reservations, Parliament in all countries has the sole responsibility for legislative decision.

What we have said above does not mean that this sole right of Parliament extends to every phase of the legislative process. Here, the succinct wording of constitutions fails to give a proper idea of the real powers of Parliament and the part it plays in the development of the various phases of the complex procedure which finally culminates in the passing of an Act: tabling the Bill, committee stage, passing by one or more Houses, coming into force and tests of whether it is constitutionally valid.

* * *

I

Introduction of Bills

The Power to initiate Legislation—Parliamentary Initiation of Legislation—The Message from the Head of the State—The Declining Trend in Initiation of Legislation by Members of Parliament

The initial phase of the legislative process is of course the introduction of a Bill, which means proposing a change in the existing legislation or the introduction of new legislation. It is what has been described as the first concept of what will ultimately become law. The power to take the step from which an Act of Parliament emerges and without which it would not exist is thus of the utmost importance. 'He who initiates legislation rules the land.'

Right from this stage, we find that the legislative monopoly of Parliament is encroached upon wholesale. Even if we except the type of system—hardly compatible with democratic government— where the executive has exclusive powers, comparative law makes it clear that the introduction of legislation is usually shared between the Government and Parliament. Indeed we may observe that this theoretical division of labour tends to give way to a system whereby the Government definitely takes the lead in the matter of introducing Bills. This is what we learn from the study of the actual right to initiate legislation, the various methods of exercising the right in Parliament, and the so-called 'message to Parliament' procedure found in some systems.

1. THE POWER TO INITIATE LEGISLATION

It is implicit in the concept of democracy that the initiative in law-making rests primarily within the elected Parliament. In fact, in all countries, Parliament is directly vested with the power to introduce legislation, though obviously it shares the right with the executive.

Since its function is to apply a given policy, a Government is better acquainted than anyone else with the needs of the country, and because of the more and more complex nature of the problems that have to be solved, it is technically better equipped than individual Members of Parliament to draft Bills which will be unexceptionable from the legal standpoint. Hence, in most countries, the Government has the right to introduce legislation, whether the ministers are Members of Parliament or not. Where they are, it can

119

be argued that Parliament has the exclusive right to initiate legislation.

In countries where there is strict separation of powers, as in the United States, the Government does not possess the right to introduce legislation and the Members of Congress alone have the right of formally initiating Bills. But this does not mean that the executive is altogether without powers in the legislative field; it can recommend Congress to examine any measures it thinks fit. In actual practice the exercise of this right amounts to initiating legislation, for in fact the President does not merely outline the general gist of legislation he would like to see enacted; he sends to Congress a complete draft. The only difference between this and formal initiation of legislation is that the draft has to be sponsored by a Member of Congress.

This universally recognized right of Parliament to initiate legislation raises a special problem in connexion with the bicameral Parliaments. There are cases where the Constitution does not place the two Houses on exactly the same footing in such matters. There is parity in the right to initiate legislation between the two Houses in Belgium, Italy, Japan, Laos, Sweden, Switzerland and the USSR; but examples where this is not the case are numerous. The position of the Yugoslav Parliament is peculiar: each House has the right to introduce legislation, but it can do so only within its own particular field, i.e. the Federal Council in general matters of state and the Council of Producers in the economic and social sphere.

On the other hand, there is a very marked difference in the Netherlands, where the First Chamber, i.e. the upper House, does not have the right to initiate legislation. The same is true in Norway of the Lagting. This may seem particularly strange, seeing that the two Houses are the product of the same election and can be regarded on the same footing as Houses elected by universal suffrage; in actual fact, the difference in treatment is merely due to the desire for increasing the effectiveness of the work of Parliament. In the Federal Republic of Germany and in Austria, the difference between the two Houses is less marked, but there is nevertheless a distinct suggestion of discrimination. The Federal German Council cannot table a Bill unless it is the outcome of a majority decision taken by its members. Similarly, the Austrian Federal Council can only exercise its right to initiate legislation collectively; furthermore, it can only submit Bills to the National Council through the Federal Government.

120

In most of the other bicameral Parliaments, the difference can be seen most clearly in financial matters, and it is based on the idea that the expenditure commitments or the introduction of taxation measures must be the preserve of the House elected by universal suffrage, on the principle that the people must give its consent to such financial burdens as it will have to bear. This is true of the French Parliament, and also of Parliaments based on the Anglo-Saxon model, which have copied fairly closely the situation arising out of the Parliament Acts passed in Great Britain in 1911 and 1949 without going quite so far, since under these Acts the House of Lords today no longer has any effective powers over 'money bills'. Thus in Australia, Burma, Ceylon, India and Ireland, as well as in the United States, Brazil and the Philippines, only the popular House can initiate financial legislation. In the Philippines, Bills of a regional nature can only be introduced in the lower House, and the same applies in Ireland to Bills designed to amend the Constitution, and in Brazil to legislation establishing the strength of the armed forces.

While the right to introduce legislation is generally exercised only by Parliament and by Governments, it can also be granted to particular parliamentary bodies. For example, in Albania, Rumania and the USSR there is a provision that the Presidium has the constitutional power to table Bills. In Poland the same applies to the Council of States. More unusual still is the right to initiate legislation enjoyed in the United Kingdom, Finland and Sweden by the Church, but it should be noted that this only applies to laws on ecclesiastical matters. Noteworthy too is the right vested in the Provincial Assembly of the Aaland Islands to introduce legislation dealing with the islands in the Finnish Parliament.

The direct introduction of legislation by the people is rare. It is based on a very strict notion of the sovereignty of the people, its purpose being to cope with any tendency towards possible slackness on the part of its representatives by inviting them to legislate on matters which the people consider important. Provision is, strictly speaking, made for popular introduction of legislation in Austria, but it is done through the Federal Government, which means that it actually takes the form of government Bills. In Italy, the Regional Councils can submit Bills in Parliament in accordance with the same procedure as is followed for government Bills or Bills introduced on the initiative of Parliament. In addition, a body of 50,000 electors can introduce a Bill in a fully drafted form. In Switzerland the same number is required, but the right of initiation in this case applies only to constitutional legislation.

In the USSR this principle has been broadened and altered in character. The Soviet Constitution provides that the initiative in regard to legislation may be taken by any public body through its central organization. The right to introduce legislation is by no means a monopoly of the chambers of the Supreme Soviet and the Council of Ministers; it is shared also with the Republic of the Union (represented by their Supreme Soviets or their Presidium), with the Supreme Court, etc. But the variety of forms which the initiative in regard to legislation can take must not blind us to the fact that it is first and foremost a right inherent in the legal rights of a Member of Parliament. Let us now see how this right is exercised.

2. PARLIAMENTARY INITIATION OF LEGISLATION

(a) Individual or Joint Initiation

In classic parliamentary practice, the initiation of legislation is the privilege of every Member of Parliament in his individual capacity. Thus, in most countries there is nothing to prevent a member from proposing any new legislation he feels would be useful. Similarly, nothing prevents several members from concerting their efforts, where they are in agreement as to a particular proposal and wish to make what amounts to a joint presentation of a Bill.

However, some Parliaments cling firmly to the principle of the right of the individual. For example, in the House of Representatives of the United States, collective initiation of legislation is prohibited altogether. In other countries, one and the same Bill may not be backed by a large number of Members of Parliament. In the Irish Seanad, the maximum number is six, in Luxembourg five, in Belgium six, in Norway ten, and in the United Kingdom twelve. In the House of Commons the rule on individual tabling of Bills is regarded as so important that where a Bill has been passed by the House of Lords, before it has been given a first reading, which is in the nature of a formality, it has to be sponsored by a member.

Some countries disregard classic parliamentary law and do not allow an individual member to initiate legislation; Members of Parliament are obliged to combine in order to introduce a Bill. The principle underlying this requirement is no doubt the desire for a pre-sifting of Bills so that only those will go forward which have the support of a considerable weight of opinion behind them and are thus worth while. Joint presentation is frequently used in some of the People's Democracies. In Bulgaria, Bills must be signed by at least one fifth of the total number of deputies; in Rumania, the consent of thirty members is required; fifteen names are required in Poland. There is a similar obligation in the Bundestag of the Federal Republic of Germany, where it is bound up with the Constitution of political groupings: a minimum number of fifteen members per group must sign the Bill. In practice the signature of the President of the group constitutes a sufficient surety. In the Austrian National Council a group of at least eight members is required. In the Spanish Cortes, any Bill must have the support of fifty co-signatories before it can be presented. In Indonesia, support must be forthcoming from at least ten members; in Japan twenty names are required in the House of Representatives and ten in the House of Councillors, or fifty and twenty respectively in the case of money Bills. As we have already seen also, collective initiation of legislation is the rule in the Bundesrat of the German Federal Republic and the Austrian Federal Council. Sometimes particular matters are deemed to be sufficiently important to need to be presented jointly. In Albania, proposals for amending the Constitution must be signed by two fifths of the members, in Turkey by one third.

(b) How Parliamentary Initiation of Legislation Operates

There would be no point in going into all the details of the way in which legislation is initiated and we shall merely consider the main aspects of this question in the light of parliamentary practice in the various countries.

In those parliamentary systems which are most jealous of the individual right of Members of Parliament in legislative matters, the initiation of legislation is purely and simply an expression of will on the part of a member, given practical expression by handing in a Bill to the office qualified to receive it. In this connexion, the French system is unusually liberal, and members of the French Parliament make full use of their right to table a large number of Bills. In the USSR and in some of the People's Democracies, members can even introduce Bills orally, and have the terms of the Bill recorded in the minutes of the House. In some cases provision is made for prior submission of proposed legislation for the views of the Chairman or Speaker. This is the case, for example, in Japan; here a Bill must also be accompanied by a memorandum explaining the background and

123

in particular the financial implications in the event of its being passed. In Egypt, a special Bills and petitions committee decides whether proposed legislation is worthy of consideration. In Spain, a similar task is entrusted to a permanent committee, and in Belgium to the House itself.

In Parliaments of the British type, tabling of a Bill consists more often than not of a request by the author of the Bill for leave to introduce it, after the title (which states the purpose of the Bill), has first been placed on the order paper. Actually, in the United Kingdom the right of members to introduce legislation can be exercised in three ways, based as always on a practical outlook which pays little heed to legal theory. There are also Private Bills which may be introduced by persons or bodies outside Parliament.

The procedure for introducing a Bill is for notification of it (including its long and short title) to be included on the Order Paper. The short title is then read out in the House of Commons and this constitutes a first reading. With regard to money Bills in particular, these are put on the Order Paper 'by order of the House'. The House, after approving a resolution adopted by a Committee of the Whole House, then decides to have placed before it a Bill founded on that resolution. In practice this procedure is only used nowadays for Bills founded on resolutions emanating from the Ways and Means Committee.

Finally we get the tabling of Bills preceded by a motion. This procedure, a survival from the past, which enables a private member who has been unable to get a Bill in which he is especially interested placed on the Order Paper as a result of the ballot, can still set the whole legislative process in motion. At the beginning of the sitting on two days a week, a ten-minute period may be devoted to this (the so-called 'ten minutes rule'). After hearing the proposer and one speaker on the opposite side, the House may, if it sees fit, give leave for the Bill to be introduced. As we have seen, this motion procedure is no longer common in the House of Commons; on the other hand, it is a regular practice in Australia and in Israel. In the latter country every Bill is submitted to the House which, after having heard its sponsor and a speaker against the Bill, decides either to reject it or to refer it to a committee. In the latter case, the committee may recommend to the House that the Bill in question be given a first reading or that it be rejected.

Regarding this procedure, a distinction must be made between motions accompanied by a complete Bill and motions which do not submit the actual terms of a Bill, but request the Government to table a Bill on a particular subject. Only the former really constitutes initiation of legislation as such. The two systems are used in the Netherlands, and in Finland where the first system has led to the passing of a large number of important Acts. But it is significant that several other European democracies of long standing, Sweden and Switzerland in particular, only make use of the second, which amounts in practice to giving the Government the monopoly in the matter of initiating legislation. In point of fact, the second system is gradually gaining ground; this is very natural, given the complex character of the problems that have to be solved. This abandoning of a constitutional right is particularly noteworthy in Norway; the Bill which the member intends to propose is first placed before the Government, which may amend it or advise against introducing it. The advice does not necessarily have to be followed, but in practice it always is.

In addition to these practical limitations, there are limitations arising out of standing orders; some are confined to specific matters, others result from the time-limits laid down for submitting Bills. In a great many countries, money Bills are subject to special rules; more often than not they are out of order unless they are supported by a message from the Head of State or the Government or at the very least by a 'recommendation' from the executive. This is true of most of the countries which have come under British influence—Australia, Burma, India, Ireland and the Sudan. There are even cases—Ceylon is one of them—where the Government has complete control of legislative operations and there is no provision for Bills to be tabled by private members.

As a general rule, the introduction of legislation goes on throughout the whole session. However, some countries have taken the precaution to lay down a deadline for tabling Bills. In Iceland, the time-limit for introducing legislation is eight weeks from the beginning of the session, unless the time-limit is waived by a vote of the House. In Finland, the rule is still more stringent—no Bill may be tabled later than mid-day on the fourteenth day following the opening of the first session after the general election, or later than mid-day on the tenth day in the case of other sessions. However, there is a safety valve here: a Bill may be submitted after that date if it is consequential upon an important parliamentary event (tabling or withdrawal of a government Bill for example) provided that the Bill is tabled within seven days of that event. In Norway, the time-limit applies not only to Bills introduced by private members (end of February) but also to government Bills (end of March). But here again the President of the House may waive the rule. Sweden has a similar system: the Government has ninety days from the opening of the annual session in which to table its Bills; the private member has only fifteen days.

(c) The Initiation of Legislation by Committees

As we saw earlier, the main purpose of committees is to help Parliament to expedite its business, especially by examining Bills submitted to them. The question thus arises whether they should be granted the right to introduce legislation themselves. In the theory of Western representative systems, definitely not, since they are considered as nothing more than working bodies and are not called upon to legislate themselves. Yet a number of countries—the USSR, Rumania, Yugoslavia, the United States, the Philippines, Austria, Iceland, Luxembourg, Sweden, Indonesia and Japan—allow them the right to initiate Bills themselves. In other words, in the four corners of the world committees are granted this right without qualification in regard to matters coming within their sphere.

In Israel, committees have on paper the right to initiate legislation, but it is little used. In other Parliaments, committees have the right to introduce legislation, but only in exceptional circumstances, and more particularly in financial matters. The Finance Committee in Finland may table Bills with a view to balancing of the Budget, just as the Bank Committee can table Bills amending the special position conferred on the National Bank. In Sweden, the Committee of Ways and Means, the Bank Committee and the Constitutional Committee have the right to introduce Bills concerning questions within their terms of reference. In Brazil, if the executive does not present the estimates within the first two months of the session, the Finance Committee must produce estimates within fifteen days. We have already discussed the initiative in regard to money Bills in the House of Commons belonging to the Committee of the Whole House, which is entitled to pass resolutions, and if these are approved by the House, they must be embodied in Bills which individual members are formally asked to draft and introduce. Similarly in Czechoslovakia committees can draw the executive's attention to the need for certain legislative measures. In the Netherlands, both committees and private members have the right to ask the Government to initiate measures which seem to them desirable. In the majority of Parliaments committees are not allowed to take direct action, but there is nothing to prevent their members from acting in an individual capacity. The result amounts to much the same thing; the ban does have the effect, however, of putting a brake on attempts by committees to embark on independent action.

126

3. THE MESSAGE FROM THE HEAD OF THE STATE

The message from the Head of the State, whether he is King, Emperor or President, outlining for the benefit of Parliament his programme of government, and more particularly his legislative proposals, is an indirect method of initiating legislation practised particularly in countries where there is strict separation of powers, as in the United States. The United States Constitution does not give the President the right to initiate legislation, but the use of the presidential message enables him to recommend to Congress the examination of the measures he requires to carry out his policy. All that has then to be done is for the members and the committees of Congress in their respective spheres to sponsor the Bills embodied in the message. In addition, the State of the Union Message, which contains both a 'balance sheet' and a programme of government action, is addressed through Congress to the American people as a whole. A similar procedure is followed in the Philippines. In Czechoslovakia, the message from the President of the Republic is discussed by the National Assembly as a whole, and is then examined in the Presiding Committee which subsequently instructs the various committees to take up the suggestions it contains; and finally, the reports submitted by the committees are put before the House.

In the Western parliamentary democracies, where the separation of powers is not complete, the Head of State's message, where the institution exists, has not the same importance as in systems where there is separation of powers, for the Government ordinarily possesses directly the right to initiate legislation. In the United Kingdom, the House can receive messages from the Crown concerning certain questions relative to the rights and prerogatives of the Crown on which legislative action is deemed necessary. It immediately examines the message, replies, possibly in the form of an 'address', and then gives orders for the preparation of the Bill envisaged in the terms of the message. The system of messages from the Government to Parliament containing recommendations to be taken up by it is used in most of the Parliaments on the British model—in Australia, Burma and Ceylon. The same procedure is also found in Switzerland. In the Netherlands and Sweden the rule is that any government Bill must be accompanied by a message recommending its adoption.

This system of messages designed to initiate legislation must not be confused with the 'Speech from the Throne' on the occasion of the opening of the session or with formal statements of national importance by the Head of State, made for example on the occasion of national or international events of some seriousness. The former are found in certain monarchies such as Belgium, Luxembourg, Laos, Sweden and the United Kingdom, where occasionally they are debated, as in Sweden, or an address in reply is voted as in Luxembourg. The latter course is sometimes found in Brazil, Egypt, France, Italy, Spain, Syria, Turkey, and also in the United Kingdom.

The message system makes it clear that whatever the circumstances, as far as the initiation of legislation is concerned, unlike the Members of Parliament the executive always has the power to take action.

4. THE DECLINING TREND IN INITIATION OF LEGISLATION BY MEMBERS OF PARLIAMENT

Although the power to legislate is regarded everywhere as belonging absolutely to Parliament, the essential phase in which the process of legislation is set in motion appears under modern constitutional practice to be the sphere of action of the executive as well as of the legislature. The division thus established by constitutions between the two powers evolves constantly in favour of the Government and to the disadvantage of Parliament. This is a palpable fact which can be observed in most countries. Let us look at the reasons for this decline in Parliament's own initiation of legislation.

In the first place it is the consequence of the complexity of modern Acts of Parliament, which require not only 'the creative imagination of a political brain but the combined knowledge of an economist and a specialist in a whole series of cognate sciences'. The Member of Parliament possesses in a lesser degree the technical facilities which the Government enjoys, and thus his Bill often has a less privileged position than that of the Government, which has the skills of numerous experts at its disposal. The tendency also reflects the small amount of time which can be devoted to the examination of Private Members' Bills, Parliament's timetable being largely taken up in the legislative sphere by the study of measures proposed by the Government for carrying out its policy.

Theoretically, even if a private member is convinced that his Bill has little chance of being taken up, there is nothing to prevent him from introducing it. In practice, if he belongs to the governing majority, he will seldom exercise his right, since if his Bill is worth while, the Government itself will sponsor it. Hence in Western parliamentary practice, legislation initiated by private members is forthcoming more often than not from the opposition benches. In this case, introducing a Bill has a special significance which is far removed from the normal one, its main purpose being to embarrass the Government. More and more, in most Parliaments, the right to initiate legislation tends to be used only by the minority party. It goes to show what meagre prospects Private Members' Bills have, even in countries where they are still numerous, as in France. Those which go through, and are finally passed, are extremely few in number and represent only a small portion of the laws enacted: one quarter in France, one tenth in the United Kingdom.

Thus the Government is by no means simply the executive agent which implements legislation enacted by Parliament; it is the dominating authority in drafting legislation. Parliament has a safeguard in the fact that it is still the deliberating body, and it alone has the right of decision in the last resort. But it loses this protection, at any rate partly, where it has occasion to delegate to the Government its own legislative power.

II

The Delegation of Legislative Power

The delegation by Parliament of its legislative powers to the executive raises one of the most complex and most baffling problems of contemporary constitutional law. Its complexity arises essentially from the difficulty of determining exactly where to draw the line between what is law and what are regulations, the two fields, according to classic theory, being the preserves of Parliament and Government respectively. Generations of writers have pondered over this question of the division of power which those who have drafted constitutions have more often than not left vague. The accidental vicissitudes of history have produced empirical and piecemeal solutions, the general tendency being an encroachment upon the exclusive rights of Parliament in legislative matters.

Ideally, in a democratic country, all laws should emanate from the direct representatives of the people. But the legal power of the latter, though constantly affirmed by constitutional instruments, does not necessarily imply their practical capacity to make laws. Technical intricacies, the daily increasing numbers of problems to be solved, and the urgency of the decisions to be taken, are less and less easy to cope with on the basis of the traditional legislative procedure. This is not readily adaptable to situations and functions which the constitutions of the past never envisaged.

This discrepancy between the work devolving upon Parliament and the means at its disposal has been well illustrated since the First World War, and it was aggravated by the economic crises which followed the war and affected a great many countries. It became a permanent state of affairs after the Second World War, so much so that it was officially recognized by some constitutions which, as it were, gave the delegation of legislative power their official blessing. This delegation of power, however it is effected, nevertheless gives rise to a serious dilemma: should one respect the democratic techniques of legislation and accept the risk of dangerously hampering the rapidity which may be necessary in enacting laws, or is it better to ensure that this task is performed as and when it is required, even if the bounds of democratic government are overstepped in doing so? Both alternatives have a democratic basis. The first is based on the traditional idea that there should invariably be a measure of national representation; the second is based on the more modern concept that the first concern of parliamentary government should be to produce legislation which will meet the wishes of the people.

Whatever the reasons adduced in its favour, the delegation of legislative power today has become current practice in most countries. There are few countries where neither the Constitution nor established practice authorizes such a transfer of power. To judge from the replies received, there would appear to be only a few countries where the delegation of power is completely unknown: Brazil, Laos (where Members of Parliament 'have always been opposed to the slightest deviation from the principle of non-delegation'), Syria and Turkey, which merely state that their Constitution does not authorize the delegation of powers. In this same category should be included the USSR and the People's Democracies (with the exception of Yugoslavia). Neither the Constitution of the USSR nor its practice permit the permanent or temporary delegation by the Supreme Soviet of the USSR to the State administration of all or part of its legislative powers. Similarly, in Bulgaria, Rumania and Czechoslovakia 'neither the Constitution nor established practice' permit of such delegation of the powers of the National Assembly. Provisional legislative power is however sometimes exercised by the Presidium which legislates by decree when the Supreme Soviet is not sitting. But it is of interest to note that this power is of a particular nature in view of the fact that the body which exerts it is the offshoot of Parliament and that the right to take over from that body is granted to Parliament, under certain other conditions, by the Constitution itself.

This practice has, in fact, been criticized fairly strongly by certain Soviet jurists, who feel that it might be a good thing to authorize the delegation of powers, if it should continue to prove necessary by amending Article 32 of the Constitution, which states that 'the legislative power in the USSR is exercised exclusively by the Supreme Soviet of the USSR'. Such authorization already exists in Albania and Poland, though admittedly it is exercised by the Presidium and the Council of State, and not by the Government. These two bodies, the direct offshoot of Parliament, are authorized to issue decrees having the force of law when Parliament is not sitting. In Poland, however, the most important spheres of political and economic life—the revision of the Constitution, finance and economic planning—are not included in such authorization. Furthermore, in either case the decrees must be submitted to Parliament for approval at the succeeding sessions.

The traditional form of delegation of powers differs from this latter type in that it is granted to the executive. This may be regarded as a more dangerous course if the supremacy of Parliament is to be maintained, especially where the Constitution has made a definite attempt to avoid it.

This contradiction between the theory of the law and the actual situation disappears in the case of unwritten constitutions under which Parliament is supreme in all fields—constitutional, legislative or administrative. One result is that the right of Parliament to delegate the power to make laws, as and when it wishes, has no limit. This is the situation in the United Kingdom in regard to the problem of the delegation of legislative power. It does not appear to give rise to any difficulty, especially as a glance at the legislation described as delegated makes it clear that most of it consists of instruments in the nature of regulations of a type which in other countries would be handled by the executive without any need for the delegation of power. Hence the primary effect of the system of delegated legislation has been to invest the Government with real power to make regulations. But this power has developed to a point where the pressure of circumstances and the application of various enabling statutes have made it a substitute in certain instances for Acts of Parliament. Since 1946 the Members of the British Parliament have felt it desirable to have under the Statutory Instruments Act a uniform procedure for the delegation of power (which previously had not followed any principle), and at the same time to keep a more effective control on the legislation delegated.

131

The statutory instruments, i.e. the decrees and regulations issued in virtue of the enabling statute, are divided for practical purposes into two categories:

(a) Those which come into force only after a resolution approving them has been passed in both Houses. This is known as the 'affirmative procedure'.

(b) Those which take effect immediately but can be annulled by a resolution of either House. This is the 'negative procedure'. The annulment must take place within forty days of the date of laying the instruments in the House, less any periods of adjournment of more than four days.

Furthermore, in view of the mass of statutory instruments which might easily escape the notice of the Members of Parliament, the House of Commons has had since 1944 a select committee of eleven members whose task is to examine such instruments and to draw the attention of Parliament particularly to all instruments which they feel warrant a more careful scrutiny, e.g. instruments concerning money matters, instruments with retrospective effect or which have been delayed or are incomplete or obscure. This committee, officially known as the Select Committee on Statutory Instruments, was originally set up for one particular session, but was set up again for subsequent sessions. It has no power to pass judgement on the expediency of any statutory instrument, its task being merely to make sure that the exercise of delegated powers is a proper one, and in particular to see to it that matters on which Parliament must maintain the upper hand (e.g. money matters and individual liberties) do not slip from its grasp by the effect of statutory instruments. The very existence of this committee has undoubtedly had a salutary effect, since in the course of its first eight years of operation, it has had occasion to draw the attention of the House to only ninety-three statutory instruments out of the 7,000 it has been called upon to examine. From this figure of 7,000 it is quite evident that most of the instruments put before the committee are in the nature of regulations. Therein lies the remarkable feature of the system. Its purpose is to put a curb on the delegation of legislative power, but in fact it amounts to a means of exercising parliamentary control over the power to issue regulations.

This confusion between the two powers is particularly marked in Australia, where for most laws, Parliament delegates to the executive 'a limited power of legislation, namely the power to make regulations necessary for their application'; and as in the United Kingdom, parliamentary control of this power to make regulations is provided by the Acts Interpretation Act. All regulations must be published and placed before each of the two Houses and they may be annulled by one or other House within fifteen days after they have been so tabled. A similar situation is to be found in India, where in general 'every principal Act of Parliament contains provisions delegating to the executive power to make rules in respect of specified matters for the practical working of the Act'. These rules must be submitted to both Houses, where they may be amended within time-limits specified by the original statute. Moreover—and this is another aspect of the British procedure—all regulations emanating from the executive are automatically examined by the Committee on Subordinate Legislation set up within the House of the People to make sure that they do not go beyond the powers conferred. A similar system operates in Burma, where both Houses of Parliament have three months in which to annul government decrees. More or less the same system appears to apply in Ceylon. In Ireland the procedure is also very similar to that of the United Kingdom, although the Constitution stipulates that only the Oireachtas has the power to legislate. The majority of the regulations enacted in virtue of a delegation of powers may be challenged within a period of twenty-one working days from the time of tabling. In addition, the ordinary courts have the power to declare void any decree made in violation of the enabling statute; and the constitutional validity of decrees may be challenged in the same way as that of Acts of Parliament. As in most of the countries which have come under British influence, it would appear that in Israel most of the delegated legislation consists of instruments having the character of regulations.

Because of this uncertainty as to where the law ends and the sphere of regulations begins, in Sweden legislation enacted by the Rigsdag extends to such matters of detail that there is little room left for the exercise of the power to make regulations. Hence the problem of the delegation of legislative power does not arise there in the same way as elsewhere. In fact, even though under the Constitution the King has the power to enact legislation of his own accord in certain spheres—over-all economy, organization of the powers of government, etc.—he delegates his own powers to Parliament in matters of importance, and asks its advice in other cases. Thus in Sweden we have the unique example in contemporary constitutional law of a limitation of executive powers, whereas everywhere else the tendency is for the executive to encroach upon the legislative function whether by practice or by constitutional prerogative.

133

In countries with fixed constitutions, the problem of delegation of the legislative function presents major legal difficulties, since in principle the right to legislate is vested in Parliament, and it cannot turn this over to the executive without infringing the Constitution. The legislation conferring full powers which transfers the responsibilities of Parliament to the Government has the effect of removing the measures out of the control of the representatives of the people. Hence it constitutes a serious challenge to the principle of national sovereignty which is inherent in democratic institutions. The logical solution would be to amend the Constitution prior to the delegation of powers.

Finland has adopted a procedure based on this concept. There is delegated legislation similar to that practised in the United Kingdom but, in addition, whenever the occasion arises to confer on the Government a general right to take measures of a legislative nature, an enabling statute must be passed under the same procedure as that required for a revision of the Constitution. But this system is not always a practical possibility, owing to the involved procedure necessary and the time it takes. For this reason it is found preferable, in countries where the delegation of powers is strictly forbidden, to stretch the constitutional provisions to their limits by questionable methods whose theoretical justification is a matter for jurists to decide. Several countries find this pragmatic method the most convenient.

The case of the United States is particularly significant. There is no doubt that a strict interpretation of the concept of defined jurisdiction and the principle of the separation of powers make the delegation of legislative powers to the President impossible. But this has not prevented him from prevailing upon Congress since 1932 to grant him powers which in fact are nothing more nor less than powers to legislate, by asking both Houses for authorization to regulate by executive orders matters which hitherto were strictly dealt with by Acts of Congress. However, the Supreme Court, which has the say in the matter of constitutional validity, keeps an eye on the limits of these delegated powers. But so long as it is willing to regard the enabling statute as regular, there is nothing to prevent Congress from giving the delegation of powers an extremely broad interpretation. A similar problem arises in Japan; while the Constitution would appear to prohibit the delegation of power, established practice authorizes it within varying limits according to circumstances. As a general rule it is permitted provided it does not reduce the status of the Diet. The courts have had occasion to state more than once that it was constitutional so long as it was done in a specific and definite manner.

France is a still more striking example than the United States, first of all because Article 13 of the Constitution states categorically: 'The National Assembly alone passes legislation. It may not delegate that right'; and secondly because of the absence of any real check on the constitutional validity of laws. The pressure of events since 1948 has obliged the legislature to have recourse to certain practices which keep strictly to the letter of the law but nevertheless do in fact grant the Government the right to legislate by executive decree in matters within a more and more extensive field, so that there is a return to a practice which it had been hoped to ban. The enabling statute defines the general principles of the policy to be followed by the Government and delimits the area and the duration of the powers delegated. In most cases, decrees must be submitted to Parliament for its tacit or express approval, and to its committees for their views. Writers have discussed at great length the constitutional validity of these new techniques, and the Council of State itself in 1953 was called upon to define the exact scope of Article 13. It came to the conclusion that Parliament had the power 'to decide that certain matters within the jurisdiction of the legislative power could be held to be within the jurisdiction of the authorities vested with the power of making regulations', provided that the matters in question were subsequently brought forward when it was thought fit and given legislative sanction. It is interesting to note that this judgement has the effect of bringing the French concept close to that of British law, where the dividing line between Acts of Parliament and regulations is merely a matter of decision on the part of Parliament. But whereas the British attitude was quite empirical and paid little heed to the theoretical justification, the result was achieved in France only after a strong case had been made out to overcome the misgivings felt by many because of the definite constitutional provision in the matter.

Belgium has been troubled by the same misgivings, for the same reasons. Many theories have been worked out to try to make it possible in exceptional circumstances to enact a variety of laws known as 'special powers' or 'extraordinary powers', giving the Head of State the right to adopt measures normally coming within the sphere of the legislature. As in France, these enabling statutes delimit the scope of the delegated powers and the duration of their validity. As a general rule, decrees must be submitted to Parliament for ratification.

The same might be said of Switzerland, with the difference that the Constitution does not actually touch upon the problem. However, all the writers on the subject agree that the full powers given to

135

the Government cannot be based on the Constitution. According to Swiss theory, the delegation of power is legitimate in such cases on the unwritten principle of compelling circumstances, which indeed is always present by implication in most countries which have recourse to the delegation of powers. In other words the concern for the safety of the State must take precedence over respect for constitutional procedure. 'Necessity knows no law,' says the proverb. Here we have the perfect illustration of it.

Because they accept this principle of compelling circumstances, a number of countries whose constitutions make no provision on the subject have admitted in practice, in the same way as Switzerland, the principle of delegation of legislative power to the executive. Denmark may be cited as an instance. But its main effect has been to give official sanction in certain recent constitutions to *fait accompli*.

There are also countries whose constitutions grant the executive the power to make laws during periods when Parliament is not sitting. Strictly speaking this is no delegation of powers by Parliament, but a direct exercise of the legislative function by the executive. A number of countries which have recently gained their independence, such as India, Pakistan, the Sudan and the Republic of Vietnam, come into this category. In India, the President of the Union may issue orders when Parliament is not sitting, where circumstances require it. These orders have the force of law, but they lapse on the expiry of a period of six weeks after the end of the parliamentary recess, unless the orders have been withdrawn earlier by resolutions passed by both Houses. In Pakistan, the President has the power to act in a similar manner. In the Sudan, the Government can enact provisional legislation when Parliament is not sitting. Likewise in case of emergency, the President of the Republic of Vietnam may enact decrees, which are transmitted forthwith to the Bureau, and they acquire real force of law if Parliament does not annul them in the course of the session following the date of their signature. There is a similar system in force in Egypt: decrees issued by the Government must be submitted to the National Assembly within fifteen days of their promulgation. In Iceland, again, the President can issue provisional decrees when Parliament is not sitting or in case of emergency, and Parliament subsequently examines them. In the same way, in Austria constitutional law allows the Federal President to issue orders when the National Council is not sitting, in the event of 'dire emergency'. However, he is required to obtain the consent of the permanent sub-committee of the National Council's Ways and Means Committee. The instruments are immediately submitted to that body, which takes the final decision. A whole series of matters such as taxation, social rights, and the protection of tenants are, moreover, excluded from the field where the President has the right to issue orders of a legislative nature.

In the cases we have considered, the idea of urgency has been the essential condition for the exercise of the legislative function by the executive in the period when Parliament is not sitting. But this condition may also apply when it is sitting. Hence most of the countries we have quoted also provide for the delegation of power when Parliament is sitting, subject to the traditional rules of authorization, i.e. definition of the extent and duration of the powers.

In Indonesia the Government may enact emergency legislation on its own authority and responsibility, i.e. without an enabling statute being required. But this must be submitted to the House of Representatives not later than the following session. In Yugoslavia, constitutional law similarly authorizes the Executive Federal Council to promulgate decrees having the force of law during a state of emergency, mobilization or war. Again in Spain, Article 13 of the law of the Cortes provides that the Head of State may enact executive decrees in the event of war or for emergency reasons, and 'account must be rendered' to the Cortes. The Italian Constitution contains a similar provision—the Government enjoys a general right to enact executive decrees in the event of 'special emergencies'. But any decree of this kind, though it has provisionally the force of law, must be submitted to Parliament on the day of its publication before it can become a law. If Parliament is not sitting, it must meet within five days. A decree not made law within sixty days of its publication is retrospectively invalidated. In none of these cases is there any enabling statute; in its stead there is *post facto* control by Parliament.

On the other hand in Luxembourg the House itself delegates its legislative powers to the Government in economic matters. The Government may use these powers only in case of urgent necessity, following a report from the committee on parliamentary business. Likewise in economic matters, in the Philippines, Congress may temporarily authorize the President to legislate in wartime or in the case of any other emergency, subject to limitations prescribed by law.

Democratic tradition looks askance at the delegation of legislative power. In Western Europe, however, two post-war constitutions have extended the practice in a way which is worthy of note. First of all, the Italian Constitution provides that delegation of powers is legitimate for a limited time and for specific purposes, provided it is accompanied by a statement of the principles and policy involved. But this safeguard of Parliament's jurisdiction may be little more than academic, since it is always possible for Parliament to lay down principles and outline policies which are so vague that the Government has ample latitude. Secondly, in the Federal Republic of Germany, Article 80 of the Constitution provides that the Federal Government, a Federal Minister, or the governments of the Länder may be authorized by law to issue 'regulations having the force of law'. The law must determine the contents, the purposes and the scope of the legislation and regulations and must indicate their legal basis. Article 81 goes still further and exceeds the framework of classic delegation of law-making. The article is concerned with 'the state of legislative emergency' in which the Government is given very wide powers, subject to certain very definite and fairly complex conditions. Suppose that the Chancellor has not obtained the necessary majority on a motion of confidence, and the Bundestag has been unable to elect a new Head of Government. If he then introduces an 'emergency' Bill and the Bill is rejected by the Bundestag, the President of the Republic may, on the request of the Government and with the consent of the Federal Council, proclaim a 'state of legislative emergency'. The Bill then comes into force on the mere strength of the Bundesrat's support. It should be noted however that these conditions have never arisen and that this procedure, which is not so much delegation of power as positive substitution of power, has never yet been applied.

The delegation of power may be kept within reasonable limits, as for example in the Netherlands, where a compromise solution has been found for the problem of delegation of legislation which appears to be satisfactory. The Constitution specifies the subjects which in any circumstances must be governed by law, and hence in respect of these there cannot be any delegation of powers. On the other hand, delegation is allowable and may be exercised freely in respect of all other questions, subject to an enabling statute embodying the general principles to be observed, and in certain cases, provided that a Bill ratifying the legislation made under the delegated power is tabled within the shortest possible time. The delegation of legislative power does not exist in the USSR. In the People's Democracies and the USSR it is held that the Government must act solely within the limits of the prerogatives laid down in the Constitution. Plenary power belongs to the supreme authority—Parliament.

So lively a concern to safeguard the exclusive right of Parliament to initiate legislation is rare nowadays. In most countries, the

Government has obtained the right to legislate either by practice or under the Constitution. In the opinion of some jurists, this is not an alarming state of affairs; it merely indicates the transformation of the concept of parliamentary democracy, while at the same time crystallizing a *de facto* situation. They argue that in view of the continuing economic and political problems in certain countries Parliament has admitted that it is frequently incapable of fulfilling its legislative function; thus the delegation of power tends to become a normal method of government, and the role of Parliament at the same time undergoes a sort of shifting of emphasis, so that its legislative function diminishes and in its stead we get wider and more powerful control over matters of policy.

The fact remains that this procedure and the new situation arising from it as far as Parliament is concerned are at variance with the very essence of the democratic system. Moreover, while legislation emanating from government departments has the advantage of being more rapid, it is by no means certain that it is of higher quality than that produced by Parliament in accordance with a procedure which, though at times it may be more complex, is nevertheless calculated to ensure the free expression of all shades of opinion.

III

The Making of Laws

The Role of Committees—Consultation outside Parliament—
The Agenda or Order of Business—Debate in the House—
Methods of Voting—Constitutional Law—Agreement
between both Houses—Royal Assent

The initiation of legislation sets in motion the whole process of law-making. Members of Parliament are notified in a variety of ways—by the posting of notices, announcements in the Chamber, insertion in the official report of the debates, or by a purely formal first reading. The Bill is then printed and distributed; occasionally it is considered either by a special committee, as in Egypt and Spain, or by the House itself, as in Belgium. The practice of distributing copies of the Bill, at any rate to Parliament and the Government, is a fundamental rule to which there are virtually no exceptions. In Austria, however, Bills emanating from Parliament are only actually distributed when the chairman of the committee empowered to examine them sees fit to have them debated. Occasionally, a Bill is

139

published before it has been examined to see whether it is in order. In Brazil, for example, when a Bill has been distributed, it is submitted to the Constitutional Juridical Committee, which is asked to report whether it is in conformity with the Constitution, and to look into its technical and legal aspects. Where a Bill is found to be unconstitutional, it is immediately reported to the House which may order it to be withdrawn. Similarly, in the United Kingdom, a Bill may be withdrawn after it has been tabled and printed. The officials of the Public Bill Office make a check to ensure that it is in conformity with the standing orders of the House. They pay particular attention to the contents of the Bill to see that they are covered by the terms of its title, and to the observance of the rules concerning public money.

Once it is decided that they are in order, Bills are printed and distributed, and they then follow a procedure the details of which may take a vast variety of forms according to the different countries, although two essential phases are found almost everywhere:

(*a*) The preparatory phase, generally entrusted to committees.
(*b*) The discussion and enactment phase, in principle a matter for the House itself.

In some cases, this division of labour is subject to fairly considerable variation—from the exclusive jurisdiction of the House itself to the less orthodox practice of handing over the jurisdiction to committees. We have already had frequent occasions to point to the tendency of committees to increase their powers, and in some cases this is sanctioned by the Constitution, as the example of the way committees function in Italy illustrates.

Article 72 of the Italian Constitution specifies that the two Houses may entrust to committees not merely the examination of Bills, but also the final enactment of such legislation. In practice, the President of the House decides on the application of this unusual procedure by which the Houses divest themselves as it were of their legislative prerogatives and hand them over to their committees, which then act with the full powers of the House. Admittedly, in all instances, even up to the final enactment of the statute, Bills must be referred to the House itself if the Government, one tenth of the Members, or one fifth of the members of the committee so require. This is what is known as 'automatic return'. It is also true that this procedure cannot apply to certain types of items—constitutional and electoral matters, legislative power, ratification of treaties, taxation or public expenditure. The fact remains that it has come to cover a considerable field and that it applies to Bills of ever-growing importance. In many spheres, it has the effect of taking the power to bring in legislation away from the House itself.

On the other hand, in Albania, Poland and Czechoslovakia, Parliament may decide to examine and discuss Bills directly in the House without reference to committees.

Between these two extremes we find first of all the British procedure by which the activities of the committees are placed under the permanent control of the House, through the medium of the successive readings by the latter, and secondly the French or American type of procedure, which leaves the final decision to the House, but grants the committee considerable powers in regard to the drafting of legislation. Thus the role of committees can be regarded as the touchstone in respect of the boundaries between the various forms of legislative procedure.

1. THE ROLE OF COMMITTEES

The importance of the role played by committees can be determined first of all by reference to the particular stage at which they are given the initiative in regard to legislation and secondly by the extent of the powers conferred on them in the course of the examination of Bills.

(a) Reference to Committees

The precise time of the committee stage of Bills is of fundamental importance. The question is which will examine the Bill first—the appropriate committee or the House itself. If it is the latter, its policy decisions will explicitly or implicitly bind the committee as far as the committee's powers are concerned. If it is the other way round, the likelihood is that the action of the committee will have a profound effect on the kind of decision taken finally by the House.

Most Parliaments have adopted the second alternative. In practice, direct reference to a committee as a rule goes hand in hand with the existence of expert permanent committees. Thus in most of the Western European countries—Belgium, France, Italy, the Netherlands (Second Chamber), Norway, Spain and Switzerland—the President refers the Bill first of all to the committee, and the House does not come into the picture. The same system applies in Laos, Turkey, the Republic of Vietnam, Brazil and Japan. Preliminary examination by the 'sections' of the House in Luxembourg and in the

First Chamber in the Netherlands, as also by the 'divisions' in Indonesia, is on much the same lines. In Sweden, Syria, the United States and the Philippines, the decision to refer the Bill to a committee is announced in the House at the first reading; (this in actual fact consists of a reading aloud of the title of the Bill and the names of its proposers, without any discussion.)

The countries where Bills are first examined by the House, before being referred to the appropriate committee, may be divided into two groups. In the first, which comprises Denmark, the Federal Republic of Germany, Iceland and Israel, committal is ordered following the first reading, which is not a pure formality, since it gives rise to a general debate during which the general principles of the Bill are made clear. The second group consists of Australia, Burma, Ceylon, India, Ireland, Pakistan, the Sudan and the United Kingdom. Committal takes place only after the second reading, in the course of which the main outlines of the Bill are defined, whereas the first reading is a mere administrative formality amounting simply to the introduction of the Bill, except in Australia, Burma, India and Ireland, where the procedure can be interrupted at this stage, if the motion for the presentation of the Bill is rejected.

In the Austrian National Council either of these procedures may be followed. As a general rule, all Bills are committed without a preliminary reading to the appropriate committees; but the Government or the sponsor of the Bill may ask for an immediate first reading, at which the general principles of the Bill will be debated, and subsequently the Bill will be referred to a committee.

Finland has an unusual system, a sort of compromise between prior examination in committee and prior examination in the House. The main feature is a double commitment. Every Bill is referred by the House, sometimes following a general debate, to a select committee, on the proposal of the President's Conference. When the Bill has been examined by the select committee it is given a first reading which consists of the presentation of the committee's report, a general exchange of views and, finally, automatic commitment of the Bill to the Grand Committee. At the second reading, the Grand Committee's report is submitted, debated in detail and where necessary amended. This debate may end in re-committal to the Grand Committee which must then submit a new report to the House. It is only at the third reading that the final decision takes place.

In the USSR and several Socialist states there are no strict and uniform rules governing reference to committees: it largely depends on the nature of the Bill. It is for the House itself or for the appropriate committee, in the event of a Bill having been referred to the latter before the opening of the session, to decide whether the Bill in question is to form the subject of a preliminary debate in the House or in committee. Any report drawn up by a committee must be distributed twenty-four hours in advance of the sitting during which it is due to be debated. In Bulgaria, both the legislative and budgetary committees must have all Bills referred to them before they are placed before the assembly. In Czechoslovakia, Bills are debated in principle in committee before being debated in the House.

In Poland, when a Bill is submitted it is given a first reading consisting of a statement by the sponsor of the Bill, a debate on its general principles, and a resolution by the Diet committing it to the appropriate committee, provided it is not rejected.

The problem of reference to committees reveals the two essential concepts of legislative procedure:

(a) In Parliaments where special permanent committees operate, they have priority in regard to the examination of Bills.
(b) In Parliaments where the examination of Bills is entrusted to a Committee of the Whole House or to select committees, the House itself plays the main role.

This preliminary conclusion is confirmed by evidence drawn from the study of the powers of committees in regard to the enactment of legislation.

(b) The Powers of Committees

The powers of committees in regard to the Bills referred to them vary considerably according to whether they belong to the British type of committee or to the Continental and American type.

In the United Kingdom, committees have relatively little power. They are regarded as bodies designed for the examination of certain matters, for the study and detailed amendment of complex Bills, the House itself being regarded as the essential working unit. They can of course amend Bills, but the latitude given them is fairly severely limited by the fact that Bills will already have been defined in their main outlines before being referred to them. It might be wondered, in the circumstances, whether they perform any useful function. Actually, they provide an invaluable help to Parliament. They engage in discussion which leads to amendments being made to most Bills, they relieve the House of all questions of detail, and they fulfil precisely the task entrusted to them, namely, the minute scrutiny

143

of both the form and every conceivable repercussion of each clause of the Bill.

In the United States the purpose of committees was originally the same, but they have become in fact the active centres of congressional supervision. In the first place they can amend or transform as they wish any Bill, including those for which the President himself stands surety. More important still, the fact that they are entirely independent of the House and the Senate, which have no way of controlling their activity, means that the future of a Bill depends entirely on their will. In practice, the key part is played by the chairman of any particular committee. If he is personally hostile to the Bill, even if the majority in the committee is favourable, he can apply a whole series of delaying tactics to prevent the Bill from being considered. Thus the Bill has no chance of success unless the chairman of the committee to which it is referred is personally in favour of it.

In France, the powers of committees are not so extensive, but they are nevertheless considerable. In the first place committees can in actual practice pigeon-hole a certain number of Bills without examining them. This may be done for political reasons, but as a general rule the reason for it is simply that the committee is snowed under by a vast number of Bills. Secondly they have the power to recast to their hearts' content any Bills submitted to them, and this recasting may go so far as to amount to a total transformation of their contents. In the opinion of some writers, granting this power to committees is tantamount to giving them the right to initiate legislation, though the Constitution expressly denies them this right.

Thus in France, as in the United States, committees play a decisive part within Parliament itself. The importance of the part they play is to a large extent the outcome of an unusual procedure known as 'voting without debate', which is somewhat analagous to the Italian system of granting committees legislative powers. A great many Bills and proposals are accepted by the House simply on the strength of the examination carried out in committee. Debate in the House is waived, and all that remains is the voting. The power of deliberation disappears and is replaced by the mere power to vote: 'The House is the place for voting, the committee for discussing.' This transfer of the deliberative function to permanent committees is particularly important in that it does not merely affect Bills which Parliament is anxious to get rid of as being of secondary importance. The procedure makes no distinction as to the importance of Bills. Its main concern is to accelerate the production of legislation, always assuming that the work has been properly done in committee and has a considerable weight of opinion in its favour. Indeed the more or less unanimous agreement of the committee members constitutes an essential condition for the use of this procedure, since the Government or any member has the right to challenge it. But committees have still the option, after examining the arguments against it, of asking for a 'short debate', which is half-way between 'voting without debate' and regular debate. In this case a summary discussion may take place in the House between the proposers of amendments which have been rejected by the committee, the Government, and the chairman and rapporteur of the committee. A single speaker for each group can speak for five minutes in explanation of their votes. There is a whole category of Bills to which the short-debate procedure cannot apply—those relating to the Constitution, standing orders, electoral legislation or amnesties.

The importance of the work of committees is one of the most characteristic features of the classic French parliamentary system. The same conclusion might be reached concerning most of the countries which make use of the institution of special permanent committees. But all committees, whatever type they belong to, have a certain similarity in regard to the internal conduct of their work.

(c) Legislative Work in Committee

As we have already seen, procedure in committee is more often than not modelled on that of the House. But its main characteristic is that it has greater latitude, both in regard to means of investigation, and in the conduct of debate.

In Austria, France, the Federal Republic of Germany, the USSR and the People's Democracies, it is the current practice to set up sub-committees, small in size and circumscribed in their powers with instructions to make a preliminary study of the work of the committee. These sub-committees add an additional operation to the procedure, but this complication is to a great extent offset by the hard work put in by these bodies, which owing to their small size can hold meetings more frequently, go into matters more thoroughly and collect the necessary data they require more rapidly than the committees themselves.

The data in question are furnished primarily by the ministers best able or most willing to furnish them. As a general rule, if a committee requests a member of the Government to appear before it, he will almost invariably accept the invitation. In Austria, the Federal Republic of Germany and Japan, in fact, he has not the option of refusing. Requests for appearance are most frequently sent direct to the ministers. In Brazil, the Philippines and Spain, it is stipulated that these requests must be made through the President of the House. In the Netherlands and Indonesia, the exchange of views between ministers and committees is done first of all in writing. A preliminary report is sent to the minister concerned by the committee, and he replies in a 'reply memorandum'. It is only when the memorandum does not satisfy the committee that the minister is invited to appear before it. In Israel, a minister is frequently represented before the committee by a member of his staff.

The problem of appearances of ministers before committees does not arise when the Bill is examined by the Committee of the Whole House, as in the countries on the British model, especially Australia, where this is the regular practice. The point here is that the Government is invariably represented. In the United Kingdom the ministers concerned also belong to the standing committees and in India, to the select committees. In Ireland they are, as a rule, members of the special and select committees. In Switzerland and Yugoslavia, it is the normal practice for representatives of the Government to take part in the meetings of committees.

Conversely, where ministers have no right, whether legally or in practice, to attend the meetings of the committees, they may be anxious to be heard by them. As a general rule, even if they do not make use of it, committees have the right to turn down any such request, except in a few countries such as Austria, Brazil, France and the Federal Republic of Germany, where the constitutional provisions or standing orders have carefully specified that ministers must be heard if they so request.

The data sought by committees are not necessarily furnished by the ministers themselves. They are often furnished by civil servants, on the authorization of the heads of the departments to which they belong. In this respect, the powers of committees are particularly extensive in the USSR and the People's Democracies. They may be exercised in respect of any branch of activity in the country, since the representatives of all State institutions and all public bodies are required to furnish committees, at their request, with any reports of proceedings or information regarding their operations. Similar powers are granted to committees in the Parliaments of Brazil, Finland and Spain.

Another means of obtaining information is the hearing of private individuals, whether they are interested parties in the problem under discussion or persons having a profound knowledge of it. For this reason, in some Parliaments private persons may be heard by committees in the capacity of 'witnesses', their function being as it were to give evidence for or against the Bill being examined. In

Burma, India, Ireland and the United Kingdom such witnesses are examined by select committees. They do not give evidence before the Committee of the Whole House nor before standing committees. In Ceylon, the witness procedure is unusually widespread, since any organization or any person outside Parliament may ask to give evidence for or against a Bill under consideration. However, the committee remains the sole judge of whether to hear them or not. The examination of witnesses is likewise one of the main features of the procedure used by committees in the United States Congress. In most other countries, witnesses can only be heard by commissions of inquiry or committees vested with powers of inquiry. This is the case in France, the Federal Republic of Germany, Iceland, Turkey and the USSR in particular. Nevertheless, committees may call upon any person they wish to hear, though the persons in question are invited only to furnish information, and do not appear in the capacity of witnesses.

The complex nature of certain problems occasionally makes the committees highly dependent on experts, and the importance of the interests involved frequently gives rise to pressure groups, whose activities and influence vary in a considerable degree from one Parliament to another. Committees have occasionally tried to free themselves from this double handicap by having experts permanently attached to them with instructions to furnish them with any clarification they need on the questions within their field. An experiment on these lines has been tried in the United States Congress, where small groups of experts are placed at the disposal of committees to help them—four per committee. In Egypt, the President may on his own authority or on the proposal of the chairman of a committee attach to the committee 'consultative members' having special qualifications, up to three in number. These have the right to attend the meetings of committees, to give advice and make comments. In its report to the House, the committee is even required to make mention of the opinions of these expert advisers, if they differ from its own.

Committee procedure, of which participation by persons outside Parliament is a marked feature, is also notable for the considerable measure of freedom allowed in debate. Any member of the committee may express his views, speak on one or more occasions, move motions, or put forward amendments on which the committee will have to vote. Thus, as consideration proceeds, the committee's conclusions on the Bill gradually emerge. They are embodied in the report, which is submitted to the House to enable the legislative procedure to take its proper course.

(d) Committee Reports

One of the primary tasks of a committee handling a Bill is to appoint a rapporteur to make a personal study of the matter, to place it before his colleagues in the committee, and then to argue it before the House. This is an extremely important part of the procedure; it affects the future of the Bill since by appointing the rapporteur the committee automatically takes a certain stand in regard to the Bill, which may give some hint as to the conclusions it will ultimately reach, and frequently as to the final decision of the House itself, since committees are as a rule constituted in accordance with a system of proportional representation of the various political groupings.

This initial identification is not found in Parliaments where committees do not appoint a special rapporteur for each particular matter. In Australia, Burma, India, Pakistan, the Sudan and the United Kingdom, and similarly in Israel, Japan, Laos and Spain, the chairman of the committee himself acts as rapporteur; in other words his function is first of all to direct the work of the committee, and then report it to the House. In Sweden, the rapporteur system also has no place. The written reports of committees are joint works containing sufficient information to make the appointment of a special rapporteur hardly necessary. This is also the case in the Netherlands, where reference is made in reports to both minority and majority opinions and where publication is conditional on the committee's approval.

In some instances the appointment of a rapporteur has no relation to the views of the committee. In Egypt, for example, any committee may nominate a permanent general rapporteur whose function is to report on all matters coming before the committee. In Brazil, rapporteurs are appointed in alphabetical order. On the other hand, in the Federal Republic of Germany and Norway, committees may appoint several rapporteurs for one and the same matter. In Switzerland there is always one German-speaking and one French-speaking rapporteur. In the Supreme Soviet of the USSR the permanent committees designate a rapporteur for each Bill if they table the Bill on their own initiative; where they present their findings concerning a Bill proposed in the Supreme Soviet by another body, they appoint a co-rapporteur, the rapporteur proper being nominated by the authority initiating the Bill in question.

The main function of the rapporteur is to be the mouthpiece in the House of the political majority in the committee, especially where—as is generally the case—he has been elected by it. This raises the question of how to safeguard the rights of the minority and how to ensure that it has a chance to express its views. Any opposition which has emerged in the committee can of course put forward its views in the House when the matter comes up for debate, but this opportunity is insufficient, and in any case it comes too late. Hence in a large number of countries the rights of the minority are safeguarded when the report is issued. In practice, when the rapporteur makes his report on the way in which the business has been conducted in committee, he will give some account of any differences of opinion which have arisen. In addition, in some Parliaments the publication of the work of the committees, and in particular the distribution of official reports of the proceedings of meetings, may make up for any defects in the committee's report. Thus for example in the United Kingdom, the United States and the Philippines, the best way of finding out what was the minority opinion is to read the committee's proceedings.

Where publication of the proceedings of committee does not give sufficient information, there are two ways by which the minority can be given a fair hearing:

(a) By the insertion of the minority views in the report, more often than not as an annex. This is the procedure used in the Federal Republic of Germany, India, and Finland. The same is true of Burma, where in addition all the members of the committee have to sign the report. In Poland, at the request of the persons concerned, minority proposals are inserted in the report.

(b) By the appointment of two separate rapporteurs, one representing the majority, the other the minority. This is permitted in the Federal Republic of Germany when differences of opinion are considerable. It is also the practice in Indonesia, Norway and Yugoslavia.

Another system is the issuing of a separate minority report. This is what happens in Italy; in Austria, if the minority on a committee consists of at least three members, it can submit a special written report. In Japan, the dissenting opinion of the minority may be submitted to the House provided a request to that effect is made by one tenth of the committee members present. In the Spanish Cortes, if a provision which has been rejected has obtained more than a quarter of the votes, it must be read in the House.

It should be noted that the concern to make known the minority view is particularly justified in Parliaments where committees do not produce an actual Bill but simply express their opinion of the

Bill submitted. This procedure is found mainly in countries where the two-party system is in force—or at any rate the Government and Opposition system. It is less evident in countries where the number of parties and their amorphous nature are such that a new majority, not necessarily the same as the majority in power, may arise in respect of every problem considered. It may very well happen in such circumstances, as the replies from Luxembourg, Denmark, France, Syria and Turkey indicate, that an Opposition rapporteur may be designated who represents the majority view on a given problem.

As a general rule a committee agrees to a report, the actual drafting of which is entrusted either to the rapporteur, the chairman, or the officers of the House. The report is printed and distributed to Members of Parliament before the topic in question comes up for debate in the House. In an emergency, provision is made (in France, Monaco, the Netherlands and Norway) for the report to be made orally, but this is an exception. Nor is the rapporteur prohibited from supplementing and commenting orally on his written report in the debate in the House. There are countries however, where the system of a mere oral report is regarded as preferable, as for example, in Israel and Spain. In Luxembourg, a written report is required where important matters are at stake, but in Switzerland oral reports are required for important matters.

Once the committee's report has thus been issued and brought to the attention of the Members of Parliament, the important question is whether the House will debate the Bill as amended by the committee as a result of its deliberations, or the Bill as originally introduced. This is the crux of the legislative procedure, and the question is largely bound up with the influence exercised by committees in any particular Parliament, since it involves the action to be taken on their work. It is unfortunately extremely difficult to gain any very clear impression of the practice adopted from the replies furnished by the various countries.

However, what does seem to emerge first and foremost is that the original Bill serves as a basis for debate in only a very small number of Parliaments, including Albania, Brazil, Bulgaria, Japan, the Netherlands, Rumania and the USSR. This amounts in fact to placing the committee which has considered the Bill on the same footing as Members of Parliament, i.e. giving it only the power to put forward amendments. The report is submitted to the House, but all it does is express an opinion on the Bill as introduced—favourable, unfavourable or suggesting modifications. However, in the USSR, amendments proposed in committee are generally taken into consideration by the Government. In a number of other countries, including Czechoslovakia, Denmark, Iceland and Luxembourg, the House itself decides at the beginning of the debate whether the original Bill or the Bill as amended in committee will be taken as a basis for discussion.

The method most commonly found is for the debate to be based on the report prepared by the committee. Here again a distinction must be made according to whether the report amounts merely to the submission of amendments or is in the form of an entirely new Bill. Clearly in any case, if no amendments are proposed by the committee, the original text will be considered. In Egypt, the Philippines and the United States, since reports embody both the original text and the amendments adopted by the committee, a mere reading gives a complete picture of the proceedings.

This is not the case in those countries—and they are the most numerous—where debate in the House is based on the Bill as amended by the committee. It means that the committees are given considerable power, varying between having the right to redraft the Bill radically and being expected to observe its principles. As we have seen, this latter alternative applies mainly to the committees of Parliaments of the British type (Australia, Burma, Ceylon, India, Ireland, Pakistan, the Sudan and the United Kingdom). As a general rule it is unknown in the Continental type of Parliament, that is in most of those of Western Europe, and also in Indonesia, Israel, Laos, Poland, Syria, Turkey, the Republic of Vietnam and Yugoslavia.

The extent of the powers of committees is frequently curtailed, where the Bill emanates from the Government, by the practice whereby the Government may request the House at the beginning of the debate to consider its own original Bill instead of the Bill as amended by the committee.

2. CONSULTATION OUTSIDE PARLIAMENT

In most instances, extra-parliamentary consultations are carried out at the committee stage, in a more or less informal manner. They are part of the work involved in considering Bills. The reason advanced in support of participation in the legislative process by persons or bodies outside Parliament is the laudable concern of committees to obtain information. The committee alone judges how far this practice is desirable. This type of participation is not in any way official, and it is effected mainly, as we have seen, by means of hearings or individual evidence; nor is it outside the power of committee, even when as in Sweden for example, committees ask interested bodies to give their veiws in writing on Bills which the committees have put before them. It can happen however that the consultation procedure outside Parliament goes beyond the scope of committee work. In this case it constitutes an encroachment upon the classic concept of representative democracy, since its essential purpose is to submit drafts to the test of opinion before any public debate takes place in the House.

This type of consultation may be arranged prior to the presentation of the Bill to Parliament. All Governments have recourse to this procedure in varying degrees and generally in an empirical and arbitrary fashion. Switzerland is one of the few countries where the process of preparing Bills has been more or less codified; a Bill is gone over carefully from the technical, legal and social angles before it is brought into the political arena. When the Federal Council prepares a parliamentary Bill, it usually appoints a committee consisting of members of both Houses, government officials and representatives of all the organizations concerned (associations of businessmen, industrialists, bankers, merchants, peasants, employees and workers) and places before this committee not only the main lines of the Bill but also its full technical details. The committee endeavours to bring into line all the various trends of opinion. The text which emerges is then transmitted to the Chancellery, where it is examined to ensure that it is compatible with existing legislation, and also to the various interested ministerial departments. The Federal Council only passes the Bill when the department responsible has given its views on the comments made. In some instances these extra-parliamentary consultations are laid down in the federal Constitution.

In Sweden a similar procedure is found where a Royal Commission is asked to prepare a Bill. It invites the representatives of the bodies concerned in the matter to submit their views to the minister who has been given the task of producing the final version of the Bill. A somewhat similar procedure to this is the consultation of representatives of the Courts, more particularly in regard to the formal drafting of Bills. Thus recourse to the Council of State is obligatory in Egypt and France in the case of government Bills. This is also the case in the Netherlands in respect of Private Members' Bills. Under this procedure recourse to the Council of State is made after both Chambers have passed the Bill. Approval is either granted or refused; in no case may the Council of State amend the Bill when it has been passed.

Where extra-parliamentary consultations are held at a stage when the Bill has already been introduced in the House, they may at times represent a particular concept of parliamentary democracy, based essentially on the concept of the sovereignty of the people. But this does not apply to opinions taken from non-parliamentary assemblies as in France, the Assembly of the French Union and the Economic Council, which are attached to Parliament precisely for the purpose of advising it on specific matters within their field.

More significant is the system used in Burma, India and Pakistan, where Members of Parliament may propose a motion for the 're-circulation of a Bill to elicit further opinion thereon'. If the motion is accepted, the appropriate ministerial department (in India, the secretariat of the two Houses) sends copies of the Bill to all the experts, to all specialist bodies and to interested organizations. The replies received are printed and distributed to members.

The most elaborate form of extra-parliamentary consultation, which presupposes adherence to the principle of popular sovereignty as opposed to the strictly representative system, is the consultative referendum. This is found only in Egypt and Yugoslavia, and seemingly in the Republic of Vietnam. Article 145 of the Egyptian Constitution provides that the President of the Republic may, on the advice of the National Assembly, consult the people on important questions concerning the higher interests of the nation. A further law may lay down regulations concerning the question on which the referendum has been held. In Yugoslavia, the Federal National Assembly can decide that a Bill before being passed shall be placed before the electorate by way of referendum. (The law specifying the details of this referendum has not yet been passed—which goes to show that the procedure presents certain difficulties in application, particularly a slowness and ponderousness which are hardly compatible with the requirements of present-day law-making.)

More effective and more realistic is the system of general public debate which operates in Yugoslavia and is a feature of the legislative procedure in the Socialist democracies. In the USSR, Bills are frequently referred for opinion to the Supreme Soviets and the Councils of Ministers of the Union Republic and also to the local Soviets and to all interested organizations. Where the Bill is of some importance, the whole people express their views on the proposed reforms. In Poland and Rumania, for example, the Constitution of 1952 was the subject of an extensively popular referendum before it was brought before the Grand National Assembly. A similar procedure applies in Czechoslovakia. In Albania and Yugoslavia, Bills embodying social legislation

F*   153

(education, public health and social security) or drafts of special interest to the people ordinarily follow this procedure. In practice this process consists in the publication of the Bill by all available means, and first and foremost the Press, so that all levels of society are informed. Discussion follows within the basic organizations, industrial and agricultural undertakings, professional and trade organizations of all kinds, people's councils, social, scientific and economic institutions, and local and regional administrations; widely differing opinions are gathered and enable suggestions, amendments and perhaps counter-proposals to be drawn up which are forwarded to Parliament and in particular to their appropriate committees. These committees examine them and may, if need be, formally take them into consideration. Before it was finally passed the Pensions Act gave rise in this way to more than 13,000 proposals from the people of the USSR. Thus country-wide discussion takes place which introduces, to some extent, a new form of direct democracy—thanks to the communications media available. The last word, however, rests with the representatives of the people, since it is for them to accept or reject the large number of suggestions addressed to them.

3. THE AGENDA OR ORDER OF BUSINESS

The power to settle the order of business is the keystone, so to speak, of the legislative process, between the preliminary consideration and the final passing of a Bill.

Once a Bill has been introduced, distributed and considered in committee, it must be debated in the House in the regular course of events. It is placed on the order papers; but this is not merely a procedural formality. Among all the various matters pending before Parliament, a definite choice has to be made. Hence the part played by the body which makes this choice, and the regulations which govern it, are extremely important, for the right to initiate legislation, either on the part of the Government or on the part of private members—and even where it is liberally recognized by the Constitution—can be seriously impaired by the method used to draw up the order of business.

If the order of business is prepared by the Government, the Government can easily get rid of awkward questions and may adopt a dictatorial attitude towards Parliament. Conversely, the order of business may be settled by Parliament. This may seem equally improper if we agree that the work of legislation is valid only in so far as the Government takes over the preliminary drafting and in so far as it is at liberty to decide when Parliament shall examine the Bills introduced by the Government. Such a prerogative, though the nature of modern legislation is an argument in its favour, is nevertheless at variance with the old democratic principle that 'Parliament is master of its own order of business'. Thus the whole difficulty—and it is not simply a matter of procedure—is to find a compromise in regard to setting the order of business which will safeguard the independence of Parliament and at the same time provide the necessary powers to enable the Government to be carried on. No system appears to meet both these conditions. Either the Government enjoys an almost absolute priority, or Parliament maintains the right to choose what matters it will deal with. To analyse the matter a little further, we find that, according to the country concerned, the order of business may be fixed by:

(a) The Government.
(b) The President or Speaker of the House.
(c) The House itself, usually on the proposal of one of its official bodies.

Here again we find an almost complete cleavage between the British system and the others. The former is the outcome of a long evolution. Until the reforms of 1832, most of the legislation in the House of Commons was proposed by private members, who had at their disposal all the time not expressly granted to the Government. But at the beginning of the nineteenth century, the House began to allow the Government two days a week to conduct its business. At present private members have ten Fridays during the parliamentary session at their disposal for putting forward Bills. In both Houses, the prerogative of the Government is exercised through the Leader of the House and the Chief Whip, who is also a member of the Government. It is they who arrange the order of business of the House after consultation with the leaders of the Opposition and other members.

This example has been followed by a number of countries, though they have not gone through the same evolution as the British Parliament in this respect. Thus in Australia, Burma, Ceylon, Ireland and Pakistan, the task of arranging the business of Parliament is given to the executive, invariably through the Leader of the House, where necessary in agreement with the leaders of the Opposition. In India, the business of the House is decided by the Speaker after consultation with the leader of the majority in the House. In Israel it is decided by the Government in collaboration with the Presidium of the Knesset, which includes representatives of the minority parties.

In practice, the power of the executive over the programme of parliamentary business is practically absolute. The time allowed for private members' business is proof of this. To give an example, in Australia such business can only be taken in the Senate on Thursday after 8 p.m., and in the House of Representatives every other Thursday up to 12.45 p.m., during which time they have priority over business introduced by the Government, unless a decision is taken to the contrary. On the other Thursday mornings, following the examination of financial matters, any member may address the House on any subject and give his views. These sittings are known as 'grievance days'. In India, every Friday a period of two and a half hours before the adjournment is set aside for private members' business. In Ceylon, the Wednesday sitting is set aside in this way, as also in Burma, though the time left over on other days once government business has been completed, is also at the disposal of private members. In Ireland, government Bills have invariably the priority, except after 9 p.m. on Wednesdays and 12 noon on Fridays.

Apart from this, the manner in which the order of bringing up Private Members' Bills is arranged is also significant. In Burma, India, Pakistan and the United Kingdom the order is simply drawn by lot. In Ceylon, it is a question of first come first served. In other words the question of urgency or importance of the problems does not affect the issue.

This method of organizing parliamentary business is completely at variance with the Continental concept of the functioning of Parliament, the essential feature under the Continental system being continuous participation in the legislative process. Actually, the underlying principle is that the executive should be given the leading role in the preparation of legislation. It is felt that the executive alone, because of the information facilities at its disposal, and because of the overall picture its position gives it, is in a position to exercise this function effectively.

Thus, although Great Britain inspired Montesquieu's celebrated theory of the separation of power, by an irony of fate, it is further removed from British practice than that of a number of other countries. In London, the principal dividing line in legislative questions is between the majority party, on the one hand, which forms the Government through which it implements its policy and with which it collaborates to legislate, and on the other, the minority party whose primary function is to criticize the action of the Government and to prepare an alternative policy. The demarcation-line between Government and Opposition is more important than that between legislative and executive.

The best proof of this is the almost official status given to the Opposition in regard to the arrangement of parliamentary business. In the first place it is consulted as to the choice of subjects for debate, and secondly it is given a fairly large number of sitting days—almost a third—during which it can exercise freely its right to criticize any matters it chooses. Theoretically, a majority party in the House of Commons, if it so desired, could take over all the time set aside for debate. In practice, and putting aside all question of propriety, the Government party would be chary of being so imprudent, as intolerant actions of this nature would merely rebound against it when through the normal democratic processes the elections went against the Government and it then became the Opposition.

The use of this system suggests two conclusions which apply to all the countries which have come under British influence in regard to legislation:

(a) The powers of the Government over the House are theoretically very considerable in this matter.

(b) The Member of Parliament as an individual has lost ground, but the official Opposition has gained, especially in the matter of keeping a check on the Government's activities.

These conclusions by no means apply in regard to other countries; in some cases the system of Government and Opposition is unknown and in its place we find shifting majorities in regard to legislative matters; in others Parliament holds fast to its prerogatives in regard to law-making and particularly in regard to settling the order of business.

It would nevertheless be paradoxical to think of the Government, which is responsible for the conduct of public affairs, being kept completely in the dark, without any weapon it could use to put its own Bills forward for debate. In theory this is most frequently the case, since in most countries only Parliament can settle the order of its own business. In actual fact, this sweeping statement requires some modification. The Government can always appeal to its majority, even if it is based on the support of different groups of opinion, to get its way.

Subject to these remarks, the prerogatives of most Parliaments in regard to the order of business are exercised in a variety of ways, all having a common feature: no official priority is given to Bills originating from the Government.

The task of arranging the order of business may be entrusted to the President or Speaker of the House. In a few European countries such as Denmark, Finland, Spain and Switzerland, and outside Europe in Brazil, Egypt and Syria, he alone is responsible. In Norway, the order of business is drawn up by the Presidency, in other words by a meeting of the Presidents of the Storting and its two Houses, the meetings of the Storting invariably having priority over those of either of the Houses. The order of business of each of these three assemblies is determined by its President within this framework. In Iceland, the same system applies.

The President may have occasion to consult certain bodies before taking his decision, e.g. the Bureau of the National Assembly in Laos, the Board of Directors of the House Management Committee in Japan, the Chairman of Committees in Monaco.

The system of giving the President or Speaker of the House the task of drawing up the order of business provides great flexibility; its avoids the introduction of political considerations; it makes it easier to take into account the requests of the Government; and frequently it has the effect of giving them a certain measure of priority (e.g. in Denmark and Finland). In Switzerland, the executive enjoys a virtually exclusive initiative in legislative matters, and is thus the body responsible for arranging the order of business of each session. The order of business may be drawn up by agreement between the heads of the parties, as in the United States Senate, or by a committee, as in the House of Representatives —the 'Rules Committee', which has in fact taken discretionary powers and is outside the control of the Government and the House itself. If a Bill has a majority of the members of the committee against it, it has little prospect of reaching the House. Conversely, if it is supported by the committee, it will have priority of debate over all others. The executive can only have its own Bills debated by arrangement with the committee. In the Federal Republic of Germany, the order of business is seldom settled by the Bundestag itself; the Bundestag intervenes only in the rare event of disagreement in the Council of Elders.

The commonest procedure is for the House itself to determine its programme of work on the basis of proposals put before it either by its President, as in Albania, the Netherlands and Yugoslavia, or by one of its directing bodies; the Presidium in Czechoslovakia, the Presidium and Council of Elders in Poland, the Bureau in Luxembourg, Bulgaria and Rumania, and the Council of Doyens in the USSR.

Frequently a special body has been set up for this purpose. As an example we have the Conference of Presidents of the French

Assemblies, consisting of the President and Vice-Presidents, and the chairmen of committees and political groups. The advantage of this procedure is that the Government can be represented on it and makes its voice heard. The practice is similar in Austria and Italy. In the Republic of Vietnam it is known as the Order of Business Board, and in Belgium the parliamentary working committee, this consisting of the President and Vice-Presidents, six representatives of groups in the Chamber, and six members appointed by the Bureau in the Senate. As a general rule these bodies meet every week, examine requests put forward by the Government on the one hand and the committees on the other, and work out a programme of business which they submit to their Houses with a good chance that it will be accepted, since the political composition of these bodies reflects in a general way that of the Houses.

The practice of settling the order of business for a fairly long period ahead makes it possible to organize the work of Parliament methodically and gives a certain stability and continuity to the debates. Casual changes are therefore hardly desirable. Apart from the confusion they are apt to introduce into the conduct of business they may give rise to argument and snap votes, which are hardly compatible with the dignity of Parliament. For this reason precautions are frequently taken to prevent the question of the order of business, once it has been settled, from being constantly re-opened. In France for example the National Assembly is prohibited from changing its order of business. Such rigidity has its drawbacks, of course, since circumstances may make it desirable to modify the order of business which has been drawn up.

In other cases, modifications are permissible, but there are conditions of varying strictness attached to them:

In Italy, where a change is proposed by a member, it must have three quarters of the votes in the lower House, and two thirds in the Senate.

In Norway, a simple majority is sufficient to pass a proposal made by the President. Two thirds of the votes are required if the proposal emanates from a member.

In the Belgian House of Representatives, changes in the order of business may be submitted by the President, the Government, the parliamentary working committee, or a member supported by one third of the House.

In the Federal Republic of Germany, an item may always be withdrawn from the order of business at the decision of the

House. A new item may not be inserted if five members present at the sitting oppose it.

The purpose of preparing an order of business, whether it gives the Government the upper hand or confirms the traditional independence of Parliament, is to cope with one of the main obstacles to the working of Parliament today—shortage of time. Modern Parliaments have always more work than they can perform. The selection of Bills for examination cannot be left to chance. If legislative business is to be effective, it must be properly organized. This need is seen in all aspects of parliamentary procedure.

4. DEBATE IN THE HOUSE

In the process of legislation, debate in the House of Bills before they are finally passed is the most spectacular phase, owing to the fact that it is in public, as well as the most complex in its operation, and the most animated, in view of the vast possibilities of developments. It may be described as a sort of contest, sometimes long and fairly exciting, between those for and those against the proposed reform, the stake being the Bill. This contest waged as a rule with the weapons of argument only, may be methodically organized or speeded up, or it may go on and on indefinitely or fizzle out without a decision.

(a) The General Features of Procedure

Parliaments can be divided into two quite distinct categories, according to whether they debate each Bill only once or carry out a series of readings of the same Bill. We must be careful not to confuse these 'readings', in the Anglo-Saxon or Germanic sense, with successive readings and examinations required by the so-called 'shuttle' procedure, by which Bills pass to and fro between the Houses in certain bicameral Parliaments, for the purpose of obtaining agreement to an identical form of words.

Subject to this reservation, it may be said that most of the countries of Western Europe and all the People's Democracies with the exception of Poland, as well as Syria, Turkey, Japan, Laos and the Republic of Vietnam, have a single stage of debate in the House itself. If we break down this single debate, we find that it invariably consists of several phases in a more or less continuous succession:

160

(*a*) Presentation of the committee's report.
(*b*) General debate in principle open to all members.
(*c*) Examination of the clauses of the bill and amendments thereto.
(*d*) Explanations of votes.
(*e*) Voting on the bill as a whole.

In actual fact, this tabulation covers a series of procedures which differ greatly in detail, and the study of this matter would be out of place here. The most we can do is to point out some peculiarities which may affect the principle of the single reading.

There is first of all the so-called 'second debate' procedure found in countries like Egypt, France and Switzerland. It consists of a reopening of the debate, prior to the vote on the Bill as a whole, on certain parts of the Bill which appear to be badly drafted or not in keeping with the rest of it. In Egypt, the request for a second debate must be made by the Government, the rapporteur or chairman of the committee, or ten members of the House. In France, the second debate is mandatory when requested or agreed to by the committee. The Bill as originally agreed to is re-committed, and the committee must present a new report. During this second debate, the House is required to make known its views only on new Bills put forward by the committee or on amendments which were made to Bills already agreed to. The House may also decide to recommit the Bill as reported by the committee for revision and consequential amendment. In this case, the committee presents its findings immediately. They are read out in the House and debate is confined to the drafting only. In the same way, in Belgium, Luxembourg and the Netherlands (Second Chamber) provision is made for a sort of second reading, confined strictly to the drafting, where the Bill has been amended in the course of examination. In Luxembourg, a second examination of any amended Bill is mandatory.

In Italian parliamentary practice we find a special type of procedure, the effect of which is to separate the debate in the House into two distinct parts. In some instances, the House may debate a Bill in a general way without touching on the individual clauses. In this case the final drafting is entrusted to the committee which has drafted the preliminary report, subject to a sort of second reading in which the clauses are agreed to without debate and there is an explanation of votes and the Bill as a whole is passed. This procedure is somewhat reminiscent of the British system, which allows the House to define the essential principles of the Bill before it is referred to the committee for the technical work of considering the individual

161

clauses. Something similar is found in the Polish Diet, where there are two readings, the first consisting of a debate on the general principles of the Bill, the second a detailed examination of the provisions and any amendments proposed by the committee. The chairman can adjourn the voting on the Bill as a whole where the amendments that have been made render it desirable to go over the Bill once more. The Indonesian Parliament also has this system of two readings, but there does not appear to be any procedural distinction to be made between them.

Most other Parliaments have the system of three readings. Here again, a distinction must be made between the European continental countries and the countries based on the British model. With regard to the former, reference has already been made to the special case of Austria and Finland in the study of legislative work in committee.[1] In Sweden there is a similarly unusual procedure. We get three readings of the committee's report following the introduction of the Bill, but no debate is permitted except during the last reading.

In Denmark, the Federal Republic of Germany, Iceland and Israel, the system is somewhat closer to the classic type. There is a first reading which starts the procedure with a debate on the general principles of the Bill, a second devoted to the examination of the committee's report, the clauses of the Bill and any proposed amendments, and a third reading confined to the final passing of the Bill on the basis of the decisions taken at the previous reading.

The British procedure is somewhat different, although in principle it consists of the same number of readings. The first reading is as a rule a pure formality. It consists simply of the introduction of the Bill. The second reading is the essential phase, for the main lines of the Bill are then determined. Amendments are in order only if they propose the rejection of the Bill *in toto* (either by adjourning the second reading to a date after the session or by proposing its rejection for certain reasons) or if they propose settlement of the matter in a way other than by allowing the Bill to go forward.

Examination in committee takes place only after this stage. Then follows a detailed debate of the Bill, as sent back by the committee, by the House. This so-called report stage constitutes to some extent a repetition of the examination made in committee, though the rules here are stricter. Its main value is to enable ministers to draft changes they had agreed to in principle in committee. During the report stage, the clauses are not voted on separately; the Bill is

[1] See page 142 (of second part).

considered as a whole. The third reading follows the report stage and as a rule takes place on the same day. It consists in reviewing the final version of the Bill; thus the debate is confined on this occasion to what actually is in the Bill. Unlike what happens at the second reading, no new suggestion is permitted. Only verbal amendments are in order and they must comply with this condition.

With some differences, especially in regard to the purpose of amendments and the time-limits for submitting them, the procedure in the Parliaments of Australia, Burma, Ceylon, India, Ireland, Pakistan and the Sudan is also based on this rule of division into three readings. In the United States and the Philippines, the three readings are more simply arranged. First there is the introduction of the Bill; then comes the examination of the report on each separate clause of the Bill and each amendment, and thirdly there is the final passing of the Bill.

Within this framework, debate, an essential feature of the democratic system, can take place. In theory at any rate, the ideal solution should emerge from this clash of ideas and exchange of views. But if the debate is to be effective and to culminate in something concrete—in this case the enactment of a law—it is frequently desirable for it to be circumscribed by strict rules. Where this proves necessary, the purpose of the rules should be both to protect the rights of the minority and to safeguard the efficient operation of the legislative process by avoiding systematic obstruction, but this is no easy task.

(b) Rules of Debate

There are two essential aspects of rules of debate: (i) limitation of the exercise of the individual's right to speak; (ii) regulation of the debate generally (indication of a definite time-limit or detailed rules governing the way in which the debate must be conducted).

(i) *Limitation of the right to speak*. Since speeches are the life-blood of parliamentary procedure, restrictions on them should be an exceptional measure. But experience shows that parliamentary rhetoric is not readily amenable to self-discipline. In one or two Parliaments there is complete freedom in this respect, and it is not abused—in Finland, any Member of Parliament or the Government can speak for as long as he pleases and can have the floor as many times as he wishes. The same is true in Bulgaria and Sweden. But this is quite exceptional. In most other Parliaments, it has been found necessary to subject the exercise of the right to speak to certain conditions, their stringency depending frequently on the status of the speaker. For example, generally speaking, members of the Government addressing the House enjoy complete freedom in regard to their speeches. However, in the Supreme Soviet of the USSR, ministers do not enjoy any special privilege in relation to other speakers, while in some countries, such as the United States and Brazil, ministers are prohibited from speaking altogether, in virtue of the principle of the separation of powers.

Another class of speakers frequently enjoying special privileges are the spokesmen of committees, the chairman and rapporteurs, especially in Parliaments where committees perform a very important function. In principle such speakers are not in any way limited, or they may have at any rate special privileges as compared with other speakers. In Iceland, rapporteurs may speak on three different occasions whereas an ordinary speaker has the right to speak only twice. In the USSR, rapporteurs may speak for an hour and a half the first time, and half an hour the second, whereas other members are allowed only twenty minutes and five minutes respectively. In Brazil rapporteurs have twice the length of time allowed to other speakers. In Austria, Italy, Poland and the USSR they are entitled to speak last, to close the debate. With regard to the right of other Members of Parliament to speak, either the number of times, or the duration of speeches, or both, are subject to strict rules in many Parliaments.

In India, members are allowed to speak only once on any subject; in Albania, Austria and the Netherlands twice. Length of speeches is limited to twenty minutes in Burma, thirty in Belgium, an hour in the Federal Republic of Germany, Luxembourg and Australia. In the last-named country there are intricate rules as to the length of time allowed for each type of subject under debate. In the Republic of Vietnam the time-limit is an hour and a half for speakers whose names are already on the list of speakers, and thirty minutes for those not on the list. In the Philippines the maximum time is two hours in the Senate and one hour in the House of Representatives. Sometimes, when two speeches are permitted, the length of each is specified—in Laos fifteen minutes for each speech, in Egypt thirty minutes, in Switzerland twenty minutes the first time and ten the second, in Poland thirty and ten minutes respectively, in Norway one hour and ten minutes respectively. In spite of the apparent strictness of all these rules, it must be borne in mind of course that in most Parliaments the President or Speaker is responsible for maintaining order during the debates, and he will ordinarily use a certain amount of discretion in exercising his authority.

In Laos, a member's right to go on speaking is interrupted when the President rises from his seat. In the House of Commons and those Parliaments which have followed its methods, the powers of the Speaker are unusually wide in this direction. The Speaker alone is responsible for deciding the order in which members are to speak. There are no formal rules on this head. The House places full confidence in the Speaker's sense of what is right and trusts him to see to it that speeches are relevant and not repetitious, and to ensure as far as possible that speakers from either side of the House are heard alternately. The authority of the President is a good deal less in other Parliaments. He has invariably the power to recall the speakers to the subject under discussion, but as a rule he is required to follow the order in which their requests to speak have been put down on a list drawn up before or during the debate.

(ii) *Limitation and Organization of Debates.* Here again, while some Parliaments such as those of Bulgaria, Czechoslovakia, Finland and Sweden are fortunate enough not to be subject to any such restrictions, most Parliaments make provision for certain types of summary procedures for dispatching business more rapidly, the main effect being to reduce considerably the length of debate. The reason for laying down a time-limit for debate may be first of all the fact that there is no disagreement on the Bill. In this connexion mention may be made of the French institution of 'voting without debate' and the shortened debate.[1] The debate may also be curtailed because of the urgency of the matter under consideration.

In some Parliaments there are special rules for speeding up the legislative procedure. This is true of Brazil, France, Ireland, Rumania, Spain and Yugoslavia, once a matter has been declared urgent. In France, the emergency debate procedure, which is subject to extremely complex rules, is decided upon by the National Assembly. Its effect is to speed up the 'shuttle' movement between the two Houses rather than actually to limit debate in either of them. The Council of the Republic has the right to resort to 'immediate discussion', a procedure not unlike that used in Yugoslavia. The main effect in both cases is to cut down very considerably the times allotted to the committees for consideration of Bills. In Ireland, in case of emergency, the Dail can decide to curtail by artificial means the time normally taken up at each stage of a Bill. In the same way, the President of the Spanish Cortes can shorten the time allowed under the ordinary procedure. In Brazil, the forty-eight hour

[1] See pages 144 and 145.

interval which must normally elapse between the first and second readings can be waived. In addition, certain matters can be examined more rapidly by being accorded 'priority' or 'preference' status.

In the House of Commons, there is a special procedure which is extremely effective, with the expressive title of the 'guillotine'. By passing a guillotine motion, the House fixes a time-limit for completion of the discussion of the whole or specific parts of the Bill or motion. A special committee known as the 'Business Committee', on which the Opposition leaders are represented, works out in detail how the Bill or motion is to be divided. When the time-limit fixed for each part of the Bill is reached, the Speaker automatically puts the question, and the House is obliged to vote forthwith. Most of the Parliaments on the British model have adopted the guillotine system; but owing to its drastic nature, where there is less urgency it is often found preferable for the representatives of the Government and the Opposition to arrive at a voluntary agreement. This is a frequent practice in the United Kingdom, Ireland and Ceylon. A practice not unlike the guillotine, though not given this name, is found in some Parliaments in the form of a decision that a debate shall not exceed a time fixed beforehand. This practice is found, for example, in Egypt, the Netherlands, the Philippines, Poland and Turkey.

But the most far-reaching procedure is that known as the 'organization of debates', found particularly in France. Once it has been decided to arrange a debate, there is a conference, attended by the President and Vice-Presidents of the Assembly, the chairmen of the political groups, the chairmen and rapporteurs of the appropriate committees, and the members whose names are on the list of speakers, along with a representative of the Government. The conference decides on the number of sittings to be set aside for the debate. Having done that, it allots the speaking time for the various political groups and in some instances it fixes the final date by which the vote on the entire Bill must be taken. Thus each group will have a definite speaking time allotted, generally proportionate to the size of its membership. It is at liberty to use its time as it wishes, but in principle it may not go beyond it. A similar system operates in the Netherlands. In the Federal Republic of Germany the initiative is taken by the Council of Elders, in Indonesia by the Steering Committee, in Israel by the House Committee, and in Japan by the House Management Committee.

All these procedures are fairly efficient, provided they are properly carried out. But their success depends largely on the observance of the rules of parliamentary procedure by the minority in particular. If the Opposition is not convinced of the merits of a measure, there are always ways to be found of delaying or preventing the termination of the debate, except under the extreme procedure of the guillotine.

(c) *Procedural Motions and Obstruction*

Parliamentary procedure places at the disposal of all parties not only the right to speak and to submit amendments, but also a whole battery of technical facilities which, while they are designed to ensure a serious and honest examination of the matters under discussion, can be distorted so that in some circumstances they are tantamount to obstruction.

Ways of avoiding or postponing a decision are found in all Parliaments except those of Israel and Sweden. The devices most frequently used are the following, in order of frequency:

(a) The motion for adjournment, which is found in virtually all Parliaments. This consists of requesting the adjournment of the debate *sine die*, or to a specific date, or until certain conditions have been fulfilled, e.g. until sufficient data have been collected, after the Bill has been distributed, or until the advice of other bodies is obtained. In the Finnish Parliament there is a special type of adjournment: at the request of a third of the members, the final passing of a Bill may be suspended, after it has been examined on third reading, until the first regular session following a general election.

(b) Request for reference back to a committee, another very common practice which is easier to apply where the powers of the committees are considerable. The argument used to justify it may be that some aspects of the Bill have not been properly studied by the original committee or need to be submitted to other committees for their views.

(c) The 'previous question', a less common device. It is proposed at the beginning of the debate and, if it is agreed to, signifies that no deliberation is called for—in other words it is for practical purposes equivalent to outright rejection of the Bill. It is used particularly in Belgium, France and Italy, where it is in order only if endorsed by ten members or fifteen senators.

(d) Proposal to change the order of business. This is similar in its effects. In Denmark, Iceland and Indonesia, it takes the form of a motion to 'take up the next item', or in Italy, to pass on to other business. In the Federal Republic of Germany, resort to this procedure, which is considered as particularly drastic, is limited by restrictive ruling.

Other less orthodox methods of prolonging the debate are also found.

Where there is no rule to prevent it from doing so the Opposition may have recourse to an endless series of amendments, or may simply prolong the speeches of its members beyond a reasonable length. The best known example is the 'filibustering' technique used in the American Senate, where any senator has the right to hold the floor as long as he can stand on his feet. Then there are other more technical methods, directly based on rules of procedure. Here are one or two examples:

(*a*) Calling for a count of the House to see that a quorum is present before proceeding with the vote. This is common in the Federal Republic of Germany, the Philippines and Turkey.

(*b*) Rising on points of order. This makes it possible, on the pretext of claiming that certain provisions of the rules of procedure should be applied to delay the debate on the subject under discussion. It is frequently practised in Egypt, France and Italy.

(*c*) Motions for the adjournment of the House.

(*d*) Request for a formal vote. This can take a variety of forms according to the particular voting methods used—request for a roll-call vote (the Federal Republic of Germany), request for a separate vote on each part of the Bill (Austria), request for a scrutiny (France).

Clearly the abuse of these various procedures, especially those last-named, is what constitutes obstruction. It is easier to challenge methods arising out of procedural motions. Actually, so long as such motions are not systematically repeated and are moved merely to indicate that a particular stand is being taken, they are not necessarily obstructive. Thus in Albania, Bulgaria and the USSR, Parliament permits motions for closure, but obstruction tactics are completely unknown.

As a matter of fact, there are always ways of countering the stock methods of abusing the rules:

First of all there are the disciplinary powers of the President or, above all, of the Speaker, who in some instances has the right to refuse to accept motions at variance with the spirit

168

if not the letter of the rules of procedure. This is true in India, for example.

More often than not the majority has the power to reject motions as fast as they are submitted, although of course this does not help to shorten the debate. Stronger action can also be taken: in France, for example, the majority can counter all delaying motions with a general motion declaring them inadmissible. In Luxembourg, and in the United States Senate, the majority can oppose debate of procedural motions by means of the 'previous question' device. In the Federal Republic of Germany, the Bundestag can as a last resort decide, with the support of two thirds of the members present, to suspend certain provisions of the standing orders, and thus put a stop to the practice of introducing large numbers of motions.

Coping with obstruction is a more formidable proposition where the Opposition makes use of procedural tactics calling a count of the House, suspension of the sitting, invocation of the rules of procedure, request for a recount, etc. Thus some Parliaments, to avoid these abuses, have taken the precaution of laying down strict regulations governing such tactics—but these regulations are not always completely effective. In that event, the majority has one ultimate weapon at its command if it wishes to curtail the debate or to cope with any attempt at obstruction—closure. The only Parliaments which do not make any provision for this procedure are those in which obstruction is entirely or almost entirely unknown, i.e. Albania, Bulgaria, Czechoslovakia, Finland, Israel, Spain, Sweden, Switzerland and the USSR.

Closure is a means by which the majority can put an end to the debate and go straight on to a vote on the Bill. In some cases short explanations of votes may be permitted. The fact that the effects of the closure system are so drastic makes it desirable to make its use dependent on certain conditions which will at least safeguard the rights of the minority. To this end, in many Parliaments the right to put forward a motion for closure may only be exercised by the President or Speaker, or by a specified number of members.

In the United Kingdom and in countries on the British model, the Speaker has the sole right to decide to put or refuse to put before the House the motion 'that the question be now put'. He can refuse to put it to the vote if he considers that it impairs the rights of the minority. Furthermore, in the House of Commons, if there is opposition to the motion for closure, the motion must be supported by at least a hundred members. Similar practices are found in many other Parliaments where the powers of the President are less extensive. In the Federal Republic of Germany, a motion to close the sitting must have the backing of thirty members, in Norway ten in Belgium ten senators and twenty members of the lower house, and in Egypt twenty members.

In Austria, France and Turkey, any member may move the closure of the debate, but only after two speakers against the original motion have been heard. In Switzerland such motions may be put only after the spokesmen of each group have been heard in the three official languages. In the Philippines, closure may be moved only after three speeches have been made for and two against the Bill. In Iceland, debates may not be cut to less than three hours. In some instances, to be passed the motion for closure requires a specific majority, e.g. in the United States Senate, and in the Swiss National Council, two thirds of the votes must be in favour.

Although there is provision for the closure motion in almost all Parliaments, it is not a very frequently used procedure, for whatever precautions are taken, it can very easily become a method of stifling the Opposition, thus getting democratic opinion up in arms against it. Indeed, the problem of obstruction goes beyond the sphere of parliamentary procedure. It can be a means of legitimate resistance where a majority tries to impose its views without regard for the rights of the minority. In such circumstances its main object is to make public opinion aware of what is going on, and the attitude of public opinion frequently determines the fate of the Bill. Such indirect interplay between the Parliament and the country indicates that, quite apart from its legal validity, obstruction is based on the sacred right of insurrection, and is recognized in the most democratic of constructions. But the relative legitimacy of obstruction must not be used as an argument for incorporating it in the rules of procedure. In virtue of an equally democratic principle, the power in Parliament must invariably rest with the majority.

(d) Amendments

The motion, as mentioned above, is a type of procedural tactic affecting the general course of the discussion; amendments on the other hand bear directly on the terms of the Bill they are designed to modify. Amendments in their turn are subject to scrutiny, first of all in committee, if they are submitted early enough, and then in the House. In both cases, the procedure is roughly the same.

170

- The right to submit amendments is universally recognized as one of the prerogatives of Members of Parliament, except in the Second Chamber in Austria and in the First Chamber in the States-General of the Netherlands. It derives first and foremost from their right to initiate legislation. If a member is entitled to introduce a complete Bill, he is *a fortiori* entitled to propose an amendment to a Bill. On the principle that the greater includes the less, an amendment is regarded as a restricted form of initiation of legislation. Again, in so far as it is exercised in meetings, the right to submit amendments may be regarded as a concomitant of the right to speak. It constitutes an essential feature of democratic practice. Hence it is allowed unusual latitude in some Parliaments, especially those of the People's Democracies.

In the USSR, the right to move amendments is unlimited for members in the Supreme Soviet. Moreover, the right to speak is sometimes granted to persons who are not members, together with the right to introduce legislation and express their wishes. Furthermore, as we have seen, important Bills are given unusually wide circulation in the Press, the idea being to stimulate comment and ideas from all citizens, as members of their various organizations, with a view to being taken up and discussed by the Members or committees of Parliament. This procedure helps to enhance the authority of the legislature and to create a sincere respect for the Bills when they are passed.

Such a method cannot be regarded altogether as a novelty, except for its official recognition, since if we look at the practice in other Parliaments, we find that it is invariably possible for a person outside Parliament in one way or another to suggest to a Member of Parliament amendments which the latter can then move of his own accord. However, the fact that such pressure can be exerted in an underhand, uncontrollable manner can occasionally give rise to severe criticism.

Where the right to submit amendments is placed on exactly the same footing as the right to introduce legislation, it means that Members of Parliament can propose the replacement of the whole Bill under discussion by another complete Bill based on different principles. In France, this system of indirect initiation of legislation is known as the alternative proposal or *contre-projet*. If such a 'counter-project' is taken up by Parliament, it is referred to the appropriate committee for further report.

On the other hand, in some cases the fact that alternative proposals are tantamount to a new Bill makes them out of order. In Spain, for example, if an amendment is tantamount to a substantive change in the Bill, it must be treated as a new Bill and go through the ordinary legislative channels. Similarly, in Denmark and Iceland, an amendment to a Bill cannot be submitted if it is so far from the original that, if passed, it would amount to the enactment of a new item of legislation, without the formality of the three readings laid down in the Constitution. In Israel, too, if an amendment proposed by a committee is challenged by a representative of the Government or a member of the committee as outside the scope of the Bill in question, the President refers the question of its admissibility to the Committee of the Whole House, whose decision is final.

Like the right to initiate legislation and the right to speak, the right to submit amendments is in many cases subject to rules designed to ensure that it is not abused and that the debate proceeds in an orderly fashion. These rules involve first and foremost the observance of certain formalities. In most Parliaments, amendments must be submitted in writing; in some, they may be submitted orally— Albania, Ceylon, Czechoslovakia, Finland, Laos, Norway, the Philippines, Rumania, Spain and the USSR. In some cases, by analogy with the provisions governing the right to initiate legislation amendments are only in order if they are supported by a specified number of members. In the Second Chamber of the Netherlands and Indonesia, the signatories of an amendment must be at least five in number; in the Belgian State two (or five after the conclusion of the general debate), and five in the House of Representatives (while the debate is still on); eight in the Austrian National Council, twenty in the Japanese House of Representatives and ten in the House of Councillors, and fifteen in the Federal German Bundestag at the third reading although one alone is enough at the second reading. In Brazil, amendments must be submitted by the leader of a party or by twenty-five members. In Italy, if they are put forward within an hour before the sitting begins they must be supported by ten members. On the other hand, in Luxembourg they may not be signed by more than five members.

As a general rule, when the Government has the right to introduce legislation, it also has the right to submit amendments. Exceptions to this rule are France, the Federal Republic of Germany and Sweden. In these countries the Government does, however, have the right to have Members of Parliament who support it submit amendments. Nevertheless, non-recognition of the right of the Government to submit amendments constitutes a considerable restriction of the right it has under the Constitution to introduce legislation. In the Netherlands however a distinction is made between 'amendments', which are always submitted by members, and 'Government modifications' which differ from them in that they may arise in the course of debate and without the agreement of the House up to the time when the provisions they aim to modify have been accepted by the Second Chamber. Should the majority oppose a Government modification, it may either reject it or make an amendment to restore the Bill to its original form. The Dutch Government thus enjoys considerable latitude in its right to submit amendments.

Notice of the terms of amendments before they are examined in Parliament would appear to be a basic necessity, since it not only makes for the orderly conduct of debate, but ensures good legislative practice. This being so, it is surprising to find that prior notice of amendments is by no means a universal requirement. It is understandable, of course, that Members of Parliament are somewhat reluctant to restrict their rights in this way. In Burma, India, Ireland, Pakistan and the Sudan, notice of amendments must be given one or two clear days before the sitting. This is also the case in Israel for amendments which have not been accepted in committee. In Egypt, Denmark, and Iceland they are required to be circulated the day before the debate is to take place. In the Republic of Vietnam, they have to be put in not more than twenty-four hours after the posting of the orders of the day which include the matter to which they relate; and in Sweden, at the latest ten days after the Bill is laid before the House, unless the House decides otherwise.

Subject to these provisions, a great deal of latitude is left as a rule to proposers of amendments. They can either propose that an entire section, a clause, a paragraph, or a sentence, or particular words should be deleted, or they can ask for part of the Bill to be amended, or for further provisions to be added.

Sometimes there are restrictions on the subject-matter which limit the admissibility of amendments—quite apart from the self-evident and therefore more or less universal rule that amendments must refer to the Bill itself. The main restrictions have to do with public money matters. Here practices differ very considerably. In the Australian Senate, proposals for new taxes by way of amendments are strictly prohibited. In India and Pakistan, amendments on money matters are admissible only on the recommendation of the Head of State; in the United Kingdom, by a 'recommendation by the Crown', and provided they are in keeping with a money resolution already passed, specifying the maximum amount to be spent in the event of the Bill being passed. In Ireland, a Member of Parliament cannot table an amendment which will or might result in an increase in public expenditure or in taxes. In the Sudan, the agreement of the Minister of Finance is required. In Turkey, amendments on money matters must have the support of fifty members, and the same number is required in the House of Representatives of Japan. In the Japanese House of Councillors twenty names are sufficient. In France amendments to a money Bill must be made within four days following the distribution of the report of the committee.

These are the main restrictions on the right to submit amendments, apart from the specific matter of the third reading in Parliaments on the British model, where in principle only verbal amendments are admissible. In Burma and India in particular, amendments which are at variance with previous decisions of the House or make the amended clause unintelligible, or which the Speaker considers frivolous, are inadmissible. In Finland and Sweden the same is true of amendments which challenge the basic principle of the matter under debate.

It would be out of place here to go into the details of the various methods of debating amendments. From the general angle, they are always examined before the part of the Bill (i.e. the clause or article) to which they refer is agreed to. They can of course themselves be modified by way of 'amendments to amendments'. Also, the debate of amendments is frequently limited, the proposer and the representatives of the Governments and of the committees having a priority right to speak.

One very important problem, since it can have a decided effect on the final shape of the Bill, is the order in which competing amendments, i.e. amendments concerning one and the same part of the text but different in scope, are called. In countries which follow the British procedure, and in the USSR and most of the People's Democracies, such amendments are taken in order of submission. On the other hand, in Western Europe, Syria, Turkey and Yugoslavia, priority is given to those amendments furthest away from the terms of the Bill, beginning with those which propose the deletion of the original words.

The powers of the President of the House in the matter of amendments may also have a decided effect on the enactment of Bills. As a general rule, the President's powers are limited to assessing the admissibility or priority status of the Bills, if his powers are actually defined. In the event of a dispute, the House has invariably the right to settle the issue in the last resort.

In the British House of Commons and also in Ceylon, India and Pakistan the Speaker has an unusually powerful prerogative, which consists of the right to select at his own discretion whichever amendments he sees fit among those which have been tabled. These wide powers of selection are granted on a regular basis only in the House of Commons. The principle has to be approached with infinite caution, since it presupposes great impartiality on the part of the Chair, as well as a profound knowledge of the subject-matter of the debate and an unusually acute political sense. The basic principle involved is too debatable, and its exercise too risky for it to be extended to other Parliaments, in spite of the unquestionable advantages it gives to the course of debate.

Once the House has reached its decision on all the various clauses, in numerical order, and on all the various amendments, its final task is to vote on the Bill as a whole. This act constitutes the ultimate step in the process of enactment of the law, except for the agreement of the other House in the case of bicameral Parliaments.

5. METHODS OF VOTING

Throughout the course of debate, and particularly when it comes to an end, Parliament has to take various decisions. The method of performing this task, which is their main *raison d'être*, is by voting. Voting is an act from which a majority emerges on any controversial issue, and the opinion of this majority, in virtue of the democratic rule, overrides the opinion of the minority and becomes binding on all citizens. Naturally enough, this crystallization of the will of the people is surrounded by a special type of ceremonial, and is safeguarded by rules designed to eliminate any possibility of chance, error or fraud, and by publication to ensure that public opinion has some control over the actions of the Members of Parliament.

(a) The Secret Ballot

Such publication is not always desirable. In fact, it is generally avoided where the House functions as an electoral body, i.e. where it makes its own appointments, either within the House itself (President, Vice-Presidents and Officers) or in the various bodies in which it is represented and for which it nominates certain members; or again where it exercises certain constitutional prerogatives, such as the election of the President of the Republic in France, Syria, and Yugoslavia, and the Chancellor in the Federal Republic of Germany. The vote is secret, which means that no one knows how any individual participant has voted. The most that can be done is to check

175

his name to ensure that he has only voted once. The secret vote is carried out by means of envelopes in which ballot papers with the names of the candidates are inserted.

Secret voting is not always confined to appointments, however. In some countries it is used for other purposes, e.g. in Rumania and Sweden for the validation of powers and questions of indemnity, in Yugoslavia for the verification of elections or the unseating of a member if the House so decides. In Laos, votes of confidence and motions of censure may be made a matter of secret voting. In Albania, the secret ballot may be used for any matter, by special decision of the House—in Austria, on the proposal of the President or twenty-five members of the National Council; in Israel, at the request of one sixth of the members of the Knesset, and in Italy, at the request of twenty members. In the Italian Chamber of Deputies, the secret ballot is the rule, as also in the Rumanian Grand National Assembly with respect to voting on Bills as a whole. In the last named two cases, the ballot-ball system is used.

(b) Anonymous Voting

Apart from appointments and the few exceptions already mentioned, decisions taken by Parliament are open and public. Most of the voting is public, in the sense that it takes place in the presence of people who have come to listen to the speeches; but as a rule the term 'public voting' is confined to the type of vote in which the names of the Members of Parliament and the way they have voted can be ascertained. Some methods frequently used because they are time-saving make this impossible and give a measure of anonymity to the decisions taken:

(a) Oral voting. Here the President calls upon the Members of the House to signify their views in turn by calling out 'Aye' or 'No'. The opinion which is expressed most loudly is regarded as being the opinion of the majority. Clearly it can be a very difficult matter at times to say what is the outcome of an oral vote. We see the proof of this in the cautious wording used by the President or Speaker: 'I think that . . .', and in the frequency with which such votes are challenged. The margin of error inherent in the system limits its use for practical purposes to cases where there is virtually no dissent. Thus it comes close to the vote by acclamation, used in Italy, and to the passing of motions by tacit consent, following the question by the chairman as to whether there are 'any objections'.

(b) Vote by show of hands. This is more reliable, since a rough count can be made of those in favour of any particular view.

(c) Vote by standing, which is not unlike the vote by show of hands, but is a sounder method.

The result of the voting in these last two cases is sometimes difficult to ascertain when the numbers are close, especially when the adherents of one particular viewpoint are not seated together on the same benches. Hence in two instances at least—in Italy and in the United States—the vote may be taken 'by division' inside the House itself, those in favour being asked to move over to one side, those against to the other, so as to simplify the counting of the votes.

(c) Public Voting

There are also other methods, more time-consuming, undoubtedly, but designed essentially to ensure that the vote of each Member of Parliament is properly recorded. These are public voting methods in the strict sense. In their different ways, they make it possible for the names of the voters and an indication whether they have voted for or against to be recorded in the official report or the minutes of the House.

However, in Laos and Syria these details are not published. In the Sudan, publication must be requested by a Member of Parliament; in Sweden by one tenth of the members. Otherwise, public voting may take a variety of forms:

(a) Voting by division, the method characteristic of the British House of Commons. Warning bells are rung throughout the building. After a few minutes, the members wishing to take part in the voting are considered to have returned to the Chamber. The Speaker then invites them to go into the lobbies on either side of the Chamber, through the 'Ayes' door, to the right of the Speaker's chair, or the 'Noes' door to his left. As they file through, the names of the members are noted by clerks, and their numbers counted by two tellers, one for the 'Ayes' the other for the 'Noes'. The whole operation lasts from ten to fifteen minutes.

(b) The roll-call vote. As his name is called out, each member replies 'aye', 'no' or 'abstain'. The replies are ticked off as they are made and the numbers in favour and against give the result. In large Parliaments the defect of this system is its slowness.

G   177

(c) The voting paper system. This is a quicker system, and where necessary it can be used for voting by proxy. Members place their voting papers, marked with their names and differing in colour according to the way they wish to vote, in boxes passed round among the benches.

Sometimes the voting paper system is combined with the roll-call. This is the so-called 'open ballot at the rostrum' common in France and Japan in particular. As each member's name is called out, he mounts the rostrum and places his voting slip in a ballot box.

(d) The electric or electronic voting machine. This is as yet little used. It is found in a few countries: Belgium, Finland, India and Sweden, and it is being installed in Burma and France. Its advantage over all the other systems is that of speed and accuracy. Votes are cast by means of a series of buttons located on the bench in front of every member. The votes are registered instantaneously, and computed, and the results are shown immediately on a lighted board on the wall of the Chamber. Simultaneously all the particulars of the vote—the names of voters and the way in which they have voted—are photographed or printed, so that the results can be published rapidly and completely.

(d) An Attempt at a Classification

The foregoing is a brief summary of the various types of voting used in Parliaments. Although they are extremely varied, a certain number of general remarks can be made regarding them:

(i) Almost every Parliament has at least one method of each kind—in the first place it uses anonymous voting, which is rapid and informal, but in case of doubt as to the result, it can resort to public voting, which is slower but more accurate. The exceptions to this rule would appear to be Israel and Switzerland (Council of State), where only the vote by standing is used. In the USSR and Czechoslovakia all voting is by show of hands. In these countries all that is revealed is the result of the voting. In contrast, in some Parliaments public voting is compulsory in regard to certain matters such as votes of confidence, motions of censure and money Bills.

(ii) One or other of two systems is found in the majority of Parliaments. In most of the countries modelled on the British system, namely Australia, Burma, India, Ireland, Pakistan and the Sudan, oral voting and voting by division go hand in hand. However, in the United Kingdom recourse may be had also to voting by standing, when the Speaker is of the opinion that a small minority is exploiting the vote by division for purposes of obstruction. Conversely, voting by show of hands or by standing, and roll-call votes, are the current procedure in continental Europe and in the People's Democracies of Albania, Bulgaria, Poland, Rumania and Yugoslavia, as well as in all countries not using either the voting paper system, as in France, or the electric or electronic machine, as in Belgium, Finland and Sweden. In the two last-named countries, in the event of a technical failure of the machine, a roll-call vote is taken instead. In Great Britain standing committees also vote by roll-call. Outside Europe, this same system is used in Ceylon, which thus differs in this regard from the other members of the British family. The Federal Republic of Germany has both the voting-paper system and the vote by division, the latter being of the anonymous type however, since no names are made public. The procedure is the very antithesis of that used in the House of Commons. The Chamber is first of all cleared. Clerks are placed at the three doors—representing 'yes', 'no' and 'abstain'—and as the members file through the doors to their seats, the count is made. Laos and Turkey are the only countries where the regular public voting is by ballot paper as in France.

(iii) Most of the voting methods require the Members of Parliament to be present in person, and hence prohibit voting by proxy. Theoretically, the proxy system is permissible in the House of Lords, but in practice the tradition is only found in France, in the form of the *boitier* system. The main objection to voting by proxy is that it encourages absenteeism; but it has the advantage of eliminating surprise votes, and where the majority is narrow, of avoiding constant travelling to and fro, which in some cases may be very inconvenient for those performing arduous ministerial duties and quite incompatible with the physical condition of some of the members. The pairing system affords some slight remedy for the situation brought about by the necessity of voting in person. If a Member of Parliament intends to be absent, he asks a member on the other side to abstain likewise from any votes taken during his absence. This system, based on a sort of gentleman's agreement, is practised mainly in Australia, Belgium and the United Kingdom. In Japan voting by proxy does not exist. However, if a Member of Parliament is present in the House but is prevented by illness or other infirmity from mounting the rostrum to take part in a vote, a clerk may deposit his voting paper in his stead.

(e) The Quorum

Whatever voting system is used, decisions are taken as a general rule by majority vote. Since, with a single exception, voting by proxy is prohibited, the size of the majority is dependent on the number of persons present, and this has its drawbacks. It is possible for a Bill to be passed in the name of an entire nation by an extremely small number of Members of Parliament. As a safeguard against this, in most Parliaments the presence of a minimum number of members is required, if not for debate, at least for the validity of a vote. In some countries—Brazil, Finland, Israel, Sweden and Spain—there is no such obligation; but normally the quorum is half the members of the House plus one, in some cases only a third (Australia, Austria and Poland). In the United Kingdom and in Ireland the requirements are less stringent. In the House of Commons the minimum is forty, and in the House of Lords three; in the Dail twenty, and in the Seanad twelve. Thus the main effect of the quorum is to ensure that in theory at least the number of votes in favour of any decision taken will be fairly substantial. In most instances the number may not be less than one quarter or one sixth of the membership of the House.

In practice, the question of a quorum rarely arises. It can only arise automatically in the case of votes involving an exact count of heads, and does not arise in anonymous votes, which are in fact the commonest procedure. When the question is brought up deliberately, it is usually ruled out of order unless supported by a certain number of members, since otherwise it could be used as a means of obstruction.

(f) The Tied Vote

As we have said above, ordinarily decisions are taken by a majority of the votes cast. The question then arises—what happens when there is no majority, i.e. in the event of a tie in the voting? Logically, it ought to mean rejection, and this is the case in most Parliaments, especially in continental Europe—Austria, Belgium, Denmark, France, the Federal Republic of Germany, Israel, Italy and Luxembourg. In the Netherlands and Indonesia, the decision is postponed to a later meeting. Another vote is taken, and if it again results in a tie, the Bill is rejected. In Parliaments on the House of Commons model, the Speaker has the casting vote. In actual practice, where he has a casting vote, he gives it in such a way as to allow the House to have the final say on another occasion. In Japan it is traditional that the President votes with the noes. In Finland and Sweden, the practice is not a matter of logic pure and simple. Drawing lots decides which way the voting shall go.

(g) Qualified Majorities

Public voting, the only type which provides for an exact count of the votes, is always essential where the passing of a motion calls for a specific number of votes in favour, i.e. a given proportion either of the votes cast or of the total number of members, or of the two together. But this requirement is quite exceptional in regard to ordinary legislation where generally speaking, subject possibly to the quorum rule, all decisions are taken by a simple majority of the votes cast, irrespective of the number of voters. However, the Egyptian Constitution requires two thirds of the members to be in favour in order to pass a fairly considerable number of Bills, namely Bills relating to the composition and method of election of Parliament, qualification of members and incompatibility of office, the exploitation of the natural resources of the State, public services and public affairs, drafting and presentation of the Budget, institution of the Higher Courts, the question of a state of emergency, and the organization of referenda. Similarly, it would appear that in Iceland, a good portion of the legislation in the joint Althing must be supported by two thirds of the votes cast. In Syria, amnesty legislation can be passed only by an absolute majority of all members. The same is true in Bulgaria of any Bills modifying the number and functions of the ministries, and in Israel of Bills in any way altering the electoral system.

There are also a few cases to which a qualified majority applies in the financial sphere: in Finland, any proposal for the creation or increase of a tax for a period exceeding one year must be regarded as rejected unless it receives two thirds of the votes cast. In Switzerland, expenditure over a certain sum must have the consent of the majority of all members. This rule acts as a brake on expenditure.

The following may be regarded as cases where a qualified majority is required in the legislative field:

(a) Prolongation of the life of Parliament in Burma (two thirds of the votes, the two Chambers voting together), and in Sweden (three quarters).

(b) Ratification of treaties in the American Senate (two thirds of the votes).

(c) The majority required for the 'shuttle' and the veto procedures. This will be discussed later.

Actually, qualified majorities are required much more frequently in non-legislative matters. The example:

(i) Matters concerning Members of Parliament exclusively, e.g. allowances (Finland), immunities (Finland, Poland and Sweden), expulsion (Japan), application of the rules of procedure (Australia, Denmark and the Federal Republic of Germany) and secret sittings (Ireland).

(ii) Matters directly concerning the relations between Parliament and Government or Head of State:

Election of the President of the Republic (France, Syria and Yugoslavia).

Election of the Chancellor (Federal Republic of Germany) and the Council of State (Poland).

Votes of confidence or censure (Federal Republic of Germany).

Withdrawal of confidence (France and Syria).

Appointment and dissolution of the Government (Poland), and in particular the impeachment of the Head of State (Burma, Finland, Federal Republic of Germany, Ireland and Syria).

(iii) Matters concerning the Constitution. Constitutional Bills being of a higher order, as a rule receive different treatment from ordinary Bills. In many countries they are enacted in accordance with a special procedure.

6. CONSTITUTIONAL LAW

The principle of the supremacy of the Constitution over ordinary law is unchallenged today. In the United Kingdom the widespread popular respect for the Constitution acts as the only real check on the theoretical ability of a simple parliamentary majority to overthrow at short notice institutions which have been built up in the course of long centuries of history. In all other countries save perhaps in Israel (which has no written Constitution), this *de facto* supremacy is reinforced by a *de jure* supremacy laid down by law, its essential feature being that all Bills for the revision of the Constitution are subject to extremely stringent rules of general law.

The methods devised by makers of constitutions to safeguard their work are extremely varied, both in form—since they can apply at every stage of the process of working out the proposed reform—

and also in their strength and effectiveness, since these are not mutually exclusive and may be combined in their effect.

The initiative in regard to any revision of the Constitution is generally a matter for the executive and the legislature together, and in the ordinary way it is similar to the regular introduction of legislation. But the right may be extended to a specific portion of the people, e.g. a body of 50,000 electors in Switzerland—or to a certain proportion of the members of a federation, e.g. two thirds of the State legislatures in the United States. Conversely, it can be severely restricted, as in Monaco, where constitutional reform is carried out by way of 'sovereign ordinances'; or its exercise may be limited: in Bulgaria, Bills making any constitutional reform must be supported by a quarter of the total number of members, in Egypt by a third, and in the Republic of Vietnam by two thirds.

In some countries, initiative in regard to constitutional matters does not mean producing a fully drafted Bill, but consists in the first instance of moving a motion of principle which must be decided before there can be any substantive debate. Thus the procedure is divided into two stages. France is a particularly good example— debate of a Bill to amend the Constitution cannot take place until three months after the resolution setting forth the principle of revision of certain articles has been passed. In Egypt the waiting period is six months. In Belgium and Yugoslavia, both Houses must approve the principle of revision before the matter can go any further.

In some cases the supremacy of the Constitution is seen in the fact that there is a special body independent of the ordinary legislature or an offshoot of it, which alone has the power to amend the Constitution. The most obvious example is the United States where, if two thirds of the State legislatures so request, a convention for the amendment of the Constitution must be convened. More often, the special body consists quite simply of a joint meeting of the two Houses of Parliament. This is the case in Laos and Norway, and also in Burma, though only after the Bill has been passed by each of the Houses. In addition two thirds of the votes must be in favour both in Burma and in Laos in the Congress, and in Norway in the Storting.

Among the most interesting systems is that found in the Nordic and Benelux countries. Parliament remains the body to whom the power is entrusted, but it has to be re-elected to exert the power. The procedure is as follows: a Bill is first debated and passes its first reading by Parliament. At this point the Houses are dissolved and general elections are held. The new Parliament takes up the Bill as passed by its predecessor, and takes a decision with the support of two thirds of the members on the whole of the Bill, with no right to make amendments. Thus popular sovereignty plays a definite part, indirectly but with full knowledge of the issues at stake, in the enactment of constitutional law. This system is found in Iceland, Luxembourg, the Netherlands, Norway and Sweden. It is also found in Finland where, however, a Bill amounting to an amendment of the Constitution may be passed in the course of one and the same Parliament, provided that the House declares its urgency with the support of five sixths of the votes and that it is approved in substance by two thirds of them. In Denmark this procedure is complemented by a further operation—compulsory recourse to the referendum. In Belgium there is a slight difference in that the initial decision, to be followed by dissolution, is only a resolution in principle. Here, the new Parliament has all the features of a body empowered to alter the Constitution.

Yugoslavia makes use of a similar procedure, at any rate inasmuch as the question of dissolution arises. The Federal Council must be dissolved if it does not succeed in reaching agreement on the Bill with the Council of Nationalities. In the Italian Constitution the provisions laid down are somewhat akin to these examples, since they call for two separate debates. Any proposed constitutional reforms must be passed by both Houses on two different occasions, with an interval of at least three months between them.

Where Parliament remains the body to whom the power to amend the Constitution is entrusted, the precaution usually taken to ensure the supremacy of the Constitution is to require a qualified majority for any decision to introduce reforms. In general the requisite proportion is two thirds of the votes cast. This is the only condition affecting constitutional law in Bulgaria, Poland, Rumania and the USSR, and also in Austria, the Federal Republic of Germany and Ceylon. In India, an absolute majority of the total membership of the House is necessary, in addition to the support of two thirds of the members present. In Czechoslovakia and Yugoslavia the only requirement is for three fifths of the members to be in favour. In the Philippines and the Republic of Vietnam the support required is three quarters.

Lastly, the supremacy of the Constitution may be safeguarded by mandatory recourse to a vote of the people. Thus in Australia, Denmark, Egypt, Ireland, Japan, Spain and Switzerland a Bill to amend the Constitution must first be passed by Parliament and then submitted to a referendum. In other countries, a referendum takes place only in the event of the Bill not obtaining a sufficient majority in Parliament; in other words, it constitutes a sort of cross-check.

Thus in France, a referendum is not mandatory unless constitutional legislation has been passed with the support of less than two thirds of the votes in the National Assembly, on second reading, or of three fifths in each of the two Houses. In Italy, the same is true if the Bill does not obtain two thirds of the votes on each reading or, if a referendum is called for within three months of the promulgation of the Bill by one fifth of the members of either House, or by 500,000 electors or five Regional Councils.

Federal constitutions may require approval of any amendment by the members of the federation. Amendments to the American Constitution must be ratified by the legislatures of three quarters of the states. In Switzerland the Constitution can be changed only with the agreement of the majority of the cantons. These additional conditions are justified by the fact that in federal states there is no single sovereignty, as it is divided between the federation and the member-territories.

Whatever procedural safeguards are taken to ensure the stability of a Constitution, they must of course be sufficiently flexible to enable institutions to evolve, as is sometimes essential. The introduction of constitutional reforms should not create such difficulties that recourse to violence proves to be the only possible solution.

7. AGREEMENT BETWEEN BOTH HOUSES

In bicameral constitutional systems, legislation is the work of both Houses. Their respective part in the operation is determined by the Constitution or the body of practice which takes the place of a Constitution. The extent of the rights of each House in legislative matters depends on how the broader problem of their relative strength in Parliament is solved. Whatever their relative strengths may be, agreement between the two Houses on a Bill puts the final seal on the legislative process. It is therefore important above all to provide machinery for reaching agreement and, of course, to provide some means of coping with constant disagreement likely to prolong the procedure indefinitely to no good purpose.

(i) *Efforts to reach Agreement.* There is no problem in Parliaments where the lower House enjoys a distinct superiority over the upper House. Thus in Australia and Laos a decision along similar lines is not in any way necessary for the enactment of legislation. In Austria the National Council alone has legislative power. While

G*   185

the Federal Council has the right to challenge any Bill by a resolution giving reasons, the National Council can override it by reiterating its original decision with at least half its members present. In Laos there is a similar system. The National Assembly in a second debate may finally pass a Bill by an absolute majority of the members present, without regard for the opinion expressed by the Council of the King. However, if the absolute majority is not reached, the council's comments and observations are regarded as agreed to. In the Netherlands, the position of the First Chamber is both more restricted, since it does not have the right to propose amendments any more than to propose legislation, and at the same time stronger, since if it rejects a Bill its decision is final and must be accepted by the Second Chamber.

Conversely, the principle of equality between the two Houses may at times make for considerable simplification of the agreement procedure. Thus the method used in unicameral-bicameral systems, such as in Iceland and Norway, follows naturally from the artificial division into two Houses. All that need be done is to revert to their original form—the joint Althing or the Storting—and the disagreement disappears. A similar procedure is found in Burma and India: when a difference of opinion arises between the two Houses and cannot be smoothed out by setting up a joint committee, the Houses are convened in joint session and examine the Bill in dispute. A decision is taken by simple majority of the votes cast. This system, although based on the principle of equality, actually gives a *de facto* advantage to the lower House because of its larger membership. Hence in Burma for example, some important laws concerning the armed forces and international treaties require the separate assent of both Houses.

Everywhere else, the relationship between the Houses is less cut-and-dried. Each House has a life of its own and hence it is essential to establish a system of relationships which will enable agreement to be reached should the need arise. There are two main methods of attaining this end:

First of all, there is the system of joint committees, known under a variety of names—'mediation', 'conciliation' or 'conference' committees, etc.—consisting of an equal number of members of each House. The function of these bodies is to come to an understanding and subsequently to submit a plan to each of the two Houses for their views. Such a procedure is moreover used in federal Parliaments when disagreement arises between the two Houses, more often than not between the representatives of the people and those of the states. The most characteristic example of this procedure is found in the Federal Republic of Germany, which has a standing mediation committee consisting of ten members of the Bundestag and ten members of the Bundesrat, with its own rules of procedure. Bodies known as conciliation committees in the USSR and Yugoslavia, or conference committees in Australia, the Philippines and the United States, operate in the same way, except that in the event of any matter giving rise to disagreement a special committee is set up. In fact non-federal states, Ireland and Japan have a similar procedure. The Swiss procedure is on somewhat similar lines. The appropriate committee of each House is brought together to study the possibility of reaching agreement. In Sweden, conciliation is assisted by the fact that there are select and permanent 'joint committees' and that in principle the legislative operation in the two Houses proceeds simultaneously.

Secondly, there is the so-called 'shuttle' system, essentially characteristic of Belgium, France and Italy. What happens here is that each House in a series of readings examines the Bill as passed by the other, until the decisions on the whole Bill are uniform. There is constant sending of the Bill from one House to the other; hence the odd term 'shuttling'. The system implies that there is no regular recourse to a conciliation body of any sort set up by the two Houses. In this respect it resembles to some extent the system of the exchange of 'messages' used in the British Parliament. The message sets out the differences in viewpoint of the two Houses. When one House receives a message, it studies the points on which differences have arisen, and motions are introduced signifying agreement or disagreement with the other Houses or proposing amendments with a view to reaching a compromise. The exchange of messages goes on until a satisfactory and acceptable Bill is passed by both Houses. The question which then arises is what happens if the points of view cannot be made to coincide exactly.

(ii) *Settling the Disagreement.* Settlement depends first and foremost on the particular brand of bicameral system involved; it differs according to whether the Houses are or are not on an equal footing in regard to legislative matters. If they are, it is quite conceivable that no decision can be reached in the face of persistent intransigence on the part of one or other House. The legislative process cannot be completed, and the Bill remains in suspense. This actually happens in Belgium and Italy when the shuttling procedure does not terminate in complete agreement. It also happens in the United States and the Philippines if the conference committee draws a blank. In Sweden, if the disagreement persists, the matter is adjourned until a later session, except in the case of Bills concerning the Budget, the National Bank or the Public Debt Administration, where a new vote is taken in each House, and the grand totals of the 'Ayes' and 'Noes' decide the issue. Thus the lower Chamber has in actual fact a considerable advantage, since it has a larger membership. These are the only circumstances in which the principle of equality of the powers of the two Houses does not apply. In Switzerland, if the compromise worked out by the two committees in joint session is not ratified by both Houses, the Bill is regarded as rejected. Thus here, the way out of the impasse caused by disagreement is of a negative nature.

There is one still more drastic solution—dissolution of Parliament. This can happen in a number of countries:

(a) In Australia, if the House of Representatives sends a Bill to the Senate on two separate occasions either during a session or in the course of two sessions, with an interval of three months between the occasions, and the Senate rejects or amends the Bill on each occasion, the Governor-General may decree the simultaneous dissolution of both Houses.

(b) In the USSR, in the event of disagreement between the Soviet of the Union and the Soviet of Nationalities the matter is brought before the Conciliation Committee, formed by the two Houses on an equal footing. Should this committee fail to settle the dispute or should its decision fail to satisfy either of the two Houses, both Houses go into the matter again. Where the disagreement persists, the Presidium of the Supreme Soviet dissolves the Supreme Soviet and new elections are held.

(c) In Yugoslavia, if after two debates of each House at an interval of seven days on the Conciliation Committee's report no positive results are forthcoming, Parliament is dissolved.

Countries where the lower House has greater powers than the upper House do not need to go so far as this. Because of the difference in power, any disagreement can always be solved to the advantage of the popular House. This is the case principally in those countries where the decision of the upper House is subjected to the time-limits of varying strictness:

(a) In Ceylon, rejection or amendment of a Bill by the Senate is effective only for one session. If the Bill is taken up again by

188

the lower House at the following session, the Senate is power-less to oppose it.

(b) In Ireland under the Constitution the Seanad has ninety days in which to examine Bills sent up to it by the Dail. After 180 days have elapsed following the expiry of this ninety-day period, any Bill passed only by the Dail is deemed to be passed by both Houses. Money Bills are deemed to be passed twenty-one days after they have been sent up to the Seanad.

(c) In Great Britain, since 1911 and more particularly since 1949, the House of Lords has had nothing more than a sort of suspensive veto. Should it reject a Bill sent to it by the House of Commons or fail to agree with the latter on the details of a Bill, its disagreement is effective only for two successive sessions of a maximum duration of one year. At the end of that time the House of Commons can pass its Bill again, and it can become law in spite of the opposition of the Lords.

(d) In France there is a system which in principle is similar, though it is a good deal more complex in its application. The Council of the Republic is allowed a period of two months for the initial examination. Once the National Assembly has taken a decision on the Bill as amended by the council, a period of 100 days begins to run during which the Bill may be referred several times from one House to the other, each having the same length of time to examine it as the other has devoted to it at each separate stage. At the end of the 100 days, if there is no agreement on the Bill as a whole, the Assembly may decide the issue finally, either confirming the Bill in its most recent version, or altering it in accordance with one or more of the council's amendments.

The position is the same where the lower House has the power to settle the issue once and for all by a qualified majority, regardless of any opposition on the part of the other House. This is the case in the Federal Republic of Germany for Bills which do not require the formal consent of the Federal Council. The latter can of course protest against a Bill passed by the Bundestag, but the latter may reject the protest by an absolute majority of its membership. If the Federal Council's protest was passed by two thirds of the votes, the Bundestag's rejection of the protest must have the same support. In Japan, if no compromise can be reached between the two Houses, the House of Representatives may pass the Bill in its original form, and thus give it the force of law, provided it is supported by two thirds of the members present.

8. ROYAL ASSENT

Agreement between both Houses, or the sovereign decision of one of them, generally places the final seal on the process of legislation. However, in the older monarchies where Parliaments function, the Sovereign—who theoretically shares the legislative powers with Parliament—is required to give his assent to the Bills passed by the House of Parliament. The existence of this procedure dates back to the time when the King was the sole legislator, and Parliament functioned merely as his advisory body.

The Sovereign, even today, continues to hold this traditional prerogative, since he is considered to form a part of Parliament. Thus, in Great Britain, the Queen in Parliament has, in principle, the right to refuse her assent to a Bill duly passed by both Houses. However, to quote the terms of the British reply, 'it is unlikely that this prerogative would ever again be invoked' as its use is incompatible with the nature of parliamentary government, having been characterized in the past by the political non-accountability of the Monarch as opposed to the accountability of the Cabinet. In Great Britain, the last withholding of Royal Assent goes back to 1707. By analogy with the British system, Royal Assent exists in Australia and is provided for, if not by name, then at least in its characteristics and effects, in Ceylon, India and the Sudan.

Royal Assent also exists in Belgium, Denmark, Norway and Sweden, and in the Netherlands, where however the Sovereign is not regarded as a part of Parliament. If assent were withheld, ministerial responsibility would be involved. But that is rather an academic problem as, in practice, the power to withhold assent does not exist, with the result that assent is, in fact, merely a formality. Royal Assent and act of promulgation, which we shall now consider, are the same process, for by promulgation is meant the signatures of the Sovereign and the counter-signatures of the ministers at the end of the Bill.

IV

The Promulgation and Publication of Acts of Parliament

Promulgation, which under one form or another is used in all countries, puts the final touch on legislation and makes it into an authoritative executive instrument. Once it is promulgated, the Bill passed by Parliament becomes a definite enactment, with binding force. Until then, it cannot be enforced. Thus promulgation is first and foremost a formality designed to make an Act of Parliament enforcible by giving a kind of official notice of it. This is essential both for the authorities which will have to apply the Act, and for the public at large, which will be subject to it.

In practice, the promulgation and publication of an Act of Parliament are more often than not one and the same thing. The Act itself may specify when it is to come into force. Otherwise, the date will be either (i) the date of publication in the official journal or gazette; or (ii) a particular day following such publication, e.g. the next day (Australia and France), three days later (Bulgaria), five days, not counting the referendum period (Switzerland), eight days (Yugoslavia), ten days (Belgium), fourteen days (Federal Republic of Germany), fifteen days (Albania), twenty days (Spain), or twenty-one days (the Netherlands). In Brazil, the period of grace before the Act comes into force varies in different parts of the country according to their distance away—from three days to four months after publication. In the USSR, laws, decrees and other legislative acts by the Supreme Soviet come into force simultaneously throughout all territories ten days after their appearance in the official publications, should no other date be specified. As these few examples show, it is difficult to formulate any general rule on the subject. The multiplicity of systems is because in some countries promulgation and publication are separate. An Act may come into force automatically the moment it is promulgated, or after an interval varying from one day (in Monaco) to twenty-eight days (in Australia).

The essential purpose of promulgation is to give the executive a final opportunity to intervene in the legislative process. In most cases this is actually the executive's prerogative—representing as it were an order to the public administration and authorities to put an Act into application, in other words it is part of the enforcement procedure.

There are few countries where the power of the legislature is so great as to do away with the act of promulgation. Where this is the case, either the actual enactment by Parliament constitutes promulgation, or it may be done by a body within Parliament itself, as in Albania, Bulgaria, Rumania and the USSR, where the President and Secretary of the Presidium are responsible for the publication of laws passed by Parliament. In Switzerland, the situation is in practice, somewhat similar, since there is no machinery for promulgation in Swiss law. The Presidents and Clerks of the two Houses sign the original copy of the Act and pass it on for publication to the Federal Council.

In most other countries, responsibility for promulgation lies with the executive. As a general rule, it is the task of the Head of State, the Monarch, or the President of the Republic, and where he does not have full responsibility, the promulgation decree must be countersigned by the members of the Cabinet. In some cases the Government itself promulgates Acts.

The real problem is whether promulgation is an obligation on or merely within the power of the executive, and whether at this point it can claim a further prerogative and again challenge the law passed by Parliament. Logically, under the democratic system in its purest form, the decision of Parliament should be final as far as the executive is concerned, and promulgation should be automatic, subject to a very short period of grace. Throughout the passage of a Bill through Parliament, the Government has any number of opportunities for expounding its ideas and getting them accepted. If it is unable to do this it must accept the Bill which has been passed, or resign. Thus, as we have remarked, the law prescribes in the USSR the publication of new Acts of Parliament in the official languages of the Republic of the Union.

On the other hand in many countries the Head of the State or the Government is allowed a certain time-limit in which to promulgate an Act. Some constitutions have provided remedies in case of failure of the executive to do so:

(a) The right of promulgation may be assigned to a legislative body—in France, if the President of the Republic fails to promulgate a new Act within ten days after it is delivered to the Government, the President of the National Assembly assumes the task. In Brazil, if the President of the Republic fails to promulgate a law within forty-eight hours, this is done forty-eight hours later by the President of the Senate (Vice-President of the Republic), or if he fails to do so after a further forty-eight hours, by the Vice-President.

(b) Promulgation may be made automatic—in Burma, any Act which is not signed by the President seven days after he has received it, enters into force just as if it had been signed. In the United States any law left unsigned by the President ten days after presentation and not referred back to Congress as a result of a veto enters into force, provided Congress is still sitting. This last restriction enables the President to exercise a kind of tacit veto on Acts presented to him less than ten days before

192

the adjournment of Congress. This 'pocket veto'—so called because the President keeps the Bill in his pocket—has been used on many occasions.

Even when promulgation is the task of the executive, the latter may have the right to ask Parliament to reconsider the new Act. The purpose of this is to give Parliament an opportunity to reconsider measures it may have taken without due reflection. The request for reconsideration, which must take place before the time-limit fixed for promulgation expires, is simply an invitation to reflect on the matter. At the reconsideration Parliament is not bound to follow any particular procedure, nor to pass the Bill by an increased majority. All it has to do is to have a further debate and to vote a second time; its final decision is then binding upon the executive. This is the procedure followed in France, Italy and Turkey. In India, the Bill is referred back to both Houses together with a message from the President in which he suggests certain amendments. In Spain the Head of State similarly puts forward his comments in referring back Bills passed by the Cortes.

The right of veto is quite a different matter. Though it has fallen into disuse in most parliamentary systems, it is still very much alive in countries which have the presidential system e.g. the United States, where it is the corollary to the principle of the equality of the powers. Just as the executive exists independently of the wishes of the Houses, so the President, precisely because he is elected by popular suffrage, is entitled to participate in the process of legislation. He does this by opposing laws passed by Congress, if he sees fit to do so. But the essential feature of this veto is that it merely suspends action. In fact, Congress can override it by passing once again the Bill rejected by the President; but it must then be supported by two thirds of the members. The same system obtains in Brazil and in the Philippines. Actually, the original *raison d'être* of the veto in the United States to protect the executive, no longer exists today. It has become a means by which the President can put before public opinion for its judgement any dispute he may have with Congress. He must therefore think twice before using it; for if the responsibility of Congress is challenged in this way and it chooses to ignore the President's veto, this has to be interpreted not only as a parliamentary defeat of the executive but above all as a sign of public loss of confidence in its policy.

A similar procedure is followed in Egypt and Czechoslovakia; here the President of the Republic has a month in which to signify his opposition to a Bill which has been passed, and to refer it back to Parliament. If it is passed a second time, it must then be promulgated—but only if it has obtained an absolute majority (or in some cases three fifths) of the members' votes in Czechoslovakia and two thirds in Egypt. In certain special circumstances, both in Finland and Ireland this veto is likewise the prerogative of the President of the Republic. In Finland, when a Bill has been passed by Parliament it is sent for approval to the President of the Republic. If the latter does not give his approval within three months, approval is deemed to be refused. On the other hand the Bill may come into force, without the approval of the President, if it is passed once more, as it stands, by a new Parliament after general elections have been held.

In Ireland promulgation may be held up if the President decides that the Bill is of sufficient national importance to warrant ascertaining the will of the people. Such a decision must be supported by a petition addressed to him by the majority of the members of the Seanad, and at least one third of those of the Dail. If after consulting the Council of State he decides that the petition is justified, he must within 18 months submit the Bill either to a referendum or to a new Parliament following a general election.

In most cases, the veto is not an insurmountable obstacle to the will of the legislators, who have only to re-marshal their forces or to bide their time in order to get their own way. But there are also examples in constitutional law of an absolute and discretionary veto which can threaten the very foundations of parliamentary government, inasmuch as the work of Parliament may be completely paralysed by it. This exceptional prerogative is enjoyed in Spain by the Head of State, subject to consultation with the Council of the Realm, the supreme advisory body of the nation, and in Indonesia by the Government, if it raises 'major objections' to the entry into force of a Bill. This type of prerogative is linked directly with the Royal Assent in its original form.

At any rate, with one or two exceptions, promulgation is the prerogative of the executive, and provides it with a last opportunity to intervene in the operation of the legislature process. In so far as it is indispensable for rounding off the process of legislation, promulgation in most cases puts the final seal on the preponderance of power possessed by the executive, as seen right from the introduction stage and throughout the discussions within Parliament.

The many varied aspects of governmental intervention and the safeguards which are frequently applied cannot conceal a steadily growing tendency for the executive to encroach more and more upon the legislative function and thus progressively to breach the exclusive right of Parliament to legislate—one of the fundamental principles of democracy.

V

Control over the Constitutional Validity of Acts of Parliament

Control over the constitutional validity of Acts of Parliament is not really as extensive as writings on constitutional law suggest. The reason for this is the practical organizational difficulty inherent in such control, even though it is the logical consequence of the principle of supremacy of the Constitution. Theoretically, it is perfectly natural that it should be so, at least in the many countries which have a written Constitution and a special procedure for its revision, giving official recognition to the superiority of the Constitution over ordinary Acts of Parliament. Any infringement of the Constitution by the legislature must be made public and appropriate action must be taken. This is the purpose of control over the constitutional validity of Acts of Parliament.

But when the attempt is made to bring actual practice into line with constitutional theory, numerous difficulties arise. Take first of all the flexible type of Constitution which can be altered by the passing of an ordinary Act of Parliament, as in Great Britain. Here, since the status of the legislators as subordinate to the Constitution is not formally laid down, control over the constitutional validity of Acts of Parliament is meaningless. It might be argued that control would be justified by the principles of jurisprudence, from which all social organization emanates. But even if this were so, its application would prove impracticable. At best it is a matter for the conscience of the legislators themselves who must set limits to their own powers.

But the very notion of control presupposes the existence of a body which is independent of the institution to be controlled, if the confusion of judge and interested party is to be avoided. This is the major difficulty. There are two objections to a controlling body outside Parliament. It is in the first place contrary to the principle of the separation of powers, recognized in many countries, which precludes any body other than the legislature itself from taking part in the law-making process. It cannot be argued that a court set up to verify that laws are valid is really part of the legislative machinery, since this is at variance with the concept of democracy. Secondly, to submit the decisions of Parliament to an external body—which would thus be superior to Parliament—would be to deny the principle of the sovereignty of the people, whose wishes must be expressed without hindrance in Parliament.

The determination that no rule of law shall prevail over the will of the people is manifested in some countries in the fact that there is no control over the constitutional validity of laws, even where there is a written Constitution formally recognized as supreme by the provision of a special procedure for its amendment. In Bulgaria, Czechoslovakia, Rumania, Poland and the USSR, since Parliament is considered to be the supreme authority in the State, no other authority is considered to have the power to pass judgement on the regularity of Acts of Parliament. In Belgium, Parliament is deemed to have decided the principle of an Act's constitutional validity by the very fact of enacting it. In the Netherlands, the oath taken by Members of Parliament to abide scrupulously by the Constitution is regarded as rendering any control over the constitutional validity of Acts of Parliament unnecessary. Absence of control is likewise a feature of the systems in Indonesia, Israel, Laos, Spain and Turkey.

Recognition of the supremacy of popular representation may at times be compatible with a semblance of control, but it is hardly likely to impose any limitation on the rights of Parliament, since the authority exercising the control is itself a parliamentary body, e.g. the Bureau of the National Assembly (Czechoslovakia) or the Presidium (Albania and the USSR). Moreover, in Albania the decisions of the Presidium have to be approved by Parliament itself. In Yugoslavia the supremacy of Parliament is asserted in a similar manner: on the proposal of the Federal Executive Council, the Federal Supreme Court, the National Assemblies and Executive Councils of the People's Republics, the elected bodies of the autonomous regions, the District People's Committees, and the interested economic organizations and independent bodies, Parliament itself may investigate the conformity of federal Acts and the Acts and constitutions of the Republic with the Federal Constitution.

According to classic theory, true control can be exercised only by a body outside Parliament. But the difficulty of reconciling the powers of such a body with the powers of Parliament is precisely what has caused the failure of most attempts to put this control into practice. Nevertheless, there are two conceivable methods of control: the first is to keep a careful watch on legislative activity before it takes place, and to nip in the bud any measures which smack of the unconstitutional; the second consists in the *ex post facto* examination of Acts already brought into force.

Prior control is exercised between the time when the Act is passed by Parliament and the time when it is promulgated. It forms, as it were, a part of the process of legislation. Hence it is entrusted to the political body responsible for promulgation, and for this reason the main feature of this system is the part played by the head of the State.

In the Federal Republic of Germany, before signing a Bill the President has the privilege and the duty of making sure that it conforms with the Constitution. However, his only concern is the formal constitutional validity of the Act, i.e. the question whether the correct procedure has been followed. Whether the President has likewise the right to examine the substantive constitutional validity of Acts of Parliament is a moot point.

In Burma, the Head of State can bring before the Supreme Court any Acts he considers to be unconstitutional before they are promulgated, and the court is asked to make a report. A similar system is found in Finland. The President of the Republic has the right to refuse an Act his blessing if he deems it to be contrary to the Constitution. He may call upon either the Supreme Court of Justice or the Supreme Administrative Court, or both, to give their opinion. But, as we have seen, Parliament may override opposition from the President by passing the same Bill again after general elections have been held. But as such a procedure does not seem ever to have been practised it remains something of an academic point.

The President of Ireland may place an Act before the Supreme Court on the ground that it is unconstitutional within seven days of receiving notice of the passing of the Act. The court must give its decision within sixty days. If it deems that any provision of the Act is at variance with the Constitution, the President will refuse to sign it. The control of legislation before promulgation is similarly catered for in France and Syria although the procedure differs appreciably. In Syria, it takes a quarter of the members of the Chamber of Deputies, or the President of the Republic, to bring an Act before the High Court on the grounds that it violates the Constitution. If the High Court considers that the law is unconstitutional, it is referred back to the Chamber of Deputies for rectification.

An unusual system is found in France: a constitutional committee is instructed to ascertain whether an Act passed by the National Assembly 'implies a revision of the Constitution'. If it does, it is returned to the Assembly for further consideration. If the Assembly stands by its original decision, the Act cannot be promulgated until the Constitution is revised. The Constitutional Committee, which may be called upon only if an absolute majority in the Council of the Republic votes in favour, and whose primary function is to bring about agreement between the two Houses, is not so much a body for checking the constitutional validity of Acts of Parliament as a body for the settlement of differences between the two Houses.

None of these procedures, despite their diversity, falls outside the scope of the framing of legislation, in its widest sense. To this extent it may be said that they do not constitute a threat to the sovereignty of Parliament, since the control is exercised before the Act is fully framed by political bodies which help to frame it, even though they are assisted in doing so by high judicial authorities.

Before it is promulgated, an Act is a political instrument; the moment it is promulgated it becomes a legal instrument. Since the problem is then to ascertain whether one legal instrument, the Act, is in conformity with another, the Constitution, it seems quite in order to entrust this task to a judge. The arguments in favour of this method of control are the impartiality and professional training of a judge, who is accustomed to settling legal disputes, and the advantages of court proceedings, which furnish valuable safeguards for the interests involved.

Once we are prepared to recognize the principle of control over the constitutional validity of Acts of Parliament by a court of law, several procedures are possible. In certain cases the power is vested in the ordinary machinery of the courts, with their own hierarchy culminating in the High Court or Supreme Court of Justice as the final court of appeal. The control then generally takes the form of an incidental plea, i.e. it assumes an action to have been brought before the ordinary courts, the latter being required to apply the disputed Act of Parliament. One of the parties to the suit may then file a plea of constitutional invalidity, asking the court not to apply the Act on the grounds that it is at variance with the Constitution. This system is officially recognized in several countries, especially Japan and Pakistan. Article 81 of the Japanese Constitution states that: 'The Supreme Court is the court of last resort with power to determine the constitutional validity of any law, order, regulation or official act.' It may do so only in connexion with a specific dispute. Similarly Article 157 of the Pakistan Constitution provides that the ordinary courts, and in the last resort the Supreme Court, are qualified to judge the validity of Acts of Parliament in respect of actions brought before them.

In most cases, control by the ordinary courts is not written into the Constitution. The best-known example of this is the United States, where control over the constitutional validity of Acts of Congress is simply a matter of case-law, based on its inherent logic. The judges have come to feel that their proper functions require them to resolve conflicts between ordinary and constitutional law in the same way as any other legal dispute. In Brazil and the Philippines similar powers are enjoyed by the Supreme Court. In the latter country the Constitution now provides for the judicial control of the constitutional validity of Acts of Parliament (although this has its origins in case-law) and stipulates that two thirds of the judges in the Supreme Court must agree before a legislative instrument can be declared unconstitutional.

Case-law has also been used for the plea that an Act of Parliament is unconstitutional in several other countries—Australia, Denmark, Egypt, Iceland and Norway. As far as Australia is concerned, there is a limited right of appeal from the decisions of the High Court to the Privy Council sitting in Great Britain. The same is true of Ceylon.

Control may also be exercised directly by the Supreme Court of Justice, disputes concerning the constitutional validity of Acts of Parliament being brought before it without having been decided by any other body. This is the system in Burma, where any person or organization sustaining a wrong as a result of a provision of the Act may appeal to the Supreme Court for a ruling as to whether or not the provision is constitutional. In the Sudan, the Civil High Court has similar powers. In Ireland, the jurisdiction of the High Court extends as far as the question of the validity of Acts of Parliament, but a decision of the High Court may be appealed against before the Supreme Court, whose ruling is final. The example of the Swiss Federal Court is often quoted in illustration of this form of control. It must be stressed, however, that this court has no control over the validity of Federal Acts; it exercises jurisdiction only in respect of cantonal Acts.

The essential feature of direct control by the highest judicial body is that it normally operates in the form of an action. What is virtually a special type of legal proceedings is instituted against an Act in question, either by individuals or a public authority. If the Act is found to be contrary to the Constitution, it is annulled absolutely, with universal application. The result is identical when the control is exercised by a special judicial body not forming part of the judicial structure, namely, the High Constitutional Court. This practice was widespread before the last war, but is rarely found nowadays.

In Austria, there is a Constitutional Court which looks into the constitutional validity of Acts of Parliament, and no other court is empowered to investigate the validity of Acts duly promulgated. The same is true in Italy, where the Constitutional Court handles disputes concerning the constitutional validity of Acts and instruments of a legislative nature passed by the State or the Regions. In the Republic of Vietnam, the Constitutional Court deals with matters concerning requests by the courts in respect of the constitutional validity of Acts or legislative decrees and administrative regulations.

A similar system operates in the Federal Republic of Germany. If a court considers an Act on whose validity its decision depends to be unconstitutional, it must withhold its decision and request the Federal Constitutional Court to decide the issue. Furthermore, if differences of opinion or doubts arise as to the compatibility of a Federal law with the Constitution, the Federal Government or a national Government or one third of the Members of the Bundestag may request a decision of the court. Again, if any person considers that the Federal Act impairs his fundamental rights as laid down in the Basic Law he may challenge the Act before the Constitutional Court within one year of its entry into force.

One characteristic which the many constitutional courts have in common is their composition. In most cases their members are chosen, at any rate in part, by Parliament: in the Federal Republic of Germany the members of the Constitutional Court are elected half by the Federal Diet and half by the Federal Council; in Italy, a third of the members are appointed by Parliament sitting in joint session. In the Republic of Vietnam, four of the nine judges are members elected by the National Assembly. The fact that the constitutional court has this type of make-up helps to overcome the drawback of having a body superior in legal authority to that which is the outcome of the popular vote.

Experience shows that no system of control over the constitutional validity of Acts of Parliament has ever been found entirely satisfactory. In view of the difficulty of putting it into effect, it may well be asked whether it serves any useful purpose. If what it implies is simple resistance to arbitrary action on the part of the legislature, the best form of control over the representatives of the people would seem to be that exercised by the sovereign people themselves. Then development of ways and means by which public opinion can express itself with the utmost frankness is the surest and most salutary method of keeping a watchful eye on the legislature.

Part Three

THE POWERS OF PARLIAMENT IN FINANCIAL MATTERS

THE POWERS OF PARLIAMENT
IN FINANCIAL MATTERS

Among the various items of parliamentary business, financial problems—first and foremost the scrutiny of the national Budget—are in a category apart. This is mainly a matter of historical evolution. Nowadays, financial law is frequently regarded as a subsidiary aspect of constitutional law, and there is a tendency to lose sight of the fact that actually constitutional law in a sense derives from financial law. In the history of representative Parliaments, the very first type of powers to make their appearance are powers in financial matters; these were the central core around which the key institutions of modern constitutional systems gradually took shape. The legislative powers of elected Parliaments, which today are regarded as one of the bases of democracy, merely followed in the wake of the acquisition of the financial powers demanded by the people, who demanded and won the right to consent to the levy of taxes before they began to bid for a share in law-making. It was the combination of this right with the right of petition that gave the House of Commons in England its power in the legislative sphere: by making the Crown accede to its wishes as a condition of its own consent to taxation, on the well-known principle that 'grievances precede supply', it gradually established its right first to suggest and then to impose legislation, and to see that its wishes were enacted in non-financial matters as well.

Thus the need to protect the nation against extortion on the part of the Monarch was what gave rise to the modern Parliament. Nowadays a strange paradox has arisen: instead of keeping a tight hold on the purse-strings, Parliaments are often apt to be free with money. Their original function of keeping expenditure within proper bounds has now been taken over by Governments, which are responsible for producing sound Budgets and fight shy of any move which is likely to jeopardize them. This has become so much the rule that in most countries, even those where democracy is strongest, severe restrictions have had to be placed on the financial powers of Parliament. Thus financial powers remain, as always, a special category apart, though for different reasons. In a number of countries, however, including the USSR, this is not the case, for there is no specific ruling restricting the financial powers of Parliament.

* * *

I

The Nature of the Budget

In a material sense, the Budget is an accountancy estimate of the over-all financial needs of the State and the resources required to cover them. It is a sort of tabular conspectus of the estimated public expenditure and income over a given period, generally a year. What is the purpose of collating all these financial data in a single document? First of all, from a book-keeping standpoint, the Budget is drawn up to enable the necessary over-all comparison of income and expenditure to be made; secondly, as a matter of financial policy, to classify expenditure, assess its relative importance and urgency; thirdly, in the light of the economy as a whole, to determine the effect of budgetary operations on the economic situation; and lastly, to facilitate parliamentary control.

Thus fundamentally the Budget is an administrative operation— a mere representation in figures of the Government's plan of action. But its legal validity only begins with the intervention of Parliament. By approving the Budget and the related estimates, the latter gives the executive authority to do two things:

(*a*) To obtain revenue. The principles of democracy require that the right to collect taxes shall be granted each year by the representatives of the people. The legislation establishing taxation is permanent, but the authorization to apply that legislation is generally speaking only temporary. This gives Parliament an essential means of control over the executive. However, in certain states, in the Netherlands for example, the majority of taxation laws remain in force indefinitely from the time they are passed. Naturally Parliament may repeal or amend them at any time, but it remains true that here Parliament's consent to the tax is, in essence, tacit.

(*b*) To spend money. Expenditure, like the levying of taxation, must be authorized by Parliament. Originally, Parliament merely voted a specific credit sum which it handed over *in toto* to the Monarch, to be used as he thought fit. The next stage was to insist on knowing that good use was made of the sums thus granted. The authority of Parliament grew stronger and stronger as the object for which the funds were voted was controlled. Today we are witnessing a steady return in the direction of the old system—a trend towards the voting of lump sums—the point being that modern expenditure is so complex that a thorough study of all its details is seldom practicable.

At any rate, the Budget may be regarded as an Act of Parliament, in the formal sense, in so far as its approval by Parliament follows the ordinary rules of legislative procedure. In a practical sense, it does not constitute an Act. An Act in this sense is a general, impersonal, mandatory rule creating rights and obligations and as a rule the Budget does not fulfil these conditions. The assessment of revenue generally speaking has no legal force, so that while in all countries the Budget embraces all taxation, fiscal resources and all manner of public income, the resulting obligations as they effect the man in the street do not derive from the Budget itself but from permanent statutes establishing the taxation system in force and having an existence of their own, quite distinct from that system. In the USSR, however, the budgetary law is of a different character: it involves directly the organs of the State.

In most countries, the expenditure estimates related to the Budget have of themselves no legal value. The authorization granted to the Government to spend funds does not *ipso facto* create subjective rights or obligations; these are the outcome of administrative legislation outside the sphere of the Budget. In view of this, several countries hold that the Budget as such does not partake of the nature of legislation. Thus in Egypt and Switzerland, it is regarded as a purely administrative measure. The Egyptian Constitution merely states that 'the measures for putting the national Budget into effect must be submitted to the National Assembly for its examination and approval', without specifying how such approval shall be given. In fact, the 1956-57 and 1957-58 Budgets, regarded primarily as administrative measures, were promulgated by decree of the President of the Republic and not in pursuance of any Act of Parliament. Similarly, in Switzerland the Budget is in the nature of a series of administrative regulations setting forth the revenue and expenditure for the year ahead, estimated in an approximate manner. The income and the expenditure are based on provisions alien to the Budget. Approval by Parliament is a separate act which does not affect the actual nature of the document to which it gives approval.

This distinction between the Budget and its approval by Parliament is also characteristic of the procedure followed in such countries as Burma, Norway, Iceland and Finland. It is a procedure that departs substantially from the traditional legislative pattern. In Burma the Budget differs from an Act of Parliament in that the Constitution does not require it to be approved by both Houses.

Article 125 of the Constitution simply stipulates that 'the Government shall prepare the estimates of receipts and expenditure of the Union for each financial year and shall present them to the Chamber of Deputies for consideration'. They are not submitted to the Chamber of Nationalities. In Iceland and Norway, on the other hand, the Budget is considered by a joint meeting of both Houses of Parliament—the United Althing and the Storting. In Finland, the Budget may not include anything but the estimates of revenue and expenditure. But if the contents of the Budget should call for the amendment of the existing law, Bills distinct from the Budget are introduced. In addition, the Budget is given a single reading instead of the three readings needed for passing an ordinary Bill.

In the same way, the British system does not regard the Budget as a Bill. It is simply a financial programme put forward by the Government. With a view to the implementation of this programme, Budget resolutions are laid before the House, and are subsequently incorporated into the Finance Act. The actual Budget does not involve legislation; only the measures needed for its application are taken by means of an Act of Parliament. This procedure, the outcome of a pragmatic conception of budgetary operations, is found in Australia, India and Pakistan. The same can be said of Ceylon: the estimates do not include the taxes and other fiscal revenue to be collected in the course of the financial year. In his Budget speech, the Minister of Finance outlines his proposals for obtaining the resources needed to meet the anticipated calls on government funds, and these proposals are in due course embodied in separate legislation.

In most other countries the formal approval of the Budget by Parliament covers more than its technical content. Since the powers given to Parliament are legislative in character, the Budget itself is regarded simply as an Act of Parliament, though a peculiar one inasmuch as its duration covers only a specific period, usually one year. In the Federal Republic of Germany, for example, the Federal Budget together with its estimates of revenue and expenditure form an integral part of the Budget Act. In France 'the Budget is approved by Parliament in virtue of the Finance Law'. In Israel, the Budget Act has annexed to it the 'Budget of revenue and expenditure'. The annex is an integral part of the Act and is passed with it. In the USSR, the national Budget is ratified by the Supreme Soviet for a period of one year. Once ratified, it has the force of law.

This practice of regarding the Budget as assimilated into a law can often be explained by the fact that in some countries—France and Belgium for example—the Budget contains provisions which amount to actual regulations and have nothing to do with estimates of income and expenditure, although the practice has often been regarded as open to criticism.

Lastly, recourse to the ordinary legislation procedure may result in a sort of fragmentation of the Budget and its related estimates, which may disintegrate into a whole series of Bills, one dealing exclusively with revenue, the rest with the expenditure of each government department. This is particularly the case in Italy.

II
Introduction and Preparation of the Budget

The primacy of the executive is made absolutely clear right from this initial stage of the procedure. We find an extraordinary measure of unanimity in the recognition that the Government alone has the right to draw up and present a Budget. This exclusive right derives from the realities of the situation.

The powers of the executive in budgetary and supply matters are based in the first place on political considerations, for the Budget is above all an instrument of policy. This vast machinery for the redistribution of the national income, with the profound effect it exerts on the economic and social structure of the country, amounts to an expression in arithmetical form of the Government's programme of action. Hence it is only proper that the executive should have a completely free hand to work out the financial implications of this programme in its minutest details. The second reason for the executive's powers in budgetary and supply matters is a technical one. Because of the administrative reports it receives, the Government is the only authority which has an accurate picture of the needs of the various services and of the amount of revenue likely to be available. The ministers alone are in a position to assess accurately the cost of running the public services; and only the finance departments are equipped to make a synthesis of all this expenditure and to try to strike a balance between it and the revenue totals.

The complexity of the Budget is such that only a small group of persons, namely the Government, can assume responsibility for it. It must first and foremost be homogeneous, and this rules out any possibility of a large deliberative assembly having a hand in it. However, the participation of Members of Parliament in the preparatory stages is not impossible. In this connexion, the experience of the United States prior to the 1921 reform is most revealing.

207

Up to then, because of the strict observance of the principle of the separation of powers, the task of working out the Budget and supply legislation fell to Congress itself. Congress handed over its powers to its many committees, which proceeded without any co-ordination, the result being a spate of legislation, often contradictory, voting funds for various purposes. Since the 1921 Budget and Accounting Act was passed, the United States has had an over-all Budget which is drawn up by an administrative body, the Bureau of the Budget, and presented in the name of the President by the Chairman of the Finance Committee.

A final argument in favour of placing the task of drawing up and presenting the Budget in the hands of the executive is that it is the executive power that has the responsibility for carrying out the provisions of the Budget.

Thus, generally speaking, Parliament does not have the right of taking the initiative in budgetary matters. The Brazilian Constitution is the only one which makes provision for intervention by Parliament, and even then only in the event of failure to act on the part of the executive. If the Government has not produced a Budget by the end of the fortnight following the first two months of the session, the Budget Committee of the Chamber of Representatives must do so. In Sweden, the Ways and Means Committee has authority to work out budgetary legislation.

All that Parliament has the power to do is to amend the Bills introduced by the Government, subject to certain conditions which we shall examine. Apart from that, it enjoys a measure of initiative indirectly, inasmuch as Private Members' Bills, when passed by both Houses, frequently have financial implications which find their way into subsequent Budgets.

Prior to the introduction of the Budget, which is the prerogative of the Government, the work of preparing budgetary estimates is an administrative matter which is in most countries carried out along similar lines. This throws light on the function performed in most countries by the Ministry of Finance, the department to which the task of estimating the revenue and suggesting any changes in taxation naturally falls. Actually, what reveals most clearly the superior status enjoyed by the Minister of Finance in relation to his Cabinet colleagues is the procedure for preparing and estimating expenditure figures. Expenditure estimates are first of all worked out by the competent divisions of each of the departments concerned, and then gathered together and forwarded to the Minister of Finance. The problem is to decide what powers the latter has in regard to the requests thus put forward. In some instances, it may merely take note of them and duly pass them on *en bloc* to the Cabinet as being the only body with power to make changes, before they are submitted to Parliament. In most countries, however, the Minister of Finance has authority, on his own initiative, to make changes in the estimates put in by the various ministries—as a rule changes involving cuts in the grants asked for. If agreement cannot be reached, the matter in dispute is referred to the head of the Government or, in the last resort, to the Cabinet as a whole. Constitutionally, the Minister of Finance has no greater powers than his colleagues, but he makes his influence felt effectively in this way. This system works empirically in many countries, notably in Australia, France, Israel, Luxembourg and the United Kingdom. In Finland, the Budget estimates are drawn up by the Minister of Finance, and examined by the Government's 'Finance Committee', and then by the Government as a whole. In the Federal Republic of Germany there is an express provision in the Budget Code for the settlement of disputes between the Minister of Finance and the rest of the Continent: all differences of opinion are brought first before the Federal Government; if the Finance Minister's view is overruled, he may enter a 'protest'; the item of expenditure or the clause in dispute may in such circumstances not be included in the Budget unless the majority of all the Federal ministers so decide, and unless the Federal Chancellor votes with the majority.

The exceptional status of the Minister of Finance may also be due to prerogatives given to him under the Constitution. In Burma, the Finance Minister is at liberty to make certain adjustments or cuts wherever he considers that they are called for, while in India he scrutinizes any new spending very closely. In Ireland all expenditure must be expressly sanctioned by the Minister of Finance, who scrutinizes all items carefully to ensure that they are kept down to a minimum. In Norway, the estimates put in by the various departments are considered by a Cabinet 'Budget conference', but the Finance Minister may himself make changes in them if he sees fit to do so.

The special status thus enjoyed by the Minister of Finance sometimes gives rise to criticism. Since the Budget is the most vital act of government policy, it is a legitimate question whether the responsibility for preparing it should not rest with the head of the Government himself. This is in fact what happens in countries organized on the presidential system, and it does ensure that the head of the Government ranks above the ministers, who are merely his executive agents. Thus in the United States, the Bureau of the

Budget is a service coming directly under the Presidency and not under the Treasury Department. Similarly, in Brazil and the Philippines, it is the President of the Republic who draws up the Budget.

Thus any intervention by Parliament throughout the preparatory phase of the Budget is virtually ruled out. Intervention is only possible at a later stage, when the time comes for debate and approval of the Budget. But here again the rules by which Parliament exercises its power differ from those obtaining in legislative procedure; in financial matters its rights are in fact most often considerably limited, except in the USSR and the other Socialist states.

III

The Budget and Public Undertakings

In virtue of the rule of universality of accounting, all income and all expenditure must be shown separately in the national Budget. According to the theory favoured by liberal economists, this rule applies only to expenditure incurred by services which are public by their very nature, and revenue designed to cover that expenditure. Nowadays, however, the State takes a hand in matters which go beyond the narrow bounds of the 'public sector' and may even embrace all economic activities, as in the Socialist states. The drawing together of 'public sector' and 'private sector' operations raises the problem of the situation in regard to the Budgets of all industrial or commercial undertakings owned wholly or partly by the State, or subsidised by it.

An over-strict application of the rule of universality of accounting would involve serious drawbacks in regard to the management of such undertakings whose activities are akin to those of similar establishments in the private sector. For this reason, they frequently enjoy a certain measure of financial autonomy; this is the case even in the USSR, where they operate on the basis of the costs they entail. The State undertakings in the Soviet Union have their individual capital, which belongs to the State and which they make use of in accordance with the provisions and overall plan of the Budget. It must be noted that in the Socialist countries the State undertakings are the very basis of the entire national economy. The State provides State undertakings with working-capital and only covers their expenses to the extent that these exceed their own earnings. Sums included in the Budget generally represent new investments, which are divided among various authorities, with due account taken of the development plan for the economy of the country as a whole. 'Profits' made by State undertakings are reserved partly to increase their production and partly for the general Budget. The budget resources of the USSR are derived in the main from the income from undertakings in the collective sphere. An important feature of the national Budget in the USSR is that revenue derived from taxation on the people themselves will continue to diminish from year to year until the time when it will no longer exist.

In countries where there is a large measure of private enterprise, the situation of undertakings in which the State has a hand may conform to any of a vast variety of types, distinguishable by the principles underlying their establishment. Some undertakings are independent merely in respect of their administration; their earnings are paid directly into the exchequer and their expenditure likewise appears as a Budget item. In the case of those undertakings which operate on a fairly large commercial scale, their accounts may take the form of an appendix to the Budget, only the totals appearing in the national Budget. This is usually true of services such as the railways or the postal services. Parliament retains complete authority in regard to both these types of undertakings.

The situation is quite different in regard to undertakings which combine financial autonomy with a legal status distinct from that of the State departments; and this is more often than not the case. The regulations governing public accountability do not in any way apply to them, and hence they are outside the scope of Parliament's powers. In such circumstance these undertakings come within the purview of the Parliament only in so far as they have to be granted subsidies to cover their deficits or to enable them to undertake new investments. Thus in the United Kingdom, for example, such undertakings only appear in the Budget 'below the line', i.e. in the part dealing with capital expenditure. Hence this type of undertaking comes into the discussion of the Budget only sporadically and partially.

The right of Parliament to know what is going on is, however, frequently within the sphere of parliamentary control, and this may be exercised in a number of ways, e.g. by the appointment of Members of Parliament to governing or administrative boards, by special supervisory bodies or by periodical scrutiny of the accounts carried out by the committees or sub-committees; by holding inquiries; or through the reports of managers of the Government, the Audit Office or the Comptroller General, and Auditor. In any event, when the battery of methods of financial control is exhausted, Parliament always has a trump card to play in regard to the executive's accountability, namely its over-all powers of political control. This will be the subject of the final part of this work.

IV

The Budget and Bicameral Parliaments

In bicameral Parliaments, it is rare for the two Houses to enjoy equality of powers. When we come to financial and budgetary problems, this fundamental inequality is as a rule still more evident, and takes the form of an even more marked restriction, amounting at times to abolition, of the powers of the Second Chamber. The effect of this is of course to alter profoundly the ordinary procedure by which agreement is reached between the two Houses, and in some instances to override it altogether.

In states built up on federal lines, the two Houses are as a rule on an equal footing. In some of these countries, they remain so even when they are dealing with financial matters. This is the case, for example, in Switzerland, the USSR and Yugoslavia, where both Houses keep the same rights and the same prerogatives in regard to all matters. The same is true of Italy, a non-federal state, where the Senate and the Chamber of Deputies have exactly the same powers in regard to financial matters. The concern to preserve equality is pursued to such a point that half the Budget proposals are submitted to each House; the half submitted first to the Chamber of Deputies one year is submitted to the Senate the following year and *vice versa*.

However, in countries where the two Houses are generally speaking on the same footing, we commonly find that the scales are weighted to some extent in favour of the lower House in regard to the Budget, even when it has to be passed by both Houses. Quite frequently this simply means that priority is given to the lower House. The system has grown up in imitation of the British budgetary procedure prior to the 1911 reform, which placed the two Houses on a different footing generally. It is applied in the United States. The Budget proposals are submitted first to the House of Representatives, which examines and approves them. It is only at this point that they go to the Senate. A similar procedure is followed in Brazil and the Philippines. In Belgium, the priority enjoyed by the Chamber of Representatives in regard to examination of the measures proposed by the Ways and Means Committee is simply a matter of tradition, since the constitutional law establishing it was abrogated at the time of the 1921 reform. In Norway and Iceland, the question of priority cannot arise, since the Budget is debated jointly by the two Houses meeting in their original form—the Storting and the United Althing. Nevertheless this still produces an element of inequality, owing to the decided disparity in the number of members of the two Houses. A similar situation is found in Sweden, where in the event of continual disagreement the two Houses take separate votes, the results being added together, thus giving an advantage to the larger body. In all these countries, the degree of inequality between the two Houses in financial matters is only slight; but its effect is more noticeable when it comes on the top of a measure of inequality in other directions.

There are few countries where the upper House does not find its already inferior powers still further curtailed when the time comes to examine the Budget. One such country, however, is Laos, where the respective powers of the two Houses are the same as in all other matters, and the final decision is taken by the National Assembly, provided an absolute majority is reached. Similarly, in the Netherlands, the position of the upper House is not appreciably more subordinate in Budget matters. It has no right of initiative or to amendment, any more than in the ordinary legislative field. It merely has the right to adopt or reject *en bloc* the measures put before it.

In most bicameral Parliaments, the fundamental lack of equality between the two Houses is greater still where money matters are concerned. This differential treatment would appear to reflect the old monarchial system where the consent of the people is needed before new taxation can be introduced. Historically the popular Houses were set up precisely to grant this consent, and frequently they make a point of preserving their privilege in the face of their upper Houses, which are handicapped by the fact that in many cases they are aristocratic in origin.

In France, the Constitution specifies that the Budget measures must first of all be examined by the National Assembly. The same is true of Australia, though, while the Senate there retains full powers to reject Bills of a financial or budgetary nature, its authority to amend such Bills is subject to certain limitations—it cannot amend Bills levying new taxes or voting funds, nor any Bill involving an increase in a prospective tax or duty. However, the Australian Senate may address to the lower House a request for tax-increase. In Japan, the House of Representatives enjoys not only priority in regard to the Budget, but also overriding powers over the House of Councillors. Where there is a discrepancy between the budgetary measures as passed by the latter body and those passed by the lower House, and no agreement can be reached through the medium of the joint committee set up for the purpose, or where the House of Councillors does not succeed in passing measures within thirty days after they are sent to it, the decision of the House of Representatives is regarded as being the decision of the Diet. This procedure is distinctly harder on the upper House than the ordinary legislative procedure.

The superior status of the popular House is still more marked in bicameral Parliaments on the British model. Since the 1911 and 1949 reforms were introduced, the role of the House of Lords in this field has been severely curtailed. All money Bills are placed before the House of Lords after they have been passed by the House of Commons, but they receive the Royal Assent after one month, whether or not they have been approved by the Lords. It is worth noting, however, that fewer than half of the Finance Bills have been money Bills within the meaning of the Parliament Act of 1911.

This curtailment of the upper House's delaying power to one month is found also in Ceylon. In the Sudan, the period is three months. In some of the other countries which have come within British influence, the House is completely bereft of powers in regard to money matters. This is true of Burma, India and Ireland. In Burma the situation is cut-and-dried; the Budget is not submitted to the Chamber of Nationalities, and approval by the Chamber of Deputies is sufficient. It is true that the various money Bills are placed before the Second Chamber after they have been passed by the Chamber of Deputies, but only for recommendation. Within twenty-one days after they have been sent up, they must be returned to the Chamber of Deputies, which may accept or reject wholly or partially the recommendations made by the Chamber of Nationalities. If they are not returned within this period, they are nevertheless regarded as passed by Parliament in the form in which they were passed by the Chamber of Deputies. It should be noted that a Bill is certified as a money Bill by the Speaker of the lower Chamber. If the Speaker's certification is objected to, and the objection is carried by two thirds of the votes, the President of the Union may appoint a privileges committee with equal membership, to decide finally as to the nature of the Bill.

A similar procedure is found in India. In the Council of States, discussion of the Budget is confined to a general debate, and the Council does not vote on estimates of government expenditure. Bills concerned with money and taxation matters are merely placed before it for recommendation, and the lower House must receive the recommendation within fourteen days. The lower House has the same powers as in Burma. Similarly in Ireland, the Seanad has a mere twenty-one days to present its recommendations to the Dail and the final decision is in any case taken by the latter.

This complete relegation of the upper House into the background in financial and budgetary matters is characteristic not only of Parliaments of the British type. It is found in Western Europe as well, e.g. in Austria, where the Federal Council is not at liberty to oppose the passing of the Budget by the National Council, and also in the Federal Republic of Germany. Here, the Budget Act is submitted to the Federal Council, but it is one of those Bills which do not require the consent of the Federal Council in order to be passed. The Federal Council's only course, if it disapproves of the Budget wholly or in part, is to appeal to the mediation commission, or if necessary to submit a protest; but the Diet may reject the protest subject to certain conditions governing the proportion of members who must vote for rejection.

Generally speaking, where the powers of the upper House in financial matters continue to be roughly identical with those of the lower House, the procedure for reaching agreement between the Houses is the same as is ordinarily put into operation in legislative matters. Thus the practice of setting up a conciliation, mediation or conference committee to find common ground between the two Houses is valid also in regard to the Budget and money matters in the following countries: Brazil, Philippines, Switzerland, United States, USSR and Yugoslavia. In Australia, the Federal Republic of Germany and Japan, the part played by such committees is less important because of the greater powers of the lower House. In Belgium and Italy the shuttle system is used to enable the two Houses to reach agreement on the Budget. In France, too, the shuttle system in budgetary matters is the same as in legislative matters generally, but the time-limit within which the Senate must complete its examination is considerably reduced.

V

The Rights of Members of Parliament in Financial Matters

While the primacy of the executive in regard to the preparation and presentation of the Budget is beyond dispute, the question does arise whether the Budget drawn up by the Government and submitted to Parliament for its approval must be accepted or turned down *en bloc*, or whether Parliament has the option of amending it more or less substantially. The considerations involved here are of two types:

(*a*) Considerations of major policy. The fundamental importance of decisions on the Budget which involve the entire nation has led democratic countries to grant Parliament powers of the most absolute kind, or in concrete terms the authority to increase or reduce as it thinks fit both revenue and expenditure, even to the point of discarding completely the Budget figures produced by the Government.

(*b*) Technical considerations. The necessity for balancing the Budget, and in any case hard economic facts, place practical limits on the powers that may be exercised by Parliament to make changes in a Budget on which the economic and social development of an entire country depends. This is a technical 'must' which no state can ignore.

Thus if Parliament is determined to preserve its prerogatives intact, it must voluntarily restrict its own powers in regard to amendment of the Budget, merely keeping a close watch on its execution or, in the event of serious disagreement, raising the question of the resignation of the Government, as the Budget is the instrument of a specific government policy. Where the self-discipline of Parliament does not appear to be equal to the task, the practice is to put constitutional limits on its powers in budgetary matters. This tendency is seen in many of the constitutional experiments of recent times. However, in a number of countries Parliament has retained the same rights in regard to the Budget as in all other legislative fields. Possibly the inference to be drawn from this is that, in such countries, freedom draws its own boundary-lines.

Most of the countries in question are in Europe, where the historical tradition by which constitutional law arises out of financial law is still alive. In all the Nordic countries, the rights of Parliament in regard to the Budget are subject only to the ordinary practice, and there is no special restriction in the financial field. The members of the Folketing in Denmark, the United Althing in Iceland, and the Storting in Norway, are at liberty to submit amendments to the Budget just as they can to any other Bill.

In Finland, any member is at liberty to propose a motion on financial matters, even if it contains proposals for the inclusion of new expenditure items in the Budget, provided such motions are submitted within seven days of the introduction of the Budget in Parliament. This apparent restriction is nothing more than the application of the ordinary legislative practice to budgetary matters. A similar power is open to members of the Riksdag in Sweden. Motions relating to revenue and expenditure are in order, whatever their intent, provided they are presented within the proper time-limits. In the particular case of proposals which require expenditure, they need not necessarily be accompanied by proposals for finding the money to cover it.

The Nordic countries are not the only countries in Europe where there is no limitation on the rights of Members of Parliament in budgetary matters. In Luxembourg and in the Second Chamber of the Netherlands, any member is entitled to put forward amendments without restriction. In Belgium, *de facto* the situation is the same, in spite of a legal provision dating from 1846, under which Bills or amendments entailing expenditure not provided for in the Budget must include an indication of means for providing the necessary funds. This precaution very soon became a mere formality, and it no longer constitutes any real restriction on the rights of members.

In Austria, and also in Switzerland, the Budget is given the same treatment as any other government Bill, i.e. all proposals by Members of Parliament are permitted, whatever their implications. Similarly, in the Bulgarian National Assembly, the Czechoslovak National Assembly, the Polish Diet, the Rumanian Grand National Assembly and the Supreme Soviet of the USSR, members are at liberty to present any proposals to reduce or increase budgetary revenue or expenditure. In Yugoslavia too, amendments in Parliament are allowed. It is the opinion in these countries that Parliament should have every latitude in deciding on matters concerning the Budget and taxation. Indeed it is considered in no way necessary that the rights of Members of Parliament should be restricted in respect of financial matters. Furthermore, the control that the electors exercise over their members makes it impossible for the latter to violate in a deliberate manner the interests of the citizens or of the State as a whole.

Outside Europe, there are few Parliaments which preserve their powers completely intact in regard to the examination of the Budget. Congress continues to do so in the United States and Brazil, since the separation of powers gives it the monopoly of the power to legislate. In Israel, the Budget is subject to the ordinary rules governing the debating of Bills. Any member of the Knesset may thus propose amendments designed to increase or reduce Budget items. Similarly, in Laos, Parliament enjoys extremely wide powers in regard to the Budget.

There are, however, quite as many Parliaments where the situation is altogether different. In some instances, the concern to safeguard the budgetary or economic balance has led certain democracies to reduce the sovereign functions of Parliament. To obviate the danger likely to result from ill-advised moves by individuals, specific rules have been made restricting the Parliament's power to make substantial modifications to the Budget as presented by the Government.

For example, for more than two hundred years, the British House of Commons in a series of standing orders, the oldest of which goes back to 1707, has virtually handed over to the executive its right to introduce Bills in the financial field. In 1713 it was decided that 'This House will receive no petition for any sum relating to the public service or proceed upon any motion for a grant or charge upon the public revenue, whether payable out of the consolidated fund or to be provided by Parliament, unless recommended from the Crown'. The effect of these rules is that the figures produced by the Government must be regarded as ceilings which Bills introduced by private members must in no case exceed.

The unique feature of the British system lies in the fact that it prohibits not merely increases in expenditure, but also increases in revenue. Any private member may propose the reduction or suppression of a tax or duty, but he may not propose that new taxes should be devised or that the rates of the old taxes should be increased beyond the limits laid down in the Queen's Recommendation. Private members of several Parliaments which follow the British tradition, particularly those of Ceylon, India and Ireland, are similarly barred from introducing such measures. The explanation of this provision goes back to the origins of the House of Commons, to the time when it met to consider demands for subsidies made by the Crown. Its task was to decide whether to comply with the demand and, if so, within what limits and by what means. This explains the prohibition on proposals to increase expenditure. The role of the British Parliament is to examine requests for funds by the Crown and to accord the minimum necessary. By virtue of this constitutional practice it is not open to Parliament to vote sums in excess of the Government's estimates. It follows that only those amendments are in order which aim to reduce the sums requested.

In actual fact, the real purpose of motions to reduce the estimate is to enable Members of Parliament to make complaints on specific points and to force the Government to furnish explanations before the sums in question are approved. Such motions, which seldom result in major amendments to the estimates since more often than not they merely propose token cuts, are a common occurrence in most of the countries which have come within British influence.

The ban on initiative from private members in financial matters is still further reinforced in these countries by the existence of a typically British institution: the 'Consolidated Fund' liabilities, consisting of sums whose annual payment is authorized by Parliament for an indefinite length of time by means of separate Acts not related to the annual estimates. Thus they are not subject to the rigours of yearly debates. They include payments in connexion with the National Debt, the civil list of the Crown (where security of payment is essential), the salaries of certain State officials such as judges, the Speaker and the Comptroller and Auditor General, who are independent of the executive and whose activities can only be criticized in Parliament through a special motion.

Although the restrictions on the rights of British private members in respect of increases in expenditure and revenue were opposed by the Constitution and reinforced by the standing orders with the aim of protecting the citizen against the Crown, it is also true to say that they serve today to protect the finances of the country against any irresponsible electioneering. The structure of the British system, based on two parties and party discipline, would in any case, even if no actual rules existed, discourage the members of the majority party from making any move in regard to measures involving the general policy of the Government, and cause them automatically to fight any suggestions coming from the Opposition. Thus, by and large, all that is involved is a voluntary renunciation of rights which have no practical effect. The efficacy of having a legal bar of this type has not been lost on the draftsmen of the constitutions of certain states who have decided to limit to a greater or lesser extent the prerogatives of Members of Parliament in respect of financial matters in order to safeguard the balance of public finances. In Egypt, Article 101 of the Constitution provides that 'the National Assembly is not authorized to make any amendment to the Budget except with the approval of the Government'. This means that, in principle, the Members of the Assembly may propose any amendments they wish, but the agreement of the executive is needed before they can take effect. In Spain, under Article 32 of the standing orders, members of the Cortes may not propose any increase in expenditure or reduction in revenue. In France, Article 17 of the Constitution stipulates that no proposal for increasing expenditure may be submitted during the Budget debate; an organic decree of 1956 specifies, in fact, that no amendment to the Finance Act is in order unless its effect would be to delete or reduce an expenditure item, to create or increase an item of revenue, or to control public finances. In the Philippines, the Constitution does not permit Congress to increase such requests for sums required for government expenditure as are submitted to it by the President; but on the other hand it may change as it sees fit the sums required for itself and for the Judicial Department. In Syria, the Chamber of Deputies may not increase either the revenue estimates or the expenditure estimates; however, in the course of the consideration of the Budget by the appropriate committee, any member is at liberty to propose an increase in expenditure or a reduction in revenue, provided that at the same time he indicates ways and means of restoring the balance originally proposed.

In the same way, several recent constitutions have tackled the problem from the angle of a balanced Budget by allowing Members to propose increases in expenditure provided these are offset by proposals for covering such expenditure. For example, Article 81 of the Constitution of the Italian Republic embodies a provision to this effect. In the Federal Republic of Germany, the task of examining ways and means of covering expenditure is left to the Budget Committee. If this committee states that the proposed expenditure cannot be made up, the proposal is deemed to have been rejected. It should be noted that this machinery does not apply solely to amendments concerning the Federal Budget, but to any Bill which may affect the state of public finances. In Japan, amendments aimed at increasing expenditure must also give some indication as to how the financial resources are to be found to cover the new debit items. Furthermore, a 1955 amendment to the law on the Diet, designed to limit the number of amendments of whatever kind to the Budget, specified that such amendments were admissible only if they were supported by at least fifty Members of Parliament in the House of Representatives, and twenty in the House of Councillors.

These last two examples show the nature of the present trend very clearly. Since the Budget is regarded more and more as an overall plan in which all the parts are closely linked together, the exercise by Parliament of its sovereign rights at its own sole discretion would appear to be hardly compatible with the principle of sound management of public finances. Hence the authority of and concentration on the policy implied in the Budget since, in judging the Budget placed before them, Parliament is first and foremost passing sovereign judgement on the basic instrument of a policy.

VI

Parliamentary Procedure in Financial Matters

*Timing—The Part Played by Committees—Special Aspects of
Debate on the Budget and Estimates*

1. TIMING

In Spain, in virtue of Article 33 of the law on public accountancy, the Budget is bi-annual. This is the only exception to the rule that Budgets are drawn up annually, which means that the Budget covers a single year; but what it means more particularly as far as we are concerned is that the Budget is submitted annually for the approval of Parliament. This practice is closely bound up with the growth of the parliamentary system. It originated as a weapon to be used by Parliament against a Government in which it had no confidence; and it has helped to secure proper parliamentary control of all government activity.

For a long time the principle of annual Budgets went unchallenged, but the issue has recently been raised, owing to the steadily growing encroachment by the State upon economic and social life. The expression in budgetary terms of long-range investment programmes cannot always be made to fit the narrow framework of a single year. The general trend towards economic planning, in accordance with the rhythm of modern life, would appear to make long-term financial Budgets inevitable.

Nevertheless, all countries—including those which have an entirely planned economy such as the USSR—have remained faithful to the principle of annual Budgets. No doubt this is partly out of respect for Parliament, which can thus make its sovereign will felt frequently; but it is also due to certain inherent financial advantages. For one thing, an annual Budget makes it possible to estimate the financial situation exactly, and thus to make forecasts with a large degree of certainty over a relatively short time. As a matter of fact, the system of annual Budgets has been applied for centuries in private enterprise, and everywhere it has become standard practice and has finally come to be regarded as a natural process, especially where the financial year coincides with the civil year.

In most countries, the financial year does actually begin on 1 January and end on 31 December. However for reasons of convenience, and particularly in order to extend the period of drawing up and debating the Budget over a longer period, it has been found preferable, in some countries, to defer the beginning of the financial year. The date on which the financial year begins in various countries is as follows:

1 March	—	Turkey
1 April	—	Denmark, Federal Republic of Germany, India, Ireland, Israel, Japan, Pakistan and the United Kingdom
1 July	—	Australia, Egypt, Italy, Laos, the Philipines, the Sudan, Sweden and the United States
1 October	—	Burma and Ceylon

Whatever the date chosen, however, the essential significance of the principle of annual Budgets is that each year the Budget can only be put into effect with the approval of Parliament. Without the agreement of the representatives of the people, the Government could not spend any money or collect any revenue for the year in question—which would mean almost total paralysis of public life. Hence it is important for the Budget to be passed in good time, i.e. before the beginning of the twelve-month period to which it refers. It may be said at once that a number of countries, including the United Kingdom and several other countries which have followed its example, have modified this principle in practice. But where its observance is regarded as essential, it raises two problems: first the problem of placing before Parliament the budgetary documents which it must pass before the beginning of the new financial year; and secondly the problem of the measures to be taken if the Budget, for one reason or another, cannot be passed in time.

In a general way, the Constitution or the law provide that the Government must submit its Budget a certain length of time prior to the beginning of the financial year, so as to give Parliament reasonable time to study, debate and pass it. The length of time given to Parliament varies according to the country, but the allowance is seldom less than two months. This is the period allowed in Finland, France, Japan, Luxembourg and the USSR. In Belgium, the Federal Republic of Germany, the Netherlands, Syria and the Republic of Vietnam, the period is three months, and it is five months in Italy, where the Budget must be submitted on 31 January, though the financial year begins only on 1 July. In most cases, the length of time allowed to Parliament runs to the very day before the first day of the new financial year. However, in Sweden under the Constitution the Budget must be approved by Parliament by 31 May, though the financial year begins on 1 July. This avoids upsetting the

222

annual pattern and resorting to emergency measures, which are extremely common in other countries.

Experience shows that it is not always easy to ensure that the Budget is passed in time, since political life is subject to fluctuations which are invariably unforeseeable and can upset the ordinary routine. In such circumstances, the problem is to bridge the budgetary gap which would otherwise exist between the end of one financial year and the passing of the Budget for the following year. A variety of methods are used to prevent any hold-up which might jeopardize the smooth running of the State machinery or even the economic life of the nation, although in some countries no machinery is provided for such an eventuality. The conclusion to be drawn from this is no doubt that the situation has never arisen, and that it has always been possible to pass the Budget in time. This is the case in Burma, Ceylon, Indonesia, Laos and Turkey. In the Philippines, the only remedy—and it appears to be seldom applied—is to convene Congress in extraordinary session.

As a general rule, special measures are taken: a provisional arrangement is made mainly in regard to expenditure, since revenue has more often than not an existence independent of the Budget, and a mere authorization is sufficient to enable it to be levied. The question is therefore to assess the importance of the part played by Parliament (which as a rule is responsible for the delay), in determining the amount of expenditure to be appropriated provisionally.

First of all, it is conceivable that in the event of Parliament temporarily failing to act, there will simply be a sort of automatic falling-back, at any rate provisionally, on the previous year's estimates. Several countries adopt this course in varying degrees:

(a) In Brazil, if the Budget Act has not been sent to the president for signature by 30 November, the current Budget is automatically continued into the next financial year.

(b) In Egypt, the Constitution provides that the Budget for the preceding year shall remain in force until the new Budget is passed.

(c) In Sweden, a similar course must be followed in the only circumstances in which the Budget cannot be passed in time, namely where the delay is caused by the dissolution of the Riksdag or one of its Houses.

The rule of automatic extension also applies in Austria, but the extension may not exceed two months. At the end of this period, a provisional Budget must be passed in the ordinary way. In the Netherlands, it is traditionally assumed that the Budget will not be ready before 1 January. Hence the Government is automatically allotted four twelfths of the expenditure authorized in the previous year's estimates to cover the first four months of the year.

Instead of a chronological deadline for automatically falling back on the previous estimates, we sometimes get a limitation by categories of expenditure. This is what happens in the Federal Republic of Germany where, under its Basic Law, the Federal Government may go ahead with any spending necessary for the maintenance of the State organizations and the application of measures laid down by law for meeting the Federal State's legal obligations and for carrying out public works projects and other productive activities provided that funds have already been appropriated for the same purposes in previous Budgets. The Constitution provides also that, in the event of the revenue being insufficient to cover all this expenditure, the Government may meet such expenditure out of Treasury funds, to the amount of one quarter of the revenue of the preceding year.

These various systems for automatically falling back on the previous Budget are somewhat reminiscent of the 'Consolidated Fund Expenditure' in the United Kingdom. It should be noted, however, that they differ from it inasmuch as they are regarded as emergency and provisional measures.

Closely akin to the system of extension of the previous Budget is that in which direct steps are taken by the executive without reference to Parliament. This makes it possible for the Government, on its own authority, to disburse the moneys needed for the functioning of the State, on the understanding that they will ultimately be included in the estimates to be approved in due course by Parliament. Several examples of this procedure may be quoted:

(a) In Syria, provisional monthly sums are allocated by decree of the Council of Ministers, on the basis of one twelfth of the funds allocated during the preceding financial year.

(b) In Monaco, the expenditure estimates are drawn up by Royal Ordinance, on the basis of the figures for the preceding year.

(c) In France, the Government may enact decrees for the allocation of funds in respect of 'services already voted', i.e. funds from the previous financial year, adjusted where necessary in the light of measures previously approved by Parliament or decided upon by the Government within the limit of the powers vested in it. This system replaced the former method of provisional twelfths in 1956.

The Republic of Vietnam goes one step further: under budgetary decrees, signed by the President of the Republic, each quarter the Government can spend one quarter of the appropriations included in the Budget, pending its final passing by the National Assembly.

In the USSR, if the Supreme Soviet has not passed the estimates by the beginning of a new year, the ministers receive from the Government the money they need until they have been agreed to. In Bulgaria, if the estimates cannot be approved before the February session, limited issues of funds are made to the various departments by government decision. In Albania, similarly, the Council of Ministers allocates funds, but may do so only for a period of not more than six months. It should be noted that in Rumania, the Budget and related estimates are traditionally submitted to the Grand National Assembly only at the beginning of the financial year. Between this date and the passing of the Budget, expenditure is voted by decree of the Presidium of the Grand National Assembly.

This unusual system is midway between the preceding system and that of provisional funds granted by Parliament in the ordinary way. Provisional funds are, as it were, votes on account, voted by Parliament more often than not under emergency procedure and subsequently included in the Budget and related estimates proper. The commonest form is that of the 'provisional twelfths'. Month by month, Parliament is called upon to vote a small vote on account so as to make it possible to carry on current business without undertaking future commitments. This is what happens for example in Belgium, Iceland, Luxembourg and the United States. The sums voted may not be strictly proportionate to a fraction of the Budget. In this case what we get is rather a 'provisional Budget' than 'provisional twelfths'. But the essential principle is that Parliament takes a hand, even where it does not do so every month, as is the case in Denmark, Israel, Norway and Switzerland. The same is true of Japan: where the House of Representatives is dissolved in the course of the deliberations on the Budget and related estimates so that they cannot be voted before the beginning of the financial year, the Cabinet convenes the House of Councillors in emergency session and submits to it a provisional Budget for one or two months. The measures taken under the procedure must subsequently be ratified by the new House of Representatives within ten days of the opening of the session. In Finland, should it prove impossible to pass the Budget and related estimates before the beginning of the financial year to which it refers, Parliament decides, following a proposal by the Government, to what extent the previous year's Budget shall be applied until such time as the new Budget is finally approved. It should be noted that in Poland and Yugoslavia, provisional sums may not be granted to the Government beyond the first quarter, and in Italy, beyond the first four months of the financial year.

The system we find in the United Kingdom and several other countries such as Australia, India, Ireland and the Sudan, is based on an entirely different principle. Contrary to the usual practice, the rule in these countries is only to approve the Budget after the beginning of the financial year. Strictly speaking, moreover, it is not the Budget itself which is passed, but a series of 'budget resolutions' and a 'Finance Bill' required to give legislative effect to the Budget. Votes on account do not constitute an exceptional procedure, but are the ordinary rule in regard to the estimates. Let us see how this system operates, taking as a stock example the United Kingdom.

It should be noted first of all that the existence of a Consolidated Fund involving certain fixed expenditure relieves Parliament of the necessity for reviewing this expenditure year after year. As regards estimates subject to annual review, Parliament determines the amount in a series of stages. The first stage consists of a vote on account, by which the funds needed by the various government departments to meet their expenses from the beginning of the financial year until the enactment of the Appropriation Act are made available. Thus the vote on account must take place before 1 April. In the ordinary way it covers five twelfths of the total amount provided in the estimates, divided up among the various departments.

The measures included in the vote on account are first of all examined by the whole House sitting as the Committee of Supply, which agrees to a resolution which is reported to the House sitting as the House for approval. Then the House sits as the Committee of Ways and Means to vote the sum required to cover the grants so far agreed to. The procedure winds up in the passing into law of the Consolidated Fund Bill authorizing the spending of the necessary public funds. This whole series of operations normally takes place in four sittings where, as is usual in matters relating to the estimates, the Opposition plays the main part, since it has the right to choose the subject for debate, usually moving that the vote be reduced by a token amount.

The items arising out of the vote on account may be regarded as advances on the main grants which will only be finally approved towards the end of July, at the close of the whole budgetary process, when both the Appropriation Act authorizing expenditure, and the Finance Act, authorizing the raising of the corresponding revenue, assume the force of law.

In Ireland, Votes on Account are calculated on a period of four months; in India, on a period of one month only, since the final decision is forthcoming only a short time after the beginning of the financial year.

All these procedures, vastly different though they are, have at any rate one point in common, apart from their object of ensuring that whatever happens the State machine will continue to function— namely the constantly widening scope of devices such as falling back on the previous Budget, the Consolidated Fund services already voted, and disbursement by decree, which give the executive a certain room for manoeuvre, by holding off the serious debate of the Budget in Parliament, which is often a sore trial for the Government.

2. THE PART PLAYED BY COMMITTEES

The difference between the British conception of the part played by committees and the Continental or American conception is strongly marked in the legislative field generally, but is particularly note-worthy in regard to the Budget and the related estimates. There are two reasons for this: in the first place, in Parliaments where perma-nent Committees operate, the committee dealing with financial matters is exceptionally important. The prior scrutiny of the finance and appropriation Bills by this committee affects the debates of the whole House profoundly. Secondly, in the present British system, the principle holds good that the financial powers of Parliament are the exclusive province of the House itself and the effect of this is to rule out entirely any reference to smaller working bodies. For practical purposes this means that, when the Budget resolutions and the Finance Bill are debated, they are not referred to a standing committee or a select committee. The Budget is dealt with by the Committee of the Whole House, which resolves itself into Com-mittee of Supply in order to approve expenditure contained first of all in the vote on account, and then in the estimates proper; it then resolves itself into a Committee of Ways and Means to vote the funds for covering this expenditure and to debate the question of revenue.

A similar system obtains in Australia, Ireland and Ceylon, though a distinction is not always made between these two bodies made up of the whole House. The system does uphold, at any rate theoretically, one of the classic principles of parliamentary procedure —examination by successive stages—since the business handled by the Committee of the Whole House must be reported to the House itself, and must be agreed to by the House.

Some of the countries which have followed the example of the procedure found in the House of Commons have seen fit to get rid of these various stages, which after all are purely procedural. In Burma, India and Pakistan, no committee is involved, not even a Committee of the Whole House. In all three countries, the Budget estimates are submitted direct to the House, sitting as a House and not as a committee. A reasonable time is of course allowed between the presentation of the Budget and its debate, to enable members to give it serious study.

In most of the other countries the debate on the Budget follows the ordinary rules governing legislative procedure, so that before the Budget and related estimates are examined in the House they are first of all referred to a committee. The usual system is for the Budget to be referred to one particular committee, which has powers to deal with all money matters. In view of the political importance of the Budget, this means that the committee in question acquires an overwhelming prestige, and frequently there is the likelihood that it may virtually take control of the debate in the House. For this reason, the part played by finance committees is frequently regarded as a vital feature of the Continental parliamentary system, especially that of France, and also of the American system.

Actually, the British method has left a decided mark on the United States Congress. The division of powers establised in the House of Commons in regard to questions of expenditure and questions of revenue is also found in the House of Representatives and the Senate. In both these bodies, there are two committees whose task is to examine the Budget and related estimates; the Committee of Ways and Means (House) and the Finance Committee (Senate) in regard to revenue; the Committee on Appropriation in regard to expenditure. In the Philippines, the Budget is examined on the same basis.

In the United States House of Representatives it is traditional for the Bills relating to taxation or the grant of funds to be debated in the Committee of the Whole House on the State of the Union. This would suggest that there is a sort of compromise between the British procedure and the Continental system. In actual fact, it leans towards the Continental system, owing to the importance of the work done by the permanent committees, especially the Committee on Appropriation, which scrutinize in detail the grant of funds for the various departments. Nor does its task end there; whenever a Bill seems likely to have financial implications, this committee must give its approval, as well as the committee which deals with the particular type of legislation involved. The establishment of a large number of sub-committees, each one corresponding to a different administrative service, helps to lighten the burden on the committee by means of a minute sub-division of labour.

This system is found also in a number of other Parliaments, particularly those of Japan, Albania, Bulgaria and the USSR. In the Soviet Union, the finance committees of the two House are split up into an average of ten or twelve sub-committees. Since there are no rigid rules, these small bodies are at liberty to carry out thorough inquiries, obtaining concrete information and enlisting the help of financial experts or representatives of the government department.

Finance committees are not always the only committees to pass judgment on the Budget and related estimates. In view of the repercussions of the Budget on all branches of public life it is sometimes found desirable to consult other committees affected by the grant and distribution of funds. But whether its powers are exclusive in regard to the substance, or whether it has the exclusive say on the Budget as a whole, the finance committee enjoys an exceptionally high status; indeed this is often regarded as the guarantee of a sound financial system.

In a number of countries, such as Czechoslovakia, France, Monaco, Norway and the Republic of Vietnam, the 'technical' committees have the right to put before the House their views on problems within their terms of reference in the form of separate reports. In many other Parliaments, their views are submitted to the finance committee, which acts as a sort of go-between. This is the procedure applied in Israel and the Federal Republic of Germany. In the latter country, the Budget as a whole is submitted to the Budget Committee; but the usual practice is for the other committees to take up such provisions as are of special interest to them and where necessary to make comments to the Budget Committee.

In Poland, a similar procedure is followed. The programme of work for the examination of the Budget is drawn up by the Committee on Economic Planning, Budget and Finance, which appoints a general rapporteur; the Budget is then submitted to several committees which study the various parts of it, either separately or in joint meetings, and these again appoint rapporteurs; the study of the over-all Budget is then taken up again by the Committee on Economic Planning, Budget and Finance, which accepts or rejects the amendments proposed by the various committees; finally, the general rapporteur reports to the Diet on the proceedings as a whole. In the Egyptian National Assembly, it is stipulated in the standing orders that the chairmen and rapporteurs of the various committees may take part in the work of the Committee on budgetary questions and accounts when questions within their particular sphere are considered.

In the procedure followed in Italy, we find a still more marked tendency to relieve the finance committee of its natural task. Both in the Chamber and in the Senate, the finance committee has the right to put forward its views on the Budget as a whole first, but the other committees then take over the separate examination of the proposals relating to their particular fields and submit written reports to the House on the issues of substance involved. In Belgium, again, there is a division of powers as to the actual substance of the Budget. We find as many committees as there are ministerial departments, and each committee is required to examine the proposals relating to its own department, and only strictly financial proposals (ways and means, pensions, national debt) are referred to the finance committee. In Indonesia and the Netherlands (Second Chamber), the study of the Budget is conducted in a similar fashion.

In Sweden, four committees are normally concerned with the Budget and related estimates: the Committee of Ways and Means in respect of revenue; the Bank Committee in regard to matters relating to the Bank of Sweden and the National Office of the Public Debt; the Committee on Agriculture as regards matters related to agriculture, forestry and fisheries; and the Budget Committee, which is the vital one, since it has powers in regard to all other matters. Where necessary, financial questions may be submitted to select committees or, pursuant to resolutions in the appropriate committees, they may be examined by a joint committee.

3. SPECIAL ASPECTS OF DEBATE ON THE BUDGET AND ESTIMATES

As we have seen, the peculiar features of Budget debates frequently have the effect of restricting in some degree the right of Members of Parliament to amend the Government's proposals and, in the case of bicameral Parliaments, of re-adjusting the relative powers of the two Houses. Subject to these reservations, the differences between financial procedure and ordinary legislative procedure tend to disappear, leaving in the main the system of rules we have described in considering the legislative function of Parliaments.

The number of countries which constitute exceptions to this general statement is very small, but reference should be made to the system found in Norway and Iceland, where the two Houses are required to hold joint sittings for financial matters, and the Swedish system, where a joint sitting is called for in the event of disagreement persisting between the two Houses. In the Norwegian Storting, the Budget debate follows a special set of rules. The debate takes place in three phases: first of all there is a 'financial debate' on the report of the finance committee. In the second phase the special reports of the other permanent committees are considered, and a number of resolutions are agreed to provisionally. These resolutions must be approved by the Storting in the third phase, on the basis of reports again drawn up by the finance committee. In Finland, too, financial procedure departs considerably from the rules followed in legislative matters. The Budget and related estimates are debated only on a single reading instead of the usual three readings. However, if amendments to the Bill presented by the finance committee are agreed to by the Diet, the estimates are referred back for reconsideration in committee and the Bill produced by the committee is submitted once again to the House in the course of a resumed debate on the single reading.

At any rate, the two essential phases of parliamentary procedure are invariably found—first of all, the general debate on the Budget as a whole and, secondly, the detailed examination of its provisions. The relative importance of each of these phases varies in accordance with the actual manner in which the role of Parliament in working on the Budget proposals is conceived, and particularly in the light of the limits on the powers of Parliament to amend them. Obviously if the power to amend the Budget is subject to serious restrictions, the 'technical' examination of the Budget items will become secondary to the general debate. This gives every Member of Parliament a general right to criticize, and the less likelihood there is of positive action being taken as a result of the criticism, the more widely this right will be exercised. Hence in all countries, stress is laid on the ample opportunities for Members of Parliament to put their own case and air their grievances in the course of the general debate. It should, however, be pointed out that there is one argument— frequently a sound one—against any over-zealous concern to avoid placing any obstacle in the way of free discussion. Time, after all, plays a vital part in financial matters, and in some cases special measures are taken—we hear of them in Belgium, Denmark, Israel and the United States—to speed up the debate and to prevent it exceeding reasonable limits.

In the British system some limits are laid down precisely. The maximum number of days allotted for the discussion of Supply in the House of Commons is twenty-six; in Ceylon the limit is twenty days, in Burma twelve. In the Sudan the debate in committee must be completed within ten days, and the second reading within three days. Similar time-limits are to be found in India, where the general debate lasts four to five days. The peculiar features of the British procedure in regard to the Budget arise out of the meaning given to the word 'Budget'. In Britain, the Budget is not a tabular conspectus of all revenue and all expenditure submitted for authorization by means of parliamentary approval. Before we can grasp the real meaning we must make a twofold distinction. In the first place, the Budget denotes the collection of proposals for adjusting the State revenue to meet the expenditure likely to be incurred, the annual rate of income tax being one of the most important sources of income. As regards the estimates, a distinction must be made between the actual statement of the amount of expenditure proposed and the method of meeting this out of public funds.

On the basis of these data, we can follow the thread of the Budget debate in the United Kingdom, complex as it may seem. The debate opens with the 'Budget statement' made by the Chancellor of the Exchequer to the House sitting as the Committee of Ways and Means. The Chancellor reviews the expenditure and revenue, and in a general way the economic state of the nation, and in the course of this review, he makes a number of proposals in regard to taxation. The statement is followed by a general debate, at the end of which Budget resolutions are passed giving effect to the Chancellor's proposals. A Finance Bill embodying the committee's decisions is then introduced, and follows the normal procedure at all its stages. Meanwhile, the resolutions passed by the Committee of Ways and Means have legal force for four months, provided they are agreed to by the House within ten sitting days and provided the Finance Bill is read a second time within twenty sitting days and receives the Royal Assent within four months.

With regard to the examination of the estimates, this is done by the Committee of Supply before the end of March, for the purpose of a vote on account, and before the end of July for the expenditure as a whole. A series of resolutions are passed by the Committee of Supply, to which the rule of twenty-six days' debate applies. Next the Committee of Ways and Means has to authorize payments out of the Consolidated Fund to meet the expenditure as thus determined. Once the resolutions of these two committees have been reported to the House and approved by it, a Bill is brought in to make the appropriation of the necessary sums. This Bill receives the Royal Assent as the 'Appropriation Act'.

In practice, approximately twenty days are devoted to the study of the principal estimates. Hence it is seldom possible to go into great detail, with the result that the debates in the Committee of Supply have undergone a change of character. The former practice of minute examination of each item has been replaced by debates on the Government's policy as revealed by the activity of one or several of its departments. On this occasion, amendments are often proposed with a view to reducing the salary of this or that minister. The *raison d'être* of this practice is to enable the House to go on to vote on the policy pursued by the Government.

This procedure cuts out a feature which is characteristic of most Continental countries, namely the thorough scrutiny of all the items of the Budget and related estimates. The debate is keen; all problems become problems of general policy. The Budget is first and foremost a matter of confidence; Parliament hands over to the Government the responsibility for ensuring the proper functioning of the State in the financial field, and thus for crystallizing in the form of a programme of expenditure and income the political views of the majority. This method, another feature of which is the transfer of the prerogatives of Parliament from the legislative field to that of control, obviates a danger experienced by many Parliaments, namely the length and technical intricacy of the debates, and frequently their disorderliness. This danger is usually manifested in an apathetic attitude on the part of public opinion towards an act of policy which after all is vital to an entire nation.

To sum up, whatever the legal position in regard to the Budget estimates and the procedure by which they are passed, in all democratic countries they constitute a financial programme which must be approved by the legislature.

Part Four

CONTROL OF THE EXECUTIVE
BY PARLIAMENT

CONTROL OF THE EXECUTIVE
BY PARLIAMENT

Essentially, the control exercised over the executive by Parliament is based on a simple concept; since Parliament is the incarnation of the will of the people, it must be in a position to supervise the way in which the policy of the State is carried out, so as to ensure that it does not stray from the path which most closely represents the aspirations of the nation as a whole. In practice this control is extremely complex, since it raises the whole problem of the relationship between a deliberate institution and the executive, and more specifically the problem of the compatability of the prerogatives of Parliament with the Government's freedom of action.

State policy is, of course, largely the outcome of legislative and financial action, and as we know, the part played by Parliament in legislation and in financial decisions is more often than not decisive. But these 'technical' tasks do not give a true picture of the real power of Parliament. The strength of a Parliament lies in the extent to which it can exercise political control. From the strictly legalistic standpoint, this is not true of systems based on the separation of power, where each arm is in principle self-contained and its effectiveness is dependent precisely on the exclusive powers it wields in its own particular sphere. But these 'presidential' systems, as they are most commonly called, are an exception; moreover, in spite of academic principles, *de facto* relationships do invariably grow up between the powers, or even a merging of the powers. However, the main difference lies in the fact that systems of the first type have no legal machinery for the settlement of any conflicts arising between the legislature and the executive.

The main point in regard to parliamentary control is not only to supervise the activity of the executive or even where necessary to issue directives, but to provide a means of bringing this activity to a halt once it ceases to be in keeping with the wishes of the representatives of the people. Thus political control and the powers that go with it constitute the essential criterion of parliamentary sovereignty. But surely then, one might say, the simplest way of keeping a firm grip on the action of the executive is to have a hand in appointing its heads.

* * *

237

I

The Part Played by Parliament in the Appointment of the Head of State and of the Executive

Appointment of the Head of State—Appointment of the Head of the Government and the Cabinet—Appointment of Certain High Officials

The problem of the structure of the executive is outside the scope of this work, but we cannot avoid reference to it if we are to understand the various possibilities open to Parliament in regard to appointment of the executive. In theory there are a number of forms of executive:

(a) Monocratic, when it consists of a single individual.
(b) Collegiate, when it is formed by men with equal powers.
(c) Directorial, when it consists of a small group of leaders forming a committee.
(d) Two-power, when there is a single individual and a committee side by side.

But constitutional practice has tended to break down the rigid divisions separating these various types of executive, so that in fact there are today only three main systems, at any rate as far as the countries studied in this work are concerned.

In the first of these systems we find, parallel with Parliament, a single power responsible for executive functions, more often than not in the person of a President whose powers are vested in him by universal suffrage. He will, of course, be surrounded by a team of helpers to assist him in his task of government, but in principle the purpose of the team is merely to prepare and to administer; it has no part in the decisions taken and its members are, in theory at least, civil servants, not statesmen. This is the characteristic feature of the 'presidential system'.

The second system has so much become identified with constitutional practice that it seems as if it were an inherent feature of it, but in point of fact it is the outcome of a long historical evolution. It is bound up with the development of the parliamentary system in England, where it came about as a result of a gradual weakening of the power of the Crown and a corresponding growth of the powers of the ministers, who were originally nothing more than the assistants of the Monarch. Its distinguishing feature is the division of the executive functions between two powers essentially independent of each other. On the one side we have the Head of State, the incarnation of the nation itself, and on the other side a Cabinet of ministers whose task is to be directly in charge of the management of public affairs.

This two-power system of government is found in most contemporary states, whether or not they use the term 'Cabinet government', and the system gains strength where one of the members of the Cabinet stands by law or in practice above the rest, in which case we get side by side with the Head of State, a Head of Government, President of the Council or Prime Minister. The system in force in most of the People's Democracies and the USSR differs considerably from the two outlined above; here, the functions of the Head of State are fulfilled by the Presidium, which is regarded not as an executive but as the supreme power of the State. This is explained by the fact that the Presidium emanates from Parliament.

Thus if we are to gain a proper appreciation of the importance of the role played by Parliament, it is essential to distinguish between the appointment of the Head of State and that of the Head of the Government and the Cabinet.

1. APPOINTMENT OF THE HEAD OF STATE

In hereditary monarchies, obviously the role of Parliament is practically negligible as far as designating the occupant of the throne is concerned. The order of dynastic succession generally follows specific rules laid down in the Constitution, or fixed by law or custom. Hence there is no occasion for Parliament to intervene, except where this is necessary to ensure that the rules are observed.

The association of the monarchy with democratic principles is characteristic of most of the hereditary monarchies still surviving in Western Europe: Belgium, Denmark, Luxembourg, the Netherlands, Norway, Sweden and the United Kingdom. Outside Europe, the only hereditary monarchies left among the countries included in the present study are Japan and Laos, unless we count Australia and Ceylon, which strictly come under the British Crown as members of the Commonwealth. It is noteworthy in this respect that the appointment of the Governor-General in these two countries is made by Her Britannic Majesty only on the recommendation of the Prime Minister. Thus Parliament preserves a certain influence, since the Head of the Government is responsible to the House. In Ceylon, for example, any Member of Parliament may put forward a motion protesting to the Queen against the appointment made by the Prime Minister.

If such a motion were carried, it would amount to a motion of censure against the Government, which would be obliged to resign or to dissolve Parliament.

As a matter of fact, in all hereditary monarchies, the time does come when Parliament is called upon to take a hand in the designation of the Sovereign. In the United Kingdom, while the two Houses no longer have to approve the accession of the Monarch to the throne or his abdication, they retain their power to settle the question of succession of the reigning Sovereign, subject to his or her assent. They can, for example, for religious or other reasons decide to change the order of succession. In Norway, Article 7 of the Constitution stipulates that if there is no Prince to succeed to the throne, the King may propose to the Storting the name of an heir, and the Storting may order its own dissolution if it does not fall in with the King's proposal. In the Netherlands, there is a provision for parliamentary intervention in the event of the House of Orange dying out. The procedure is very unusual and is worth mentioning: along with the two Houses of Parliament in joint session, an equal number of members would be elected by the people to form an electoral college which is entrusted with the task of choosing a new King. In Sweden, the Riksdag alone has the power to designate a new royal line in the event of the Bernadotte dynasty dying out. It is also empowered to elect one, three or five Regents in the event of the King dying before the heir to the throne has come of age. In Belgium, Parliament is called on to play a part in various circumstances specified in the Constitution:

(a) If the King has no male descendant, Parliament designates a successor, on the proposal of the King, by two thirds of the members of both Houses voting in a proportion of two to one in his favour.
(b) If the heir is a minor, i.e. under 18 years of age, or in the event of the King's incapacity, the two Houses meet and arrange for a Regency and for guardianship.
(c) If the throne should fall vacant, both Houses meet in joint session and provisionally institute a Regency system until such time as a new Parliament meets to fill the vacancy permanently.

It should also be noted that the new Sovereign is required to take the oath before Parliament. The same is true in Luxembourg.

It is clear from these few examples that the role of Parliament in the case of an hereditary Monarch is considerably curtailed. This is still more true of certain republics where the President is elected by the people, a system designed to build up side by side with the legislative power an executive power which will have at least as much authority, since it too may claim the consent of the people.

This system of equality of status between the powers, more often than not involving a merging of the functions of Head of State and of Head of Government, is the characteristic feature of the classic type of presidential system as practised in the United States, Brazil and the Philippines, as well as to some extent in Egypt and the Republic of Vietnam. Other countries such as Austria, Iceland, Indonesia and Ireland have likewise felt it desirable to give the authority of the Head of State a more solid foundation by basing his election on direct universal suffrage—which, of course, rules out any action by Parliament.

In the United States, admittedly, the people do not designate the President himself, but only the presidential electoral college. But this procedure is a pure formality since the presidential electoral college has no choice in the matter. The result of this is that the presidential election, i.e. the vote recorded by the electoral college has become a mere legal formality of which the man in the street is hardly aware. It is only at this stage of the procedure that Congress comes into the picture, since the counting of the votes must be done in Congress. Its task ends there, except in the improbable event of none of the candidates obtaining an absolute majority of the votes. If this should happen, the House of Representatives must hold a referendum among the delegations of the various states, each delegation having a single vote; the candidate mustering the largest number of votes is then elected President. The Senate fulfils a similar function in regard to the Vice-President, who must be elected at the same time.

In Egypt, Iceland and Ireland, Parliament plays a more important role. In Egypt, the National Assembly chooses the candidate for the Presidency of the Republic by an absolute majority of its members. The candidate thus proposed then faces the electorate and becomes President of the Republic provided he obtains an absolute majority of the votes. Otherwise, the Assembly puts up a new candidate and the same procedure is repeated. In Iceland the part played by Parliament is somewhat peculiar. The Althing does not elect the President of the Republic, but it has the authority to divest him of his powers by an adverse vote of two thirds of its membership, provided this move is confirmed within two months by a popular vote. In Ireland, a candidate other than a former President or the outgoing President must be presented either by twenty members of either House of Parliament or by the Councils of four administrative committees.

There is only one country where the election of the Head of State is the outcome of indirect universal suffrage, namely Finland. Here the election is entrusted to a special electoral body consisting of 300 members elected at separate general elections. Parliament takes no part in it. The resemblance to the presidential system stops there. In Finland the President of the Republic is a parliamentary Head of State whose constitutional prerogatives are exercised in practice by the President of the Council and the ministers. However, the manner of his election gives him an authority and an influence greater than that enjoyed in the classic type of parliamentary régime, where the role of the Head of State is very slight indeed.

In the period between the two wars a number of constitutions, under the influence of a school of thought which wished to rationalize the parliamentary system on an academic basis, got rid of the Head of State altogether as being superfluous. Actually, the republic tradition has not always looked with favour on this institution, which perhaps seemed dangerous inasmuch as its electoral support gave it a great measure of power which might easily slip over into dictatorship. But political circumstances have militated in favour of the retention of the system. Nowadays it is regarded mainly as a moral leadership not easily dispensed with, but the tendency to resist any division of executive power is still strong, and one of the means used to prevent any autocratic leanings on the part of the Head of State is to place his appointment in the hands of Parliament. The system of election by Parliament also has the advantage of being simple and rapid. Hence in eighteen states of the republican type, the primary manifestation of parliamentary control over the executive consists in the appointment by Parliament of its head.

In states with a fairly marked federal structure, the action taken by Parliament may be robbed of some of its significance by the fact that a number of representatives of the various regions may take a hand. This is what happens in the Federal Republic of Germany. The Federal President is elected by the Federal Convention, which consists of the Members of the Bundestag and an equal number of members elected on the proportional representation system by the Parliaments of the Länder. The concern which this indicates to take account of the will of the electoral body at the particular moment, along with the opinion previously expressed by Members of Parliament elected earlier, is not unlike the Netherlands' procedure for choosing a new Sovereign.

In India, the President of the Union is elected by an electoral college comprising the members of the two Houses of Parliament and those of the legislative assemblies of the states. In Pakistan, the provincial assemblies join with the National Assembly in designating the President of the Republic. In Italy, those who take part in the election of the President of the Republic include, in addition to the members of the two Houses in joint Congress, three delegates from each region, elected by the Regional Councils. In all the other countries, Parliament alone has the authority to choose the Head of State.

In bicameral Paliaments, the election normally takes place with both Houses sitting jointly in the form of a 'Congress'. This is true of Burma, France and Yugoslavia. In the last-named country, the President of the Republic is first and foremost the Head of the State, but he is also President of the Federal Executive Council, i.e. the Head of the Government. This fusion of the two functions in a single person might perhaps suggest a parallel between the Yugoslav Constitution and the presidential system. In actual fact, the two systems are poles apart, since the President is elected by Parliament and is answerable to it, and he does not enjoy the independence characteristic of a presidential chief executive. In Czechoslovakia, Israel, Syria and Turkey, the single-chamber Parliament elects the President of the Republic.

The practice in the USSR, Albania, Bulgaria, Poland and Rumania is to place the functions of Chief of State in the hands of a collective body known as the Presidium (or in Poland the Council of State), a body which is actually complex in character. This curious type of body bears no direct resemblance to anything existing in the Western countries. Its President, Vice-Presidents, Secretaries and ordinary members are elected by Parliament from among its own membership, or if necessary by both Houses jointly. It has two types of powers, first of all those normally enjoyed by a parliamentary Head of State, and secondly powers of a greater importance as 'directing body' of Parliament, for which it substitutes when Parliament is not sitting, for example in regard to the Council of Ministers (accountability, dismissal and appointment). But its own authority proceeds directly from Parliament to which it is at all times responsible for its actions.

Equally unusual is the constitutional organization of Switzerland. Here the executive power as a whole is in the hands of a Federal Council elected for four years by both Houses in joint session. One of the members of the Council is elected in the same manner, but for one year only, as President of the Confederation. He acts as Head of

State, but he has no authority over the other members of the Council, who are all on an equal footing; he is merely *primus inter pares*. The Federal Council wields governmental authority as a body. This system is the practical embodiment of the unity of the executive, and it throws light on the importance of the functions of government, which are generally greater than those of the Head of State. Indeed, the desire to ensure the primacy of Parliament is more effectively shown in the choice of the particular procedure for designating the Head of the Government and the members of the Cabinet.

2. APPOINTMENT OF THE HEAD OF THE GOVERNMENT AND THE CABINET

In systems of the presidential type (United States, Brazil, the Philippines, Egypt and the Republic of Vietnam), the functions of Head of State and Head of the Government are fused and carried out by one and the same person, elected, as we have seen, by universal suffrage. The strict separation of the legislative and the executive powers thus excludes any intervention by Parliament, at any rate as regards the President. In the United States, in fact, the appointment of the members of the Cabinet by the Head of State is not at his discretion— it requires the approval of the Senate. This unusual prerogative— unusual in view of the separation of powers—makes sense if we regard it as having no political character whatsoever but as being what it really is—an administrative act, for we must remember that Secretaries of State are in principle civil servants. In the Philippines too, the appointment of the members of the Cabinet must also be approved by a parliamentary body—the Committee on Appointments, consisting of twelve Members of the House of Representatives and twelve Senators, with the President of the Senate as Chairman.

Subject to this reservation, which does not amount to a great deal, since in practice it is difficult to do anything but ratify the choice of the President, the influence of Parliament in presidential systems is therefore insignificant in this direction. This is equally true of Spain, where the Government is designated by the Head of State, and in Monaco, where the Head of the Government and the three Counsellors are selected and appointed by the Prince.

Everywhere else, the procedure for designating the Head of the Government and the Cabinet brings out the part played directly or indirectly by Parliament. This takes various forms, which ensure to a greater or lesser degree the overriding power of Parliament in relation to the Government. The most straightforward method is direct election, since it ensures a close dependence of the Government on Parliament. This dependence is particularly marked in Yugo-slavia, since the Federal Executive Council, which fulfils the tasks of government, is legally the executive agent of Parliament itself before being the executive agent of the State. Actually, in spite of this peculiarity, it is largely independent of Parliament, and the nature of its powers distinguishes it clearly from the strictly parliamentary type of machinery. It is nevertheless the agent of Parliament, which alone has the power to elect or dismiss it at a joint sitting of both Houses.

Government by delegation by Parliament is in fact a legal feature of the present Soviet Constitution and those which have taken it as a model, namely Albania, Bulgaria, Poland and Rumania. In the USSR the Supreme Soviet, in a joint sitting of both Houses, appoints the President of the Council of Ministers of the USSR by an absolute majority of votes in each Chamber. The members of the Government are proposed by the President of the Council of Ministers, and approved by the Supreme Soviet according to a procedure identical to that governing the nomination of the President of the Council of Ministers himself. In Rumania, names of candidates for the position of President of the Council must come from the Presidium, the Bureau of the Grand National Assembly, or a group of at least thirty-five members.

Side by side with the power of appointment are equally broad powers of individual or collective dismissal. This machinery throws light on the procedure of the downward delegation of powers found in the Soviet system. The highest authority is the Supreme Soviet. When it is not sitting it delegates its powers to the Presidium which exercises them, particularly in regard to the Council of Ministers, whose legal status is merely that of a part of the State administration and not a supreme authority of 'State power', though the personality of the President of the Council frequently helps to raise its prestige as an institution.

The constitutional structure of the Czechoslovak Republic de-parts quite markedly in this respect from the system described above. The institution of President of the Republic has in some respects something in common with the rules governing the Western type of parliamentary system. The President enjoys real authority, as is seen particularly in the power he has to appoint the Head and the other members of the Government prior to any action by Parliament. The latter is not rendered altogether impotent, however, for before the Government takes office it must appear before Parliament, outline its programme and obtain a vote of confidence. This is of course the usual procedure for government investiture under the cabinet system.

There are two features characteristic of the cabinet system: (i) the formal appointment of the Head of the Government and ministers by the Head of the State, and (ii) the necessity for parliamentary approval before the appointment becomes effective. The problem is to decide when and how this approval is to be given, whether it should come before or after the formal act of appointment, and whether it should be explicit or simply a matter of tacit consent. The replies to the questions on these points emanate from two differing concepts of the role of Parliament; one is more academic, and might almost be called radical; the other more empirical and traditionalist. .

In some countries, the intention is clearly that the Cabinet actually be elected:

(a) In Israel the Head of State consults with representatives of the various parties and then entrusts a member of the Knesset with forming a Government. Once formed, the Cabinet comes before the Knesset and asks for a vote of confidence, which must be obtained before the Cabinet may legally take office. In France and Laos, the system used is roughly the same.

(b) The Federal German procedure is particularly complex: the Chancellor is elected without debate by the Bundestag, by an absolute majority of the membership, on the motion of the Federal President. But the Bundestag is not bound to agree to this motion. It can set aside the proposed candidate and elect another within fifteen days following the first vote, and likewise by an absolute majority vote. If the Bundestag does not succeed in electing a Chancellor in this way, another vote is taken immediately, and the candidate obtaining the largest number of votes is elected. However, appointment based on this majority is not final. The Federal President then has two courses open to him: within seven days, he can either appoint the person elected, or dissolve the Bundestag.

(c) A number of unusual features are also found in the Japanese Constitution. Here the Diet appoints the Prime Minister from among its own members. Investiture takes place in both Houses, but where the House of Representatives and House of Councillors are not in agreement as to the person appointed as Prime Minister, the will of the former prevails. In addition, the Prime Minister himself appoints the members of his Cabinet, and he must choose the majority of them from the membership of the Diet.

246

Approval by Parliament before appointment as such is likewise a feature of the procedure followed in Ireland. The Head of the State appoints the Prime Minister only on a resolution of the Dail. Similarly, he appoints the other members of the Government, on the recommendation of the Prime Minister once the latter is installed, but again subject to the prior approval of the Dail expressed in a resolution.

This method of appointment does not conform to British practice, which is based on an entirely different set of principles. In the United Kingdom, the principle is simple—the members of the Government must be appointed by the Crown, i.e. by the Head of the State. Strictly speaking, Parliament takes no part in the matter. In actual fact, this only gives a true picture of the situation if we regard it in the light of the tradition which tends to strengthen the links between the members of the Government and Parliament, in particular the tradition by which the Monarch chooses the Prime Minister from the party which has a parliamentary majority. The scope of the royal prerogative is often merely theoretical, since the political parties tend to elect their own leaders. Even the Opposition party designates its own leader—in fact it may even select all the members who will make up the prospective next Cabinet (everyone has heard of the 'Shadow Cabinet'). This system constitutes a compromise between the old forms of government and modern democratic techniques. It is hardly surprising that in its essentials we find it in most of the hereditary monarchies of Western Europe; Denmark, Luxembourg, the Netherlands, Norway and Sweden, as well as in Australia and Ceylon because of their allegiance to the British Crown. In certain countries, however, and notably in the Netherlands, the method of appointing the Head of Government differs further from the British system as a result of the existence of a multiplicity of parties and of the Sovereign's right to choose a Prime Minister from outside the States-General—though anyone so chosen must still have the confidence of Parliament.

A number of states of the republican type have also seen fit to make the Head of State solely responsible for designating the Head of the Government—Finland, India, Indonesia and Pakistan. The essential feature here is that the Government does not have to obtain a vote of confidence from Parliament before taking office. The necessity for majority support is merely a matter of practical politics.

Other systems are based on this inasmuch as the mere decision of the Head of State is sufficient for the Government to take office. But all of them are qualified by the obligation on the part of the Government to present itself before Parliament. This is the practice in

247

Belgium, where the King names a person to form a Cabinet, and once the ministerial team has been picked, actually appoints those whose names are submitted to him. As soon as the Government is in office, the Prime Minister outlines his programme before both Houses. If the programme does not obtain the approval of a majority there, the Prime Minister hands in his Government's resignation to the King. In Italy also, the Government is appointed before there is any vote by Parliament. But this does not mean that Parliament is robbed of its powers, for the Constitution provides that the Government must have the confidence of both Houses and that a resolution of confidence must be passed within ten days of the appointment of the Government. It is interesting to note, in regard to these last two examples, that the Cabinet must be acceptable not only to the lower House but also to the upper House, which constitutes a departure from the regular practice in bicameral government.

However different the procedures for the appointment of the Government, they have one fundamental feature in common: all Governments must have the confidence of Parliament, whether this is forthcoming beforehand or afterwards. This is one of the principles of parliamentary government. Hence the particular aspect of parliamentary control we have just considered leads into the more general problem of ministerial accountability, which is the very marrow of parliamentary life. Before we discuss this, however, let us glance quickly at another tool, although uncommon, available to Parliament to extend pressure on the executive.

3. APPOINTMENT OF CERTAIN HIGH OFFICALS

Since the administrative power is the province of the executive, the appointment of administrative agents is one of its functions. This is a general rule and there are few exceptions to it. Paradoxically enough, the few exceptions that exist are to be found in the countries which otherwise follow most faithfully the principle of the separation of powers. Thus in the United States, appointments of senior officials, especially ambassadors, are made by the President only upon the advice and consent of the Senate, expressed in the form of a majority vote on the reports of the committees concerned.

This departure from the rules of the separation of powers deserves some explanation. The executive function thus given to the Senate derives from the conception of the function of the Senate that the draftsmen of the American Constitution had in mind. Originally, the Senate was to have been not merely a legislative body, but also a sort of executive council set up alongside the President to assist him in his task. This idea was very soon outmoded by constitutional practice. But the prerogatives have been preserved, in particular the unusual sharing of a privilege which should normally be the province of the executive. On the analogy of the American procedure, the Brazilian Constitution grants this right to the Federal Senate. In the Philippines there is an unusual feature: the appointment of high officials is subject to the approval of a joint committee of both Houses. Apart from the three countries just mentioned, Japan is the only other important exception to the general rule. The Diet must approve the appointment of a very long list of high officials, for it includes all the officials who have to be appointed by the Prime Minister or the Cabinet.

In other countries the exclusive nature of the executive's powers in regard to the appointment of officials is to some extent shown by the fact that as a rule Parliament does not take a hand in regard to appointments except for posts where independence in relation to the executive is desirable—i.e. in the judiciary and the control of public finance. Examples are not hard to find: it is the general practice in regard to the Supreme Courts of Justice, and the occasional practice in regard to the lower courts—in the Federal Republic of Germany, for example, the Bundestag takes part in the election of the judges of all the Federal courts—and again in regard to the State Prosecutor's Office, as in Albania, Bulgaria, Denmark, Finland, Rumania, Sweden and the USSR.

Bodies concerned with financial control are an offshoot of budge-tary control and their purpose is ordinarily to help Parliament in this important and delicate task. Their status is thus, in general, not comparable with that of officials.

II

The Accountability of the Government to Parliament

The Meaning of Ministerial Accountability—The Political Accountability of the Government—Accountability and Dissolution

Constitutionally or in practice Parliament and Government are linked as partners in the conduct of public affairs by a whole network of relationships; but the partnership is seldom an equal one, even when the draftsmen of the Constitution have intended that it

I*   249

should be so. An analysis of these relationships should make it possible to assess accurately the influence exerted by the one on the other. We have seen how in certain countries the executive has got the upper hand in certain aspects of legislative and financial matters. At the same time, we have stressed the general tendency for the prerogatives of Parliament to move over in the direction of the control of government activities. By means of such control, Parliament can safeguard its essential powers. Frequently, the primacy of Parliament begins to make itself felt, as we have seen, in the procedure for appointing the members of the Government and it can make itself felt even more decisively in the procedure for their dismissal. This poses the problem of ministerial accountability, which is an extremely complex phenomenon with a vast number of facets; as constitutional practice shows, it is frequently bound up closely with the complementary phenomenon of dissolution.

1. THE MEANING OF MINISTERIAL ACCOUNTABILITY

Theoretically there are three types of ministerial accountability:

(a) Personal financial accountability, i.e. the obligation on ministers to make good financially any harm caused through their fault to the interests of the tax-payer. We shall not go into this question here, first of all because it has nothing to do with the relationship between the executive and the Parliament, and secondly because it is largely an academic problem.

(b) Penal accountability, i.e. the obligation upon ministers to answer for criminal acts such as treason, misappropriation or extortion, corrupt practices and encroachment upon the freedom of the individual. This question, although it is at the root of political responsibility, raises the broader issue of political trials, which will be considered later in so far as it gives rise to intervention by Parliament. It is, however, of considerable importance in states where political accountability has ceased to apply.

(c) Political accountability. This is based not on criminal acts or civil offences determined objectively, but on essentially subjective factors to be assessed by Parliament. Its scope is infinitely vast. It may apply to any act performed by a minister in the exercise of his duties, or by his outlook, his actions or failure to act, or even his intentions, the minister's conduct being regarded in the light not of its legality, but

250

simply of its political wisdom in the face of the views expressed by Parliament.

Viewed in this light, the political accountability of ministers is the essential machinery by which the will of Parliament can make itself felt. Clearly, in systems where the separation of powers is the rule, the ministers are politically answerable only to the Head of State, and he alone can dismiss them where he disapproves of something they have done. Elsewhere, political accountability implies for practical purposes the obligation on the part of the Government to act constantly in accordance with the views of the majority group in Parliament. What gives this obligation force is the threat of loss of office by the minister if his conduct is disapproved by the representatives of the nation.

This type of accountability and the penalties that go with it were not directly the brain-children of theorists on constitutional law. They are the fruits of a long evolution characteristic of the British institutions and originating in the penal procedure known as 'impeachment'. This procedure made its first appearance as early as the sixteenth century. It consisted of the arraignment of a minister by the House of Commons, and his subsequent trial by the House of Lords. In this form it was used to attack those ministers whose intimacy with the Sovereign was considered undesirable and who, under the terms of the laws obtaining at the time, could not be made the subject of legal action. In so far as ministers depended for their office on royal favour, impeachment served as Parliament's last recourse in the matter of imposing its will. But as the minister's accountability to the Sovereign gave way to their accountability to Parliament, less and less recourse was had to impeachment until today it has disappeared. This gradual transfer of the seat of power began with the accession to the throne of the House of Hanover and became complete in 1782 when, for the first time, a British Cabinet had to resign before a hostile vote on the part of the House—and political accountability was born. It has had prodigious influence, for it established the power of modern Parliaments. Once the principle is accepted that a ministry can only continue in power so long as it complies with the will of Parliament, there is nothing to stop the latter from laying down the conditions governing the confidence they place in it. Here we have the very substance of democracy, inasmuch as Parliament is the embodiment of the sovereignty of the people.

This incidentally explains why in many bicameral Parliaments only the lower House, elected by direct universal suffrage, has the power to call ministers to account. This is the case in Australia, Austria, Burma, Ceylon, France, the Federal Republic of Germany, India, Ireland, Japan, Laos, the Sudan and the United Kingdom. Where the upper House is on the same footing electorally as the lower House, it enjoys the same powers as in Norway, Iceland, the USSR and Yugoslavia. In Belgium, Italy and Sweden, however, the upper House enjoys exactly the same prerogatives as the lower House, even though it is not exactly the same in origin. Theoretically, the same is also true of the Netherlands; but, in practice, the Dutch Government is answerable primarily to the Second Chamber of the States-General.

The fact nevertheless remains that political accountability is the reflection in the Government—Parliament relationship of the principles of genuine democracy. Clearly it is meaningless where the executive itself comes to power through universal suffrage, since this gives it the same authority as the legislature. This is what has happened in the United States, Brazil, the Philippines and the Republic of Vietnam. However, the position in Switzerland is proof enough of the fact that democracy is perfectly compatible with the principle of ministerial non-accountability. Here the Federal Council is elected for four years, and cannot be dissolved by Parliament. Parliament can express serious disagreement by refusing to approve a report submitted by the Federal Council, but this does not imply the resignation of the Government. Actually, the Federal Council is not so much a 'Government' as an agent for the implementation of decisions taken by Parliament. Although it is not answerable to the Federal Parliament, the Federal Council is subordinate to it, and Parliament can give it instructions or amend or annul its decisions. Each session the Federal Council must give an account of its administration to Parliament. It submits to the latter a report on the state of the Confederation. At the end of the debate there is a vote on resolutions laying down the directives with which the Council must comply.

However, ordinarily speaking, ministerial accountability is regarded as the only weapon capable of ensuring the exercise of real parliamentary control.

Parliamentary control can take two forms. It may be individual or collective, according to whether the matter which gives rise to parliamentary censure implicates one single minister or the entire Cabinet. In practice, there is hardly any act performed by a minister which is not more or less directly linked with general policy. Hence in several constitutions ministerial accountability is conceived of only as a collective matter. If Parliament expresses a lack of confidence in a single one of the ministers, the entire body of ministers is called upon to resign. This at any rate is the practice in the systems of Cabinet Government built up on the British model. It does not, in fact, rule out the possibility of the resignation of a minister in the face of parliamentary opposition, but such resignations are extremely rare.

On the other hand, individual accountability is the general rule in countries where ministers are the direct instruments for the execution of the policy laid down by Parliament. Thus each one may be asked to give an account of the way in which he is carrying out that policy within his own department. Ministers are answerable for the acts of the Government only in their own particular sphere. There is no 'one for all and all for one' rule.

2. THE POLITICAL ACCOUNTABILITY OF THE GOVERNMENT

The principle of the political accountability of ministers to Parliament carried to its logical conclusion would imply recognition of the principle that Parliament has the right to appoint the ministers and to remove them. Dismissal, an act of authority which leaves no latitude for interpretation on the part of its victims, is the power which enforces ministerial accountability in the parliamentary type of government where all powers stem from the representatives of the nation and are exercised in their name.

Dismissal is a separate decision which can be directed at the Government as a whole just as at any individual minister. The power of dismissal is self-contained. It need not necessarily be linked with any other form of parliamentary activity. Since Parliament is kept informed as to the activity of the Government through the reports regularly submitted to it, it can at any moment pass judgement on this activity and draw whatever conclusions are necessary as to the composition of the Government.

Powers of this kind are to be found in the Supreme Soviet of the USSR, the National Assembly in Bulgaria, the Grand National Assembly in Rumania, the Polish Diet, and of course the Yugoslav Federal Assembly—since the executive here is legally a branch of the Assembly. In all these countries, the intention is to ensure that the will of Parliament is done at all times. In view of the length of the periods between sessions, control of the executive when the Parliament is not sitting is assured by their Presidium, which in that case acts not as Head of State but as a delegate-body of Parliament. In the USSR the Council of Ministers is responsible to the Supreme

Soviet, which has the power to alter its composition at any time. During recess, however, ministerial appointments are made and revoked by the Presidium conditionally on the subsequent endorsement of the Supreme Soviet.

The power wielded by Parliament on account of the political accountability of the Government is less drastic in those countries which have been directly inspired by the British tradition. The Cabinet nominated on the responsibility of the Prime Minister enjoys an existence in its own right, and its members are not regarded as mere agents for carrying out the will of Parliament. The question of dismissal no longer arises. The Cabinet is not 'dismissed'—it resigns the moment it finds that it has lost the confidence of Parliament and can no longer govern effectively and legitimately. The margin of choice left to ministers in this respect is extremely narrow, either because of the political context in which it is expressed, or because of the legal framework surrounding it in some countries.

Generally the procedure by which the question of ministerial accountability is raised is not in any way cut-and-dried. The way in which disagreement between Parliament and Government is expressed is unimportant. It is of course possible for Parliament to pass an explicit motion of censure which brings the disagreement out into the open in unequivocal terms. Provision is made for this procedure in the House of Commons, where the motion is usually tabled by the Leader of the Opposition, and in practice the Government usually agrees to debate it immediately. If the motion is carried, the Government must resign, or ask the Queen to dissolve Parliament. In practice, owing to the two-party structure which is a fundamental feature of the British system, there is very little likelihood of a Government being defeated, since it is sure of the support of its majority. In the event, however, of a substantial reduction in that majority, resulting from exceptional circumstances, the Government may in effect fall, as exemplified by the resignation of the Chamberlain Cabinet on 8 May 1940.

It is of course equally possible for the Government to ask for a vote of confidence which will enable it to demonstrate the fact that it has a strong majority in Parliament. This procedure is more or less complementary to censure motions, and it follows the same rules.

Ministerial accountability can, however, arise at any moment in respect of any question whatever in which the views of Parliament differ from those of the Government, such as the adoption of legislation or taxation or the voting of funds. The practice today in the United Kingdom and generally speaking in all the countries influenced by Britain is to regard any vote hostile to the Government's policy or administration as a matter of confidence. This is the case, for example, of the vote on adjournment motions. In accordance with a special procedure, the House of Commons can take up 'definite' matters of 'urgent public importance' and discuss them forthwith. It is left to the Speaker to decide whether the questions raised at the beginning of the sitting are definite and urgent. Subject to his agreement and provided a sufficient number of members consider that the matter is of public importance, the debate takes place in the evening between 7 and 10 p.m. and all other business is deferred. Technically speaking, all that the motion calls for is the adjournment of the House, but a defeat of the Government could well force the Government or the minister primarily responsible to resign. This procedure, which is fairly rare, is reminiscent of the French 'interpellation'; it is also found in the Australian House of Representatives, and in Ceylon and Pakistan.

In many other countries, for example Denmark, Iceland, Israel and Norway, the devices available for raising the question of government accountability are no less numerous than in the United Kingdom. As a general rule they extend beyond explicit motions of confidence or no-confidence to all parliamentary activity, legislative or financial; frequently the passing of the Budget constitutes the essential criterion of parliamentary confidence in the Government. In Sweden the absence of a specific procedure in regard to ministerial accountability is seen in its most striking form; there the system of motions of censure and matters of confidence is unknown. All attempts made so far to introduce any such system have failed. The question of accountability of the Government arises before the Riksdag only when Bills or proposals are brought up for examination by it. In Finland, lack of confidence in the Government on the part of Parliament is expressed in a similar manner, usually by a hostile vote on a Bill, grant of money or other measure, approval of which is regarded by the executive as particularly important.

A feature of these various procedures would appear to be a measure of permanence in regard to accountability, owing to the very fact that there are no specific rules for invoking it. Theoretically there is a grave danger involved in such an absence of concrete rules, since any vote implying a lack of confidence, even implicit, would mean the fall of the ministry at any time or on any occasion during the debate, however small the majority in favour of the motion and however small the number of members present in the House. This subordination of the Government is hardly compatible with a system of collaboration between the powers of the State,

255

which postulates a certain measure of independence for the executive; but actually in most instances the subordination is largely offset by the political factors inherent in the two-party system. The fact that there are only two sides makes for a bond between the Government and the House which it is extremely difficult to break. It gives the executive a strong feeling of security to know that it has a solid majority behind it.

In countries where the political situation cannot be reduced to such simple terms and where the large number of parties militates against the establishment of a comfortable majority, the problem of government stability becomes a matter of great concern. A number of unfortunate experiences in this respect have led certain countries to lay down more or less strict regulations governing the invoking of ministerial accountability with a view to obviating hasty or thoughtless votes of censure on the part of Parliament. This is an instance of what has been called the 'rationalization' of the parliamentary system.

The underlying intention may be merely practical. For example, in Belgium, a number of rules have been worked out to define more precisely the circumstances for invoking ministerial accountability. In principle, before the Government can be forced to resign, its difference of opinion with Parliament must: (i) be fairly serious; (ii) be on a general policy issue and not an isolated administrative matter; and (iii) be raised categorically as a matter of confidence; the Government may take the initiative itself, or the Members of Parliament may do so, by making use of the 'interpellation' procedure which invariably ends in a vote of confidence or censure.

In several countries, established practice is replaced by statutory rules to ensure that invoking ministerial accountability does not degenerate into an 'off with his head' attitude.

The Austrian Constitution provides that the National Council can express a lack of confidence only by means of an explicit resolution passed in the presence of at least half of its members. In Egypt, a censure motion can only be passed following an interpellation if it is signed by at least one tenth of the members of the Assembly; no decision can be taken until three days after the motion has been tabled; and the vote of no-confidence is only carried if there is an absolute majority of the members. In Syria, a motion of censure must be tabled by at least fifteen members, and the voting can only take place after an interval of two days.

The present Constitution of Czechoslovakia has in the main taken over the provisions in force before the War. There are two procedures, one set in motion by the Government, the other by Parliament, and these alone can bring about the fall of the Government. A question of confidence may be raised at any time; and it is debated immediately. A censure motion, on the other hand, must be signed by at least one hundred members, and is handed to the President of the Assembly, who must report on it within a week. A vote must then be taken by roll-call, with half the members present, and an absolute majority is required for the motion to be passed.

This system is somewhat similar to the French constitutional rules under which the question of political accountability of the Government cannot be formally raised except under two conditions: (i) after the question of confidence has been put by the President of the Council (the vote not to be taken less than one clear day after this), and a vote of no-confidence has been passed by the majority of the members in the National Assembly; or (ii) by the adoption of a motion of censure, put down by Parliament, the same majority rule applying.

Regulations governing the invoking of ministerial accountability are also laid down in the Italian Constitution. Here again the intention is to obviate the constant fall of the Government—a precaution made all the more necessary by the fact that the Cabinet is subject to a vote of no-confidence in either House. A distinction is made between any vote which happens to be against the Government and an explicit vote of no-confidence. The former does not automatically entail the resignation of the Cabinet; only the second type requires it to resign. The rules are designed to eliminate any possibility of a snap vote. Motions of no-confidence must be signed by at least one tenth of the members. In addition, the reasons for the motion must be stated and the vote must be taken by roll-call; moreover, it cannot be debated until three days have elapsed from the date on which it was tabled.

Both in its aim and in the methods used this system is somewhat similar to the one in force in France. But they are also analogous in that both are in practice ineffective, since in Italy and in France alike the Government always has the option of resigning even if there is no adverse vote on the part of Parliament to require it to do so, in fact even without any vote at all. In other words, if it lacks the support of Parliament, even if the lack of confidence is not expressed in so many words, the Government is rendered impotent and has to resign, so that legal regulations lose their meaning. However ingeniously they are drafted, they cannot of themselves solve the problem of government stability, which bursts through the bonds of constitutional organization and is dictated rather by hard facts.

The spirit of the parliamentary system would appear to be inimical to an over-rigid apparatus of rules.

Nevertheless this is the way things work out in the Federal Republic of Germany, where the Constitution has combined the traditional rules of ministerial accountability with a type of machinery which would certainly seem to be effective even though it may not be in line with parliamentary orthodoxy. Unquestionably the Bundestag has the power to overthrow the Government; it does so by a vote of no-confidence. But such a vote does not of itself entail the fall of the Cabinet. The Assembly must elect a new Chancellor by a majority of its membership. Only then can the Federal President relieve the defeated Chancellor of his office. By thus making the effectiveness of a vote of no-confidence conditional upon the appointment of a successor to the Chancellor in office, the basic law has endeavoured to cope with the danger of repeated and insoluble crises such as took place during the Weimar Republic. Its aim is as it were to make a majority in opposition present a coherent and constructive purpose. In such circumstances it is extremely difficult in practice to overthrow the Federal Chancellor.

Furthermore, the concern to ensure the stability of the Government is seen in the fact that here, more than anywhere else, ministerial accountability is linked with the dissolution of Parliament, in the event of the question of accountability and resignation being raised. In other words, if a motion tabled by the Federal Chancellor with a view to obtaining a vote of confidence is not passed by a majority of the members of the Bundestag, the Federal President, on the advice of the Chancellor, may dissolve the Bundestag within twenty-one days. Meanwhile, however, the Bundestag may appoint a new Federal Chancellor, again by a majority of its members, and thus prevent the dissolution from taking place.

In the light of this example we see the connexion between ministerial accountability and dissolution of Parliament, a connexion which some consider to be the cornerstone of the classic parliamentary system based on balance between the powers.

3. ACCOUNTABILITY AND DISSOLUTION

According to parliamentary theory, dissolution is for the Government what the invoking of ministerial accountability is for Parliament. It gives the Cabinet which finds itself without a majority in Parliament the right to have its difference of opinion with Parliament settled by the electors. Actually, the dissolution of Parliament is not always a means of settling disagreements between the Government and Parliament. We must of course leave aside the case of Parliament dissolving itself, which does not constitute any challenge to the executive. The power to dissolve itself would appear to be one of the primary corollaries of the independence of Parliament. But it does not always have this power—the German Bundestag, for example, does not have authority to decide on dissolution of its own accord.

There is another instance where dissolution raises, not the problem of the relationship between the Government and Parliament, but that of the relationship between the two Houses of one and the same Parliament. We saw, for example, that in the USSR, Yugoslavia and Australia, dissolution is the final recourse for putting an end to a conflict in legislative matters between the two Houses.

Thus there are many facets to a dissolution, since it has a meaning only in relation to the political context of the country where the question arises. The right of dissolution has no value in itself, but only in relation to what it is designed to bring about and the way in which it is used.

Dissolution of Parliament is not a coherent creation of political thinking, any more than is ministerial accountability, of which it is the corollary. In England, it first made its appearance as a means of taking action against Parliament. It was used by the Monarch to get rid of a House after he had got from it what he wanted. It became the counterpart of ministerial accountability only from the time when national representation was established on a permanent footing and the authority of the Cabinet replaced that of the Crown. This established the balance between the executive and Parliament. If the Government was dismissed by the House, the Government could reply by dismissing Parliament. This system enabled the Cabinet to avoid total subjugation, and by opposing two equal forces to each other it made collaboration between them possible. Thus side by side with accountability, the power to dissolve Parliament has become one of the essential cogs in the parliamentary machine. Following the British model, it was incorporated during the nineteenth century into most constitutional monarchies, being regarded first and foremost as a royal prerogative. Looked at from another angle as a vital principle of the parliamentary system, it was adopted by a larger number of republican constitutions. From still another angle, it was regarded by a number of countries as lowering the standing of Parliament vis-à-vis the executive, and was therefore not adopted by Albania, Austria, Bulgaria, Israel, Norway, Poland, Rumania, Turkey, USSR and Yugoslavia. In the Socialist states it is considered as a violation of the sovereignty of representative assemblies. The advocates of the power to dissolve Parliament argue that it is not a question of subjecting Parliament to the wishes of the Government, but to the wishes of the people themselves, and on these grounds they consider this procedure admirably democratic.

In its classic form, the power to dissolve Parliament is strictly speaking one of the prerogatives of the Head of State, the Monarch or the President. In the event of Parliament losing confidence in the Government, theoretically the Head of State has two possible courses: he can either dismiss the Government, or he can dissolve Parliament or one of its Houses. His freedom of choice is extremely limited, since in actual fact it is the Government that takes the decision to dissolve Parliament. There are few countries, though Burma, Indonesia and Ireland are examples, where the Head of State is not obliged to take the Prime Minister's advice. In Italy the power to dissolve Parliament is the prerogative of the President. In most countries the Government takes the initiative, when it finds that Parliament has no confidence in it. This is what happens in Australia, Belgium, Ceylon, Denmark, Finland, Iceland, India, Japan, Laos, Luxembourg, the Netherlands, Pakistan, the Sudan and Sweden.

In the United Kingdom, where the system originated, dissolution today has lost much of its character as a means of arbitration between the Cabinet and the House of Commons owing to the tendency towards the *de facto* merging of the executive and the legislature. The union of the two powers is the outcome of the single majority party system. This does not mean, however, that the power to dissolve Parliament no longer exists; but it is dissociated from the problem of accountability. Nowadays dissolution takes place only in four cases:

(a) To bring the life of the House to an end when it is approaching the end of its legal term—this is the most frequent case.
(b) Where the Government feels that a new situation or problem has arisen which requires that the electorate should be consulted.
(c) Where the Government hopes to strengthen its own position by a new general election.
(d) Where the Government, having suffered a defeat in the House of Commons, requests that the House be dissolved and the Sovereign grants the request. It should be pointed out that in these circumstances the Sovereign has a certain latitude in the matter of accepting or rejecting the recommendation made to

him. Two factors in particular will influence his decision: on the one hand, the practicability of a new Cabinet being formed immediately; on the other, the length of time the current Parliament still has to run.

None of these cases involves any challenge to the will of Parliament and the classic notion of dissolution is thus completely transformed. The purpose of dissolution is no longer to regulate the relationships between the Government and Parliament, and its only object is to strengthen the links between the party in power and public opinion by recourse to a general election. Viewed from this angle, the power to dissolve Parliament no longer appears as a threat to democratic institutions.

In some countries, on the other hand, it is regarded as an anti-democratic measure, and the conditions surrounding its exercise are such that for practical purposes it has become inoperative. In France, for example, dissolution must be decided upon by the Council of Ministers, on the advice of the President of the National Assembly. Dissolution cannot take place during the first eighteen months of the life of the legislature. Thereafter, it can only take place if two governments have fallen within a period of eighteen months, and their fall must have arisen following a majority vote of the Assembly on a question of confidence or a motion of censure. These very severe conditions actually have the effect of making the exercise of the power to dissolve Parliament dependent on Parliament itself. Thus it is no longer the counterpart of the involving of ministerial accountability, since Parliament always has means at its disposal to overthrow the Government without running the risk of being itself dissolved.

The classic system is still more drastically altered in the Federal Republic of Germany, where dissolution does not have the effect of settling a conflict between Parliament and Government by means of an appeal to the electorate. What it does rather is to act as a threat calculated to force the parties to form a majority in the Bundestag. It can only take place in two circumstances:

(a) Where the Bundestag does not succeed in electing a Chancellor. In this case the Federal President can either appoint the person who has received most votes as Chancellor or dissolve Parliament. Thus it is not a matter of settling an issue between the executive and Parliament, since in this case there is no executive. Moreover, dissolution is therefore to some extent dependent on the Bundestag itself. All it has to do is to elect a Chancellor by an absolute majority, and the exercise of the power to dissolve is ruled out.

(b) Where the Bundestag has not adopted a motion of confidence put forward by the Chancellor. In this case the Chancellor may ask the Federal President to dissolve but, as we have seen, the Bundestag cannot express an effective vote of no-confidence unless it elects a successor. Thus the power to dissolve can only be exercised in the event of the Bundestag voting the Chancellor down without being able to designate a successor—which brings us back to the first case.

The power to dissolve would seem to be therefore not so much a weapon in the hands of the executive as a procedure for strengthening the authority of the Bundestag by compelling it to constitute a solid majority.

The diversity we find in these few examples illustrates the extreme complexity of this basic feature of the Constitution, the principle of dissolution, and the various ways in which it is bound up with the problem of ministerial responsibility. The invoking of ministerial accountability and the fall of the Government and dissolution of Parliament which that entails, constitute the most dramatic and acute phase of the control exercised by Parliament over the executive. Parliamentary control of the Government also has other less drastic devices at its disposal, but all of them are designed in their various ways to keep Members of Parliament aware of the policy of the Government by giving them right of access to information and the right to explanations in affairs of concern to them.

III

The Machinery of Parliamentary Control

*General Debate and 'Interpellation'—Questions to Ministers
—Parliamentary Inquiries—Parliamentary 'Procurators' and
other Ad Hoc Bodies of Control*

If Parliament is to be in a position to keep an eye on the Government and to place and maintain its confidence in it or withdraw its confidence, as the case may be, it is essential that they should be kept fully supplied with information. Keeping Parliament informed has been rendered both more necessary and more difficult by the increasingly broad scope of government activity. In every country, Parliament has a variety of means of investigation at its disposal, forming a network of links with the executive. In view of the tendency for Parliament to lose its powers in legislative and financial matters, it is important that these various control devices should be sufficiently effective to restore, in one way or another, the full substance of those powers to the representatives of the nation. The primary problem is to adapt the control machinery to fit its purpose. This presupposes that the activities of the Government lend themselves to the type of supervision which large non-specialist bodies can exercise. All in all, constitutional law provides Parliaments with a vast selection of ways and means of accomplishing its task. In fact the real problem is how to use these devices judiciously, since each one of them has been conceived with a particular task in mind—control of overall policy, supervision of the administration, protection of the individual, or bringing to light and eliminating abuses and injustice.

1. GENERAL DEBATE AND 'INTERPELLATION'

In some countries the provisions of the Constitution require the executive to render to Parliament periodically an account of its stewardship, thus providing an opportunity to exercise effective control. This system is primarily characteristic of constitutions based on separation of powers; it helps to make up to some extent for the fact that the executive is not accountable for its actions. In the United States, for example, the President each year reports to Congress on the state of the Union, and all the points in his speech are the object of minute scrutiny on the part of the members. Similarly, in the Republic of Vietnam, each year at the beginning of the second regular session the President of the Republic furnishes the National Assembly with a statement on the general state of the country and the Government's domestic and foreign policy. The best illustration of this regulatory procedure is Switzerland; here the presentation of the annual report of the Federal Council to both Houses is followed by a debate. A report is published and distributed by the Chancellery, and it is examined by the administrative committee of each House, and then debated in the House itself. It is a detailed statement, describing not only the policy pursued by the Federal Council, but also, with supporting figures, the activities engaged in over the previous year by each of the seven ministerial departments and their subsidiary bodies, the two Federal courts and the Federal Chancellery. The debate on the report lasts on an average three days in the National Council and one and a half to two days in the Council of States.

In countries where the Government is accountable for its actions, an annual report of this kind is not so essential, since Parliament usually has a number of other means of putting pressure on the executive. It should be noted however that in Finland this method does much to help Parliament maintain control over the public administration. Each year a report on the measures taken by the Government is submitted to the Diet.

The same result is obtained, in the ceremonial form of the Speech from the Throne followed by the voting of an Address in reply to the Speech, in certain monarchies, particularly in the United Kingdom and Australia, Laos, Luxembourg, the Netherlands and Sweden. In Belgium, this institution was very much alive during the nineteenth century, but it now appears to have fallen into disuse.

Something similar is found in the USSR and the People's Democracies in the system of 'progress reports' frequently made to both Houses by the ministers in the course of the session. These reports are not mandatory, and they are not required to be made at any particular intervals; but in practice some reports are submitted to each session. They may be asked for by both Houses or volunteered by the ministers themselves and are followed by a debate culminating in the passing of the necessary resolutions. In Yugoslavia however, the executive Federal Council is required to present to both Houses annual reports on its work and on certain important questions relating to all aspects of public life.

In most other countries, the over-all problems are not automatically subject to periodic examination. They may be raised on the initiative of the Government in the form of 'communications' or 'statements' to Parliament, as for example in France, without being subject to debate, or they may simply arise out of a general debate on the political situation, notably on the occasion of the President of the Council taking office. This is not, strictly speaking, control, but there is no doubt that it is useful to both of them for the executive and the legislature to have a regular exchange of views.

In the majority of countries, this only happens in connexion with the parliamentary prerogative known as the 'right of interpellation'. This is the stock procedure for obtaining information and exercising control in the Continental parliamentary system generally, and the French system in particular. A Member of Parliament calls upon a minister to explain something his department has done or questions the Head of the Government, who is obliged to reply, in regard to

264

national policy. Interpellation has two essential features: in the first place it starts off a general debate in which all members can take part; and secondly it constitutes a weapon against the Government, since the debate culminates in a vote on a motion expressing either the satisfaction or the dissatisfaction of the House with the explanations furnished by the Government. Thus interpellation can be extremely effective, especially since it enables the question of ministerial accountability to be raised.

Interpellation is not, therefore, a mere device for obtaining information, but a very direct form of control; indeed the institution is bound up with the history of the parliamentary system. In France, it goes back a long way; as early as 1791 the Constitution specified that 'ministers shall be heard when they are required to give explanations'. Actually, interpellation only became a regular practice under the monarchy of 1830. Today, interpellation debates are circumscribed by a number of procedural rules; for example, it is stipulated that before the debate can take place on the substance of the question, the date for holding it must be debated, and the Government can ask for any awkward interpellations to be 'held over'. In practice, the debate on the date for the substantive debate always gives the initiator of the interpellation an opportunity to develop his arguments at this initial stage of the procedure, in spite of the time-limit on speeches laid down in the rules of procedure. It should be noted that the vote which winds up the debate does not involve any obligation on the part of the Cabinet to resign even if it is defeated, so long as there is no formal question of confidence or motion of censure. The fact that the interpellation makes it possible to invoke the question of ministerial accountability explains why the device is not allowed to be used in the Council of the Republic, though this body in practice by-passed this prohibition by the adoption of a similar procedure, as regards form at any rate, known as the 'oral question with debate'. In the National Assembly, the tendency to overdo the requests for interpellations has lowered the prestige of the procedure in principle; it should be kept for problems of national scope.

The same thing has happened in Switzerland, where the interpellation procedure is more often than not used for the debate of minor issues. Although an interpellation requires the support of ten members in the National Council and of three in the Council of States, members appear in the main to make use of it not for the purpose of exercising real control, but rather to put forward claims and criticisms of private or local interest in a way which will give them the maximum amount of publicity.

This aspect of the interpellation procedure would tend to bring it closer to the parallel process of the parliamentary 'question'. Nevertheless, the interpellation system does maintain its prestige intact, in a great many countries, where unlike the question procedure it is reserved for important issues. This is the case, for example, in Belgium, where it is the essential means of dealing with the question of confidence. There are strict rules designed to prevent it from being misused—the interpellant may not speak for more than half an hour. Should the minister reply, only four speakers may be heard, for not more than ten minutes each. If the minister does not reply, the interpellation is closed, and the interpellant alone can speak for fifteen minutes. All interpellations must be disposed of at the sitting at which they are brought up. However, these strict rules are waived when the House decides that the problem under discussion warrants priority and urgent treatment.

In the Federal Republic of Germany, although there is no rule restricting the scope of the interpellation system, it would appear to be used only for matters relating to general policy. Any interpellation must be submitted to the President of the Bundestag in writing. It must be concise and specific, and it must be signed by at least thirty members. The President forwards it to the Government with the request for a statement as to whether it proposes to reply, and when. The Government is not obliged to reply to an interpellation, so long however as it continues to accept its accountability, whether it replies or not. The text of the interpellation is distributed to all the members of the Bundestag. In general, the debate is put down on the order paper after a sitting designed to suit the Government. One of the sponsors outlines the arguments, and the Government replies. The minister's reply is followed by a debate, provided that thirty members present at the meeting ask for one. If the Government refuses to reply or is not prepared to do so within the fifteen-day period allowed, the Bundestag may take the initiative and place the discussion on the order paper, provided thirty members present at the meeting call for it, and a representative of the Government may be required to be present if a motion to that effect is passed.

In Finland, interpellations must be tabled in writing and supported by twenty Members of Parliament. A reply must be furnished by the minister concerned within fifteen days, or if the Government does not intend to reply it must notify Parliament to that effect within the same period, explaining why it does not intend to do so.

In Denmark, Luxembourg, the Netherlands and Sweden, it would appear that recourse to the interpellation procedure is conditional upon the problem in question being of general importance. In Luxembourg, the Government may reply in the course of the sitting or at another sitting of its choice. In the Netherlands, the House will authorize one of its members to introduce an interpellation only if it considers that the matter warrants it. The same authorization is granted in Denmark and Sweden by the House without debate.

Interpellation is practised in accordance with a variety of procedures and with varying degrees of success in a large number of other countries, including Austria, Iceland, Italy, Laos, Norway, Syria and Turkey.

It is sometimes difficult to make a sharp distinction between the interpellation and the question. In the USSR and some of the People's Democracies, the two procedures both follow similar rules, especially in regard to the time-limits for ministerial replies to be given (three days in Rumania and the USSR, seven days in Poland, and the duration of the session in Bulgaria). In the British type of system, interpellation is practically unknown, though the 'adjournment motion' is not unlike it. The adjourment motion made prior to the beginning of the parliamentary recess gives an opportunity for putting a whole series of questions to the Government, but no voting takes place; on the other hand, the adjournment motion on a 'definite' question of 'urgent public importance' may end in a vote in the same way as the Continental type of interpellation. But in the second instance it is not a separate proceeding; it is often linked with the essential machinery for parliamentary control in the United Kingdom which is questions to Ministers.

2. QUESTIONS TO MINISTERS

The practice of putting questions to ministers is a type of control used in Parliaments in all countries where the Government is politically accountable, although theoretically no legal requirement to answer is involved. For this reason it is used also in a number of other countries, e.g. in Spain, where the executive is not accountable to Parliament. Questions may be either oral or written; which means that the person asking the question requests the appropriate minister to reply orally or in writing. Questions are more often than not tabled in writing if only so that the Speaker can transmit them to the Government.

Like so many other pieces of parliamentary procedure, the question system originated in Britain. As in the course of the nineteenth century the transfer of legislative power took place from Parliament to the Government, and as administrative business

267

increased, members began to ask more and more questions, and these gradually replaced the public petitions to the House, which had fallen into disuse. The question system did not become paper until 1835. In 1902 the practice of written questions was introduced. Today several thousand questions are asked every year. The question is a request by a member of the House to a minister for explanation in regard to some specific point. Its purpose is to elicit concrete information from the administration to request its intervention, and where necessary to expose abuses and seek redress. Many of the questions are routine, but they furnish the Opposition with a means of discovering the Government's weak points, and because of the publicity given to them, they invariably have a salutary effect on the Government.

In the House of Commons, a member wishing to ask a question must first of all put the question in writing and hand it in to the Clerks at the Table. If he wishes for an oral reply, he marks it with a star; for starred questions, two days' notice must be given at least (Monday for Thursday's sitting, Thursday for Monday's sitting, for example). If he is in a great hurry, the questioner may make a special request by which he can gain a day; this is the so-called 'expedited questions' procedure. In the case of unusually urgent matters 'private notice questions' can be taken after the time laid down in the standing orders for oral questions has expired. A member wishing to take advantage of this privilege must give notice of his question to the minister concerned and to the Speaker before 12 noon of the day on which he proposes to put the question. This type of question must fulfil a number of conditions, and the Speaker is the final judge, especially in regard to urgency. In any event, the private notice question must not anticipate another question already tabled on the same subject. All questions other than private notice questions are printed and circulated, and no member may ask more than three questions to which an oral reply is requested on a single day. Ministers invariably reply to oral questions on the day fixed, but they have more latitude in regard to written questions, the replies to which are published in Hansard. If answers are not forthcoming within a reasonable time, the member may repeat his request.

Written replies are often preferred in regard to questions on personal matters or on administrative details. Oral questions are put at the start of the sitting on Mondays, Tuesdays, Wednesdays and Thursdays. Question time continues until 3.30 p.m., so that approximately an hour is devoted to questions. Since it is impossible for a reply to be given to all the questions put on any particular day, the order in which they are taken is extremely important. In addition, the ministers follow a sort of rota, each one answering questions on a particular day or on certain days of the week. Replies to oral questions which for shortage of time cannot be reached are printed in Hansard along with the replies to written questions, except where members ask for their questions to be put down afresh for oral answer.

The Speaker calls upon each member whose question is on the order paper in turn. The name is called out; the member stands up and says: 'Question No. so and so' and sits down again. The minister then answers by reading the reply prepared by his department. The member has the right to put a 'supplementary question' to which the minister again replies. The exchange of views may go on for some minutes, with other members taking part also, until the Speaker decides that it is time to pass on to the next question. The brevity and speed with which one supplementary question and answer follows another can be gauged from the number of questions disposed of in the course of an hour—often in the region of fifty. The oral question procedure is in very active use, especially because of the 'supplementaries' device, which can easily embarrass the ministers, since they may have to be answered without the help of papers prepared beforehand.

This answering of questions on the spur of the moment is one of the chief differences between the British system and the French system, the latter being a good deal more inflexible and formal. In the French National Assembly, written questions put by members are answered in replies published in the *Journal Officiel*. If a reply has not been given within a month, the question may be asked orally by the person who put the original question. Ten oral questions are automatically included, in order of notification, at the head of the order paper every Friday. No question may be placed on the order paper for a particular sitting unless it was handed in at least two days beforehand. The only persons allowed to speak are the minister concerned and the member asking the question, each being allowed five minutes. Owing to the large number of questions asked, the fact that they are taken in chronological order frequently prevents the more topical questions from being taken up. But since 1955, it has been possible for two oral questions to be taken out of their turn, at the head of the order paper for Wednesday or Thursday afternoons.

If a Minister should be absent on three successive occasions when an oral question is put to him, the member asking the question may change it on the spot into an interpellation and move a motion for a vote by Parliament. But this rarely happens. In French parliamentary practice, oral questions have not the prestige they have acquired in countries of the British type, no doubt because of the competition from the interpellation procedure, which is regarded as a more forceful measure. As to written questions, there is more often than not little suggestion of an over-all parliamentary control. Their main use to Members of Parliament is as a means of obtaining administrative information on particular individual cases. In 1957, 4,715 written questions were tabled in the National Assembly.

In all the countries based on the British model—in Australia, Burma, Ceylon, India, Ireland, Pakistan and the Sudan—Questions Time, arranged on roughly the same lines as in the House of Commons, is an extremely important aspect of parliamentary control. In the Australian House of Representatives and Senate, approximately three quarters of an hour at the beginning of each sitting is devoted to questions; the variety of questions asked gives an opportunity of surveying a very wide field of government administration. In Burma and India, question time is one hour at the beginning of every sitting. In Ceylon, supplementary questions are limited to three.

The question procedure is extremely varied according to the country in which it is practised. In Italy, it takes its cue directly from the British system. With the exception of questions designed to call forth written replies, questions are placed on the order paper for the next sitting but one, after they are handed in and in the order in which they are handed in. In the Chamber the first forty minutes, and in the Senate the first hour, of each sitting is taken up with oral questions. For written questions the ministers have ten days in which to reply.

In the Federal Republic of Germany, written questions must be supported by fifteen members of the Bundestag and must be accompanied by a short explanation. If the questioners are not satisfied with the written reply of the Government, or have not received a reply within fifteen days, they are at liberty to put the question orally. At least once a month, on the motion of the Council of Elders, an hour is set aside for oral questions. These must not deal with any subject which would make them in effect interpellations, i.e. they must be confined to problems of local or regional importance. The President draws up a list of such questions in the order in which they are handed in. The list is printed and distributed, and it must be brought to the notice of the ministers at least three days prior to the date on which they have to reply. No debate is allowed, but the questioner may put two supplementary questions.

In Belgium, again, written questions must be answered within a certain time and the replies are published in a special bulletin known as the 'Bulletin of Questions and Answers'. Under the rules of procedure a member may also put an oral question to a minister by means of a point of order in the course of a sitting, and the minister may reply to it if he so desires; but no debate may take place.

In Finland, questions must be answered, either verbally or in writing, at the choice of the minister concerned, within thirty days. In Israel, all questions are asked in writing and the appropriate minister is required to answer orally within twenty-one days. The questioner then has the right to ask, orally, one supplementary question. In Sweden too, questions must be answered orally, without prior notice being given. The questioner and the minister concerned alone have the right to speak, unless the House decides to hold a general debate on the subject. In Japan, the period allowed for replies is only a week in the case of written questions. The oral question procedure is kept for urgent matters subject to the consent of the House.

In the Netherlands, both written and oral questions must be answered within a specified period. Otherwise they are published in an annex to the official proceedings of the debate under the heading 'Questions to which no reply has been given'. Ministers do not willingly run the risk of having questions published in this time. The number of questions per session is relatively small, seldom more than two or three hundred. The fixed criteria governing the admissibility of questions form an interesting feature of Dutch procedure. The President of either Chamber of the States General is empowered to reject any question which bears on a matter outside the responsibility of the minister, or which is phrased in offensive terms, or which concerns a matter due to be debated in Parliament in the near future.

Questions are undoubtedly one of the most widespread procedures in parliamentary practice. Apart from the countries mentioned above, they are found also in Albania, Denmark, Egypt, Iceland, Indonesia, Laos, Luxembourg, Norway, Syria, Turkey and Yugoslavia. Emphasis is often placed on the problem of the period allowed to the Government to furnish its reply. For example, this is three days in Rumania and the USSR, and thirty days in Czechoslovakia, while in Bulgaria the Government has the whole session in which to reply. But the fact that such time-limits exist in most countries means that the Government is under the obligation of furnishing the information asked for, and this obligation, whether it is based on the Constitution, the law, standing orders or mere established practice,

271

is what gives the question device its real strength, although in most Parliaments it is open to ministers to invoke reasons of public interest in order to refuse to reply.

The popularity of the question procedure is largely due to the fact that in making use of his right to ask questions the Member of Parliament is a completely free agent. The only limits on his freedom of action are those which his conscience dictates, since any rules which may govern all admissibility of questions are purely formal in character.

3. PARLIAMENTARY INQUIRIES

A function similar to that performed in regard to control of government and administrative business by the interpellation in France and the 'question in the House' in the United Kingdom is performed in the United States by the parliamentary investigation. Inquiries on behalf of Congress can be conducted either by permanent committees or by committees specially set up for the purpose—'investigating committees'. We have also seen that in some countries the 'legislative' committees enjoy, either as of right or on their request, powers of inquiry in regard to matters coming within their terms of reference. In the United States, although the rule is that such committees can only undertake investigations vital to the legislative business referred to them, they are in the habit of carrying out research which in many cases has only a very remote connexion with the matters they are set up to handle. Conversely, in countries like the Federal Republic of Germany, Italy, the Netherlands, Syria and Turkey, legislative committees may not carry out inquiries which involve powers of a judicial character. In the Federal Republic of Germany, for example, committees can only take up questions referred to them by the Bundestag itself. The only exceptions to this principle are the Permanent Committees set up under Article 45 of the Constitution to safeguard the rights of the Bundestag *vis-à-vis* the Federal Government in the interval between dissolution and the meeting of a new Parliament, and the Defence Committee. These alone possess the permanent powers of a judicial nature characteristic of special commissions of inquiry.

Whereas the powers of legislative committees to carry out inquiries are frequently challenged, or at any rate made subject to the formal authorization of the House itself, there is provision for committees of inquiry to study specific issues in most Parliaments. The committee of inquiry system means that a Parliament instructs a number of its members to collect such information as it needs to enable it to

272

exercise proper control, and to submit a report on which, if he sees fit, the House will take a decision. The right to institute an inquiry is a natural corollary of the principle that Parliament must have the right to obtain clarification in regard to any questions on which it is called upon to take a decision. In some countries, such as Finland, Norway and Sweden, Parliament has been refused the right to set up committees of inquiry vested with special powers.

On the other hand, the system has found fertile soil in the United States, where it is one of the essential characteristics of parliamentary government. The investigating committees of Congress have extremely wide powers which they do not hesitate to use. They can, for example, call before them any person whom they feel they should hear, and they have the right not merely to punish persons who fail to respond, but to oblige them to appear by issuing subpoenas against them. The activities of the American investigating committees are wholly directed towards the administration. Frequently it is the Secretary of State who is the target of an attack on a service or department. When this is the case, the supervision exercised by the investigating committee is somewhat akin to the classic form of parliamentary control. The parallel is even closer where the Secretary of State of his own accord asks to be heard by a committee, since it implies that he is anxious to obtain its assistance or the power to pursue his policy. Some writers regard this procedure as an indication of an evolution in the direction of the classic parliamentary system.

Clearly, in countries where the executive is politically accountable, commissions of inquiry have less significance, even when the means of investigation open to Parliament are as ample as they are in the United States. The prerogatives of the Belgian Parliament for example are unusually wide, since under both the Constitution and the law, both Houses are at liberty to hold an inquiry, with the same powers as are given to an examining magistrate by the Code of Criminal Procedure. Yet unlike the American Congress, the Belgian Parliament only exercises its right in quite exceptional instances. Similarly, in the Federal Republic of Germany, the Bundestag rarely makes use of its right to appoint committees of inquiry, and in fact these must be moved for in a motion signed by a quarter of the members.

As in Belgium, so too in France, the powers of inquiry granted to a parliamentary committee by the House are mostly along the lines of judicial procedure. Any person whom the committee feels it would be useful to hear is obliged to comply with the summons, which is served on him by a bailiff or police officer at the request of the chairman of the committee. Should he fail to appear as a witness, he is liable to a fine unless he can produce a legitimate reason. Furthermore, on a requisition by the committee, he may be subpoenaed. Refusal to take the oath, false testimony or the suborning of witnesses are offences punishable by penalties laid down in the Penal Code. Similar provisions are laid down in Syria in the case of witnesses summoned to appear.

In some countries it is difficult for committees of inquiry to exercise their functions. In Iceland, for example, a committee cannot force anyone to appear or to take the oath or to reply to its questions. If a witness who is called is unco-operative, the House is obliged to ask the Government to summon him to appear before the courts, which thus to some extent take over from the committee and impose penalities in the event of a refusal to give evidence.

The best way of making a parliamentary inquiry effective is by taking evidence on oath, with all the judicial consequences this implies, and the machinery of taking the oath is provided for by most Parliaments which make use of the inquiry procedure. Not all witnesses are required to take the oath, particularly in the countries which have come under British influence. In Poland, special leave is needed, and must be given on the merits of each particular case by the House. The practice of taking evidence on oath is completely unknown in Albania, Bulgaria, the USSR and Yugoslavia; nevertheless witnesses who give false testimony are criminally liable. In Denmark, Iceland and Switzerland, committees of inquiry are not entitled to ask witnesses to take the oath.

The question of evidence given by government officials to committees of inquiry raises a special problem, since civil servants are the subordinates of the minister in charge of their particular department. The question arises how far the Government is at liberty to order them not to reply to questions put to them by parliamentary committees. Actually, it is a question which has seldom been properly settled in law. The only noteworthy instance is Japan, where it is catered for by a number of legislative provisions to the effect that if an official refuses to give evidence, the reason for his refusal must be explained to Parliament by the ministerial department employing him. In the event of an explanation to the effect that for the official to speak would be prejudicial to the vital interests of the nation, Parliament can demand confirmation of this from the Cabinet. If the Cabinet makes no reply within ten days following the request by Parliament, the witness is required to give his evidence. In the Federal Republic of Germany, the consent of the department concerned is required, but such consent may not be withheld unless

the fact of furnishing the information required would be 'prejudicial
to public security or liable to jeopardize or make difficult the carrying
on of the public service'. This is the course usually adopted, even
where there are no written regulations governing such matters.

Authorization or refusal by the minister raises a problem of
political accountability which is a pragmatic issue rather than
one based on legal principles. The British House of Commons,
admittedly, has the power to have a civil servant who refuses to
reply imprisoned for contempt. But apart from the fact that the
House would generally be reluctant to go so far, it is extremely
likely that if a civil servant obeying instructions refused to give
evidence, the question raised would not be his own liability but the
political responsibility of the minister concerned, indeed that of the
Cabinet as a whole. In other words, the effect of the inquiry would be
to raise the problem of the political relationship between Parliament
and Government.

It should be noted that whatever the system, the committee set up
to conduct an inquiry is nothing more than an investigating and
fact-finding body whose only function is to prepare a report for
submission to the House which has set it up. It is always a matter
for the House itself to draw the necessary conclusions from the
inquiry and the data elicited by it and a committee of inquiry can
never of itself take a decision concerning the matter it is asked to
investigate. For this reason, the efficacy of the inquiry procedure is
extremely variable. Where inquiries are of a technical nature, and
particularly where they constitute a sort of inspection by Parliament
of the administrative services, the results are frequently excellent.
On the other hand, the value of the inquiry system is more debatable
where, on the pretext of throwing light on a particular issue, it is
used for political ends, which may not stop short of party-political
manoeuvre.

4. PARLIAMENTARY 'PROCURATORS' AND OTHER AD HOC BODIES OF CONTROL

The Swedish Parliament has had since the beginning of the eighteenth
century a special means of control in regard to the Government
through the so-called 'Riksdag Procurator' (*Ombudsman*). This
office originated in a royal decree of the year 1713 and it was designed
to ensure that the Government and the Ministry of Justice observed
the law in force at the time and that the public service in general was
run properly. The Constitution of 1809 merely took over and
reinforced a tradition which was already firmly established. By 1915

the work-load was so great that it was decided to divide the office and to appoint a Procurator for Civil Affairs and another for Military Affairs. These two officials are appointed by Parliament in accordance with a special procedure, and they must be persons eminent in the field of law and of recognized integrity. Each House appoints from among its members a group of twenty-two electors, who meet within ten days and choose the Procurators. These hold office for four years, but there is a proviso for dismissal on a recommendation by one of the three legislative committees which is called upon to supervise the activities of the Procurators. Thus they are *prima facie* parliamentary officials, but as far as public opinion is concerned, they are regarded mainly as 'tribunes of the people' who keep a permanent watch, and act as 'an indispensable factor in ensuring legal protection against the abuses and shortcomings of the Government'. The most striking of the functions of the Procurators is to defend the ordinary citizen against the powers that be, this defence not being provided as in other countries by administrative tribunals. However, the Procurators may also act on their own initiative, even where no move is made by a private individual to safeguard his rights, and it is here that their activities, backed by the delegated authority of Parliament, are seen to be an effective means of control by Parliament over the whole field of government activity. This control takes the form of annual reports which are published and submitted to Parliament. No doubt the office goes distinctly beyond the traditions of the classic type of parliamentary system, but nevertheless it has certain inherent virtues—above all it is flexible; it works quickly; and it is eminently democratic.

For these reasons, it has been imitated in two of the other Nordic countries—Finland and Denmark. In Finland, the single Procurator is elected for a term of three years. Each year he places before the Diet a report on the way in which the laws have been observed by the courts and all public authorities. In Denmark, the Folketing Procurator for Public Affairs supervises the civil and military administration of the State in the name of Parliament. He too submits a report on his findings each year to the Folketing.

Two other institutions may be cited as akin to this unusual type of office: in the Federal Republic of Germany there is a Defence Commissioner, elected by the Bundestag, his duty being to safeguard the fundamental rights of military personnel and to assist the Bundestag in controlling the armed forces; secondly, there are the functions performed in the USSR, Albania, Bulgaria and Rumania by the 'Procurator-General'. This official is elected by Parliament and his powers of control cover the whole of the activities of the public administration. However, in these countries the Procurator-General is at the head of a vast corps of officials. In Poland we find an institution of an unusual character: the Supreme Chamber of Control. This is a permanent body nominated by and solely accountable to the Diet itself. Under the terms of the Constitution the Supreme Chamber is responsible for ensuring the legality, efficiency and expediency of the economic, financial and administrative work performed by the central and local department of the State. It is empowered to supervise the Government itself together with the services, institutions and undertaking for which the latter is responsible. It peforms its functions by virtue of a recommendation by the Diet or a decision to the same effect by a Parliamentary Committee. In addition the Supreme Chamber is required to report to Parliament each year on the implementation of the Budget and the economic plan and to submit its comments regarding the financial statements made by the Government. It is obliged to supply the parliamentary committees, should they so request, with all relevant information concerning the work of any minister, institution or establishment.

The exercise of control over the Government and the administration by the representatives of the people is regarded as vital by all countries which hold firmly to the democratic ideal. Hence the importance of the various procedures described above not only for those Parliaments where the right of initiative in legislative and financial matters is subject to certain restrictions, but also for those which in their relationship with the executive come up against the abstract bar of the separation of powers. But over and above the relations between the powers, the real meaning of parliamentary control is to be sought in the safeguard it ensures for liberty, individual and collective alike. Hence it has been rightly said that parliamentary control, whatever form it takes, is literally 'democracy in action'.

IV

Parliamentary Control Over Finance

Control over the manner in which financial provisions are carried out is a separate aspect—and by no means the least important—of the general powers of control exercised by Parliament over the

277

activities of the Government. Its importance is justified by the purpose it serves, and its separate character is the result of the special features of the procedure by which it is exercised.

Since public finance is regarded as the special preserve of the legislature, quite clearly the rights of Parliament do not end with the voting of the Budget and the related estimates. It has still to make sure that the financial provisions have in actual fact been carried out in accordance with the authority it has granted. It is only when this has been verified that Parliament can feel satisfied that the Budget operation has been carried out properly and can be regarded as disposed of. Thus Parliament takes a hand both at the beginning and at the end of the financial cycle. For practical purposes there is no divergence of opinion as to what control should cover, but unanimity has by no means been reached in regard to the method of achieving it. In actual fact, it is extremely difficult to analyse the control devices open to Parliament, owing to the way in which other devices designed to achieve the same purpose but coming within the administrative or judicial field exert an influence on them. At any rate, action by Parliament is the rule, whether this takes place directly or through the instructions given to special bodies, and whether it coincides with the implementation of the Budget or comes later. In most cases there are several systems side by side to help to make Parliament more effective in this field.

The first type of financial control is based on the over-all supervisory powers normally enjoyed by Parliament in all matters, and is exercised through such devices as interpellations, questions or inquiries. These various procedures apply in exactly the same way in regard to finance as to any other matters. Hence the very fact that they are political devices as a rule makes them ill-fitted for the purposes of technical supervision, one might even say a supervision at the accountant level, of the activities of the Government.

Another form of control exercised with great frequency is one which belongs to financial procedure proper. The Budget and the related estimates are after all not drawn up by a rigid, cut-and-dried decision. Whenever the Government comes to Parliament with a request for some modification of the estimates Parliament has *ipso facto* occasion to review the manner in which its original grant was used. New or supplementary grants asked for by the Government are ordinarily made in accordance with the same procedure as that followed when the grants were voted. Thus Parliament has an opportunity not only to obtain information as to how expenditure has been handled, but also to put pressure on the Government, if the out-turn has not been in keeping with the original decisions, by refusing any further funds. This method of control, an aspect of the overall financial powers of Parliament, tends more often than not to become identified with approval or disapproval on political grounds. But since impartiality, which is an essential feature of control over the implementation of the Budget and the related estimates, demands that this control should be based on technical data, it is important that suitable means of information such as are not furnished by the ordinary procedures for political control should be at the disposal of Parliament. Supervision by Parliament therefore necessitates first and foremost a whole intelligence apparatus designed to keep it informed as to the manner in which government expenditure is being made. Its task is then to draw conclusions from the information it receives.

With this in mind, the practice in several countries especially in Eastern Europe, is for general reports to be submitted by the Government or the administration. For example, the People's Assembly in Albania and the National Assembly in Bulgaria can at any time ask for an oral report on the way in which the State Financial programme is being implemented and take decisions accordingly. In Poland, it is the duty of the Council of Ministers to submit to the Diet an annual report on the use made of the grants of funds which have been made. The report is submitted first of all to the Economic Planning, Budget and Finance Committee, and then to the Diet as a whole. Similarly, the Supreme Soviet of the USSR receives reports, which may be debated at any time, on the way in which the financial policy is being carried out. In Czechoslovakia, the Government is required to submit a progress report on the economic plan regularly to the National Assembly.

In Finland, Parliament can exercise a measure of control over the management of public finances on the occasion of the annual review of the Government's report on the state of the exchequer. But the country where this method of control is organized most systematically is Japan. The Japanese Constitution stipulates that 'at regular intervals, not less than once a year, the Cabinet shall report to the Diet and to the people on the state of the nation's finances'. The finance laws further stipulate that 'the Cabinet shall report to the Diet and to the nation at least once a quarter on the use made of the exchequer and on the general financial situation'. Although these general reports are extremely useful, they are nevertheless not sufficient to give an effective picture of the day-to-day details of financial management, where any irregularities would tend to be found. Hence the various devices for providing general information are supplemented by fact-finding machinery entrusted directly either to certain parliamentary bodies or to special supervisory commissions functioning under the authority of Parliament.

In Parliaments where the system of permanent committees is the rule, the part played by finance committees in this respect is particularly important. Apart from eliciting general information, these committees have ways and means of obtaining more specialized information through their rapporteurs or through sub-committees set up to deal with specific matters and sometimes including in their membership members of other committees. In the French Parliament, for example, there are sub-committees whose function is 'to exercise permanent supervision over the use made of national defence funds' or 'to supervise and assess the efficiency of the administration of nationalized undertakings and corporations partly dependent on Government funds'. These bodies are empowered to supervise—'with access to documentary and other evidence'—the use made of voted funds, and have as a general rule full powers of investigation. In Switzerland, in the same way, the implementation of the estimates is supervised by the 'finance delegation' consisting of six members of the finance committee of each House.

In the Federal Republic of Germany, the Bundestag Budget committee takes a hand, while the Budget is being applied, in approving certain grants, subject to conditions laid down by the Budget law. It also chooses from among its own members a sub-committee to audit the accounts, and this body examines all accounts submitted to the Bundestag as well as the statements made by the Audit Office, and subsequently reports back to the Bundestag. In Sweden, supervision by the Budget committee is permanent, and it may take the form of statements or directives likely to have repercussions on the way in which the financial programme is implemented. Similarly, it would appear that in the USSR and the People's Democracies, the task of carrying out a systematic control over the way in which the Government and the Administration have applied financial decisions falls essentially to the finance committees.

Outside Europe, it is interesting to note the equally important part played by the appropriations committees of the United States Congress. But the activities of these committees are paralleled by those of a body outside Parliament, a body essentially characteristic of the Anglo-Saxon method of control—the 'Comptroller General'. In the United Kingdom, the Comptroller and 'Auditor General' is appointed by the Crown. However, he can be relieved of his duties by an Address passed by the two Houses. He enjoys complete independence from the Treasury, his task being to verify the

280

regularity of all expenditure, both from the Consolidated Fund and from funds voted by Parliament, and he submits periodic reports on the findings of his investigations to the House of Commons. As liaison between the Comptroller and Auditor General and the House there is a special committee, the Public Accounts Committee, which fulfils a somewhat similar function to that of the permanent committee on finance in other Parliaments. The Public Accounts Committee consists of fifteen members, the chairman being by tradition a member of the Opposition. The Financial Secretary to the Treasury is a member *ex officio*, although he seldom attends its meetings. In practice, the committee's essential function is to scrutinize matters drawn to its attention by the reports of the Comptroller and Auditor General. Where it appears that some irregularity has been committed, the committee investigates the matter and decides whether the incident should be brought before the House. Within a fairly short time it issues a report on the over-all execution of the government expenditure, and there may be a debate in the House, but only if the Opposition so requests.

The main features of this system, based on permanent control by officials outside Parliament, but under the auspices of a Select Committee, have been taken over by a number of countries of the British type—Australia, Burma, Ceylon, India, Ireland and the Sudan. It may be mentioned that in Australia and in India the Public Accounts Committee is a joint committee of both Houses, consisting of seven members of the House and three members of the Senate in Australia, and fifteen members of the lower House and seven members of the upper House in India.

In the United States the main controlling body is the General Accounting Office, the head of which, the Comptroller-General, is appointed for a fifteen-year term by the President subject to the agreement of the Senate. He can only be removed by Congress, and only in the circumstances prescribed by law. His office is extremely important, since he exercises control over expenditure before it takes place. Throughout the year he scrutinizes all documents concerning expenditure, and he is at liberty to stop payment and to call the officials concerned to account. He issues periodic reports on the financial administration of the various departments and submits a report on the financial situation to Congress at the end of the financial year. Owing to the separation of the executive power from the legislature, the actual organization of control prevents Congress from censuring the administration of the ministerial departments. Nevertheless, the supervision exercised by the committees on appropriations is greatly simplified by the work of the Comptroller-General.

One particularly useful function he fulfils is to advise congress on the desirability of including certain items in the following year's Budget.

A more important role is played by Parliament where the auditing of the accounts is in the hands of a body chosen by itself, as in Denmark, Finland, Iceland, Norway and Sweden. In these countries, the controlling body is all-party in character, so that its membership is representative of the various political trends. For example, the Danish Folketing each year appoints four accounts commissioners, the United Althing in Iceland three, elected by proportional representation; and in Norway, five auditors are appointed by the Storting. In Israel, the Comptroller-General is appointed by the Head of State on a recommendation by the Knesset. In the Netherlands, the three members of the General Accounts Board are appointed by the Crown, but on the nomination of the Second Chamber of the States-General. In Sweden, the main financial control is in the hands of twelve 'auditors', six being elected from each House by proportional representation. Thus the Opposition is automatically represented and takes its turn in providing the chairman of the Board of Auditors. This fact does not prevent the Board from carrying out its duties efficiently and in a non-party manner. It is required to submit a printed report not later than 15 December each year. The report is submitted first to all the government departments which have come in for criticism, and their observations are annexed to it. The report is then placed before the Riksdag and it is referred to the Budget committee, which itself produces a report embodying recommendations which are moved in the Riksdag for endorsement. In the next session, the Government must indicate to Parliament what measures it has taken in compliance with the recommendations thus made.

There is one final method of control, by which Parliament formally approves the whole of the accounts for the financial year. This system has the virtue of being logical in that it has a certain symmetry—it completes the cycle which began with the voting of the Budget and related estimates; also theoretically, it offers Parliament considerable safeguards. In actual fact, it is effective only if approval by Parliament is forthcoming in a relatively short time so that adequate attention can be given to the problems under discussion and, if necessary, action taken against the ministers responsible for any shortcomings.

Formal approval of the accounts by Parliament, as required in Austria, Belgium, Bulgaria, Denmark, Egypt, France, the Federal Republic of Germany, Iceland, Italy, Japan, Laos, the Netherlands,

Rumania, Syria and Yugoslavia, can take a variety of forms. In Denmark and Iceland, Parliament passes resolutions; in Japan the approval of the accounts is done by each House separately. The decision of each is final and it does not necessarily coincide with the other House's decision, unlike the procedure in regard to the approval of the Budget. In most cases approval is given in the form of legislation; the Government submits a Bill relating to the public accounts, which follows the ordinary legislative routine. In Bulgaria the occasion for passing the Budget by the National Assembly is also the occasion for approving the financial accounts for the previous financial year.

In a number of countries, including Austria, Belgium, France and Italy, the Accounts Act is only passed after an initial audit has been carried out by a body with the status of a high administrative tribunal, the 'Audit Office'. As a rule, this body is made up of officials who have the status of irremovable judicial officers. However, in Belgium its members are appointed by the Chamber of Representatives itself, and their main task is to make a prior check of all expenditure, whereas in most instances the control carried out by the Audit Office is only done *ex post facto*. The idea underlying the Audit Office is that the operation of auditing the public accounts should be in the hands of an independent and impartial body, free from any political influence. In this way any action it may take is a guarantee of regularity, which is a vital necessity in all Budget operations. At the same time, however, it does introduce an element of delay, sometimes a considerable one, which distinctly lessens the value of the passing of the Accounts Act. The whole approved expenditure for the year has to be carried by the Government and the administrative departments, and the administrative control bodies and the Audit Office have to audit the regularity of the operation. It is only at this point that the effective expenditure and income are summarized in a document for Parliament to approve. The result is that more often than not the vote of approval is a mere formality. At any rate this is the case in France, where the Accounts Act is passed in accordance with the 'no debate' procedure. In Belgium the Audit Office transmits its general report to Parliament, in the year following the closing of the accounts audited. Despite this the Accounts Act is usually passed several years later, and it is passed without debate. But the acceptance of this state of affairs by Parliament must not be taken as a relinquishment of its sovereignty; it is rather a tribute to the effectiveness of the network of controls carried out by other bodies, administrative or judicial, whose impartiality cannot be questioned.

Furthermore, a close examination of the control procedures makes it clear that the interest shown by Parliament in regard to the execution of financial decisions varies in inverse proportion to the part taken by Parliament in the preparation of the Budget and the related estimates. This shows that in most Parliaments there is, in practice if not in the Constitution, a certain balance between their financial function and their controlling function, the essential point being to maintain their prerogatives, whatever the field of activities.

V

Parliament and Foreign Policy

The Direction of Foreign Policy by Parliament—Parliamentary Control of Foreign Policy—Authorization to ratify Treaties

For a long time, foreign policy was not regarded as among the prerogatives of Parliament, on the grounds that 'diplomacy is the province of Princes, not of commoners'. But after two world wars, the problem of war and peace and the paths leading there has been brought home to every individual; so much so that the attitude prevalent in the past appears to be completely outmoded. However, there is no gainsaying the fact that the progress of democracy has long been held up by this traditional stumbling-block, and its achievements are by no means proportionate everywhere to the magnitude of the objective sought. This state of affairs is the result of all of the thinking of early writers on constitutional law, who tended to fall in with the ideas handed down to them and to rule out any idea of participation by the people in the conduct of international affairs. Admittedly it is only recently that the man in the street has become aware of such matters, and the politically enlightened groups in the various countries have not made any particular effort to awaken this interest. It might of course be claimed that international politics is a specialist subject and too complex to be debated publicly. But after all, there is hardly any problem—political, economic or social—which does not have its technicalities and does not demand enlightenment and understanding. And there is surely no problem which is more closely bound up with the needs of the community than the problems of peace, security and international relations.

Obviously there can be no question of entrusting the conduct of foreign policy to the whole body of representatives of the people, particularly as they are quite likely to have divergent or even antagonistic views. But the same thing is no less true of domestic affairs, and there is no more reason why the one type should be entrusted solely to the Government than the other. With regard to the right of Parliament to supervise the activities of the executive, this should apply in the same way whether the subject is foreign policy or domestic policy. In actual practice, if we look closely at the various institutions and constitutional practices we find that in most countries the executive enjoys, in practice or by the Constitution, an independence which is hardly compatible with the principle of popular sovereignty and its representation in Parliament. Thus the part played by Parliament, whether it takes the form of previous consultation, of subsequent supervision or, in the case of treaties, of parliamentary authorization to ratify them, is distinctly limited.

1. THE DIRECTION OF FOREIGN POLICY BY PARLIAMENT

The conduct of foreign policy is as a rule regarded as the prerogative of the executive. In practice it is, of course, hardly practicable for Parliament to participate in arriving at decisions on international issues, if only because of the frequency and suddenness with which they occur, to say nothing of the secrecy surrounding certain types of negotiations; on the other hand it is extremely questionable whether they should be kept in ignorance of the over-all policy on which the diplomatic activities of the State are based. Yet few constitutions provide formally for Parliament to play any part at this stage; and even when they do, it may mean no more than outlining general principles, and the interpretation of these principles may leave the Government a great deal of latitude. Thus, the Supreme Soviet of the USSR lays down the principles of foreign policy and treats of the problems of peace and war and, moreover, settles concrete questions regarding the State's foreign relations. The position is similar in Albania where the National Assembly lays down the 'principles' of the country's foreign policy. In Bulgaria the National Assembly lays down the 'essential lines' of Bulgarian foreign policy. The Rumanian Grand National Assembly gives 'directives' to the Government which the latter is expected to observe in its relations with other states. In Czechoslovakia the basic problems of the country's foreign policy are debated in the National Assembly whose directives are binding on the Government.

In most of the other countries, there is no provision for entrusting such a role to Parliament. In actual fact, however, the situation is not appreciably different, since the gap between the two systems is largely filled by the pragmatic workings of Parliament, at any rate in so far as this is based on the political accountability of the executive. Hence it can be argued that there is no need to lay down formally the rules for the part played by Parliament where these arise in practice out of its ordinary prerogatives, particularly its right to apply various procedures such as interpellations, resolutions, etc., in order to bring such problems of interest into the limelight and to make known its views on the issues involved. Moreover, in several countries the procedure for the investiture of the Head of the Government gives Parliament an opportunity to approve the programme outlined in his speech, and this programme invariably includes a number of points concerning the way in which the State's foreign policy will be conducted.

Whatever the system, the part played by Parliament would appear to be generally a discreet one. The general nature of the principles laid down by Parliaments or worked out by Governments makes it impossible to regard the part played by Parliament in the preparation of foreign policy as an effective one. At the very best it is seldom more than a question of giving general directives. Thus since Parliament is denied a real hand in policy-making, that is all the more reason why its powers of control should be well safeguarded.

2. PARLIAMENTARY CONTROL OF FOREIGN POLICY

In regard to the Government's foreign policy, Parliament has of course all the usual means of control, whether exercised by the House itself (in the form of debates, approval of grants of funds, or resolutions), by fact-finding or advisory committees, or commissions of inquiry, or by the Members of Parliament themselves in the form of questions. In practice the efficacy of these various devices is considerably blunted for foreign policy problems, since unfortunately they have a negligible value for election purposes and differences of opinion on them are not so likely to be expressed with vehemence.

The Budget debate is an indirect means of control. Theoretically it is confined to the financial implications of the foreign policy carried out by the Government, but in fact it is used to challenge the basic principles of the policy. Motions for reductions of grants of funds, whether token or otherwise, to say nothing of general debate, are devices used by Members of Parliament to oblige the Foreign Minister to give explanations on specific points.

Foreign policy debates in the House itself can take a variety of forms in different countries. First of all there are the statements and communiqués volunteered by the Government and the summaries and reports which may be statutorily required from time to time. This is the case in some of the Easter European countries such as Bulgaria, Rumania, USSR and Yugoslavia, as well as in Switzerland, though here the reports are concerned only with the economic measures arising out of agreements concluded with foreign states. Parliamentary control may also be exercised on the initiative of Parliament itself, and indeed it is likely to be more effective, since as a rule, it gives rise to a general debate. This is what happens in interpellations, which actually culminate in motions approving or disapproving the action of the Government. In the French system, as also in Austria, Belgium, Luxembourg and the Netherlands, the interpellation is the most widely practised method of control. In particular, in Austria, the Federal Republic of Germany, Israel, Poland and Yugoslavia, the views of Parliament may also be expressed in the form of resolutions moved by private members, though without any coercive force in regard to the Government. Finally, we have the general debate, as in the United Kingdom, which enables the Government to take the measure of parliamentary opinion.

The system of questions put to the Foreign Minister can be extremely valuable, provided it is flexible enough, so that the course of international events can be followed closely. It is an interesting fact that the question procedure was introduced in France specifically and precisely in order to facilitate the supervision of foreign policy and to make that supervision a practical possibility. It was felt that general debates would be dangerous owing to their public character and the extempore nature of many statements made; whereas the question system, since it gave the minister time for reflection, was felt by those who advocated it to have a great deal in its favour. In practice, the subsequent evolution of this procedure seems to owe very little to the considerations which led to its introduction, judging from the extremely small number of questions asked on foreign affairs.

On the other hand, the sober and dispassionate nature of the work of parliamentary committees would appear to be particularly suited to this type of problem. Indeed the establishment of a special committee such as exists in the French and American systems has evidently been found technically attractive, since all the Parliaments which have permanent committees today have a Foreign Affairs

287

Committee. The practice has had its advocates in the United Kingdom, but it has not been adopted. The establishment of a separate committee for foreign affairs makes for a type of control which, *mutatis mutandis*, can be compared with the control exercised in its particular field by the finance committee.

In the first place, a foreign affairs committee is better equipped than the House itself to collect information furnished by the various government departments. It is as a rule kept informed as to the trend of the international economic situation, either at its own request or on the initiative of the minister. In Finland one of the tasks of the foreign affairs committee is to consider a report submitted each year by the Government on relations with foreign Powers. In Israel, similarly, the foreign affairs committee hears periodic reports by the Prime Minister, the Foreign Minister, or the Defence Minister. Sometimes, though less frequently, a foreign affairs committee can act in an advisory capacity. Since its views will reflect fairly accurately those which the House itself would put forward, it may be valuable to the Government to know what those views are before embarking on a particular policy it regards as opportune. The difference between the two functions which such a committee can fulfil is particularly noteworthy in the Netherlands, where the foreign affairs committee of the First Chamber is merely empowered to receive information, whereas the Second Chamber's committee has the further privilege of being consulted by the Government.

The practice of prior consultation of committees, always on an informal level, is found particularly in Czechoslovakia, Denmark, the Federal Republic of Germany, Norway, Syria and Yugoslavia. In the Federal Republic of Germany and Sweden there are also special bodies worth mentioning. The German Bundestag has an advisory council in regard to agreements on commercial policy, consisting of nine members of the committee on external trade and four representatives of the Bundesrat. It ensures close co-operation between the Bundestag and the Government when trade agreements are being drawn up. The drafts of agreements are submitted to it, and it gives its views as to whether a particular agreement requires the consent of Parliament as a whole or not. Sweden has an advisory council on foreign affairs. This is a committee of the executive; in fact the King himself presides over it, but it includes a number of members of the foreign affairs committee of the Riksdag, side by side with the representatives of the Government. The council does not take any decisions or give opinions as a body; all it does is put forward the individual opinions or recommendations of each of its members.

Here we have, in a nutshell, the various types of control used by Parliaments. Certainly they are hardly calculated to hamper the freedom of action of the Government, which is left completely independent except for such limits as arise out of its political accountability in general; what is more, Parliament will think twice before challenging the Government in this field. In some countries, once this type of control has been exercised, the task of Parliament is finished. In other countries, it continues when international relations are crystallized in the conclusion of treaties.

3. AUTHORIZATION TO RATIFY TREATIES

Treaties are as it were the formal expression of the relationships established between states, the concrete embodiment of their foreign policies. In general it is not possible, either legally or practically, for Parliament to take part in the negotiations leading up to the conclusion of treaties; nor can they, except on rare occasions, force the Government to embark on such negotiations. On the other hand, it would seem to be a relatively simple matter to establish their right to exercise *ex post facto* control over treaties after they have been signed, but before they are ratified by the Head of the State. It might even be argued that democratic principles would require that no treaty acquired the force of law until it had been approved by Parliament. But any such rule is far from being observed everywhere in law. In some countries, Parliament has no prerogative in regard to treaties. In India and Pakistan, for example, there is no provision for participation by Parliament in the ratification of treaties. Similarly, in Israel, there is no obligation on the Government to submit treaties to the Knesset before ratifying them. In Syria neither the Constitution nor the law nor the rules of parliamentary procedure require the Government to keep Parliament informed as to its foreign policy and hence as to any treaties it has concluded.

In some countries the authorization of Parliament prior to ratification is required in the case of specific categories of treaties enumerated exhaustively in the Constitution or by law. The length of the list gives theoretically the measure of the power of Parliament. In the United Kingdom, Burma, Ceylon and Ireland, the approval of Parliament is necessary only if the proposed treaty involves changes in domestic legislation or has financial implications. In the United Kingdom, the principle as thus stated does not altogether reflect the real situation for under a recent agreement any treaties concluded are debated only if a request to that end is made by the Opposition

289

or by a fairly large group of members of the government party, and even when such debates do take place, they seldom end in a vote.

In some countries the list of treaties requiring the approval of Parliament before they are ratified is longer. In France it comprises 'treaties relating to international organization, peace treaties, trade agreements, treaties involving State funds, treaties relating to the legal position and property rights of French citizens abroad, treaties affecting French internal legislation, and treaties for the cession, exchange or acquisition of territory'. The Belgian list is somewhat similar. In Iceland, emphasis is laid on treaties which affect the integrity of the territory or of the territorial waters, and those which will involve constitutional amendments. In Finland the consent of Parliament is required before any treaty can come into force if it necessitates legislative measures or the grant of funds, or entails changes to the nation's frontiers, or constitutes a peace treaty.

It would be a mistake to assume that such provisions place any real curb on the independence of the executive, since even the apparently full lists often leave out major political treaties and treaties of alliance—incontestably the ones which exert most influence over the destiny of a nation. It is noteworthy, however, that some constitutions have repaired this omission. In the Federal Republic of Germany, treaties requiring the agreement of Parliament expressly include those which regulate the 'political relations' of the Federation. The same is true in Austria of 'political treaties', and in Yugoslavia of treaties concerning 'political or military co-operation'. The same would appear to be true in Bulgaria of 'major international treaties' and in Sweden of 'important treaties', which may not be ratified without the consent of the Riksdag except in case of emergency.

In principle, all treaties require parliamentary authorization before they can be ratified in Czechoslovakia, Denmark, Indonesia, Japan, Laos, Luxembourg, the Netherlands, Norway and Switzerland, but there are some special points to be noted. In Japan, for example, the Constitution provides that when the Government concludes treaties, the approval of the Diet may be given beforehand or afterwards, according to the circumstances. In the Netherlands, the approbation given by the States-General may be either explicit or tacit. In the former case, a Bill to secure approbation is introduced, debated and passed in accordance with the ordinary legislative procedure. In the case of tacit approval, the Government lays the text of the treaty before both Houses, along with a letter asking for their agreement. Approval is assumed to have been given if within a period of thirty days no request has been made for approval to be given in an explicit manner, i.e. in the form of an Act of Parliament. Such a request must be sponsored by at least one fifth of the members of either House. Although somewhat more cut-and-dried, this system is not unlike the procedure followed in the House of Commons. In Switzerland, on the other hand, ratification of treaties requires not merely the prior approval of the Federal Parliament, but the approval of the nation as well, by way of referendum with optional voting, if the duration of the treaty is unlimited or exceeds fifteen years.

In countries where the ratification of treaties is a function reserved for the Presidium, the ambivalent nature of this body makes it possible to regard its action as taken not merely as Head of State but also as a delegate-body of Parliament. In the USSR, however, the Supreme Soviet has power to ratify even the most important treaties.

The most notorious example of the intervention of a parliamentary body in regard to treaties is found in the American Constitution. The freedom of action of the President of the United States is decidedly curtailed, since before any treaty can be ratified it must have the assent of the Senate, given by at least two thirds of the members present. This might appear to be an excessive prerogative, especially if we consider that in practice the representatives of a mere twelfth of the population can in this way impose their wishes on the nation as a whole. But it makes sense if we remember that the Senate is not supposed to be a body representing the will of the people, but rather the champion of the independence of the states belonging to the Federation. All the same, the fact that the Senate takes a hand makes it incumbent upon the President, if he wishes to avoid the risk of being rebuffed, to canvass senators whose influence carries weight in foreign affairs circles. Thus, paradoxically enough, it is a system of separation of powers that gives us the most effective manifestation of parliamentary control. In the Philippines this same control is exercised by the Senate, and in Brazil by both Houses.

The famous example of the treaty of Versailles will not easily be forgotten. Nevertheless, the part played by Parliament in the ratification of treaties must not be over-stated. Its freedom of action in this respect is qualified by two types of factor. The first is a technical matter—it is not the text of the treaty that is subject to debate, but simply the authorization to ratify the treaty; and, even where this authorization is requested in the form of legislation as in Austria, Belgium, France, the Federal Republic of Germany and the Netherlands, Parliament has no power to amend the treaty in question—they must simply accept it or reject it as it stands.

291

Secondly, there is the political argument—to refuse to ratify a treaty is an act of the utmost gravity. It is not easy publicly to disavow the Government of one's country and to go back on pledges it has given to other Powers. Thus Parliament is faced with a *fait accompli* to which it was not a party, yet for which in the ultimate analysis it will have to take the responsibility.

There are two points to be remembered: first of all the procedure for ratification by Parliament does not embrace all treaties; secondly, treaties as such represent only a small proportion of the diplomatic measures (declarations, agreements, arrangements, the 'executive argreements' of the United States, etc.) at the disposal of the executive. Most of these do not come within the control afforded by parliamentary authorization.

Thus in foreign policy the role of Parliament is to approve and ratify rather than to take charge and lead the way. Clearly democracy has a long way to go in this direction, assuming we accept the principle that diplomacy should no longer be the affairs of Princes but of the people.

VI

The Judicial Function of Parliament

The penal liability of the members of the executive before Parliament is at the root of their political accountability. Today, this penal liability is no more than a survival of ancient monarchic institutions, but it is still alive in a number of contemporary constitutions, even though its utility is strongly challenged; from the theoretical point of view, it raises the more general problem of political justice, which is outside the scope of this study. It might be argued at any rate that since any crimes committed would be political crimes involving high officials, these would hardly come within the jurisdiction of the ordinary courts. From the practical point of view, in the parliamentary system political accountability has completely supplanted penal liability, at any rate as far as the members of governments are concerned. Penal liability does of course still constitute a weapon for use against the Head of State unless he is completely exempt from accountability for his actions, as in the case of Monarchs, or as a substitute for political accountability, the absence of which is the important feature of systems of the separation of powers type.

292

As far as we are concerned, the problem is what part Parliament can play in the procedure by which the Head of State and the Government can be arraigned and brought to justice. We find in law three main systems in which a role of varying importance is played by Parliament:

(a) First of all we get the system in which the task of trying the accused persons is entrusted to the supreme judicial court of the country, but they must be brought before it by a decision of Parliament. This system is followed in Belgium. The Constitution lays down that 'the Chamber of Representatives shall have the right to bring charges against ministers and to arraign them before the Court of Appeals, which shall have the sole right to judge them in joint session . . . A law shall be enacted defining the liability, the penalties to be imposed on ministers and the proceedings to be taken against them'. It should be noted that this law has never been passed and that the 'provisional arrangements' instituted by the Constitution of 1831 are still in being. The Chamber of Representatives has discretionary power to bring charges against a minister, and the Court of Appeals to try him, stating the nature of the offence and imposing the penalty. Similarly, in the Netherlands, the Second Chamber can, in theory, bring ministers before the Supreme Court on the charge of violation of the law, but this right has never in fact been exercised.

In Austria, on the strength of a decision by the National Council, the members of the Federal Government can be charged with committing crimes or other offences in the exercise of their functions. Their case is tried by the Constitutional Court, which can sentence a minister to dismissal from office, with loss of his political rights. In Iceland, charges brought against ministers are a matter for the United Althing, and they are tried by the Court of Arraignment. With the agreement of the Althing, the President may withdraw the accusations against the ministers or absolve them from the penalities imposed on them. In Finland, Parliament may decide with the support of three quarters of the votes cast to bring the President of the Republic before the Supreme Court of Justice for treason or high treason—the only crimes of which he can be accused.

(b) Under the second system the trial of the accused is in the hands of a special court, usually known as the 'High Court'. Here Parliament, or one of its Houses, has the exclusive right

293

to initiate the arraignment procedure. In addition, it takes a fairly significant part in the arrangements for appointing the members of the High Court.

In Denmark, part of the membership of the High Court of the Realm consists of a certain number of judges elected from outside by the Folketing. In Finland, the High Court consists of *ex officio* members and judicial officers designated by the parliamentary 'electors'. Its function is to try members of the Government brought before it by Parliament on the strength of a simple majority decision. It should be remembered that the President of the Republic must be brought to justice before the Supreme Court and that a charge against him requires a decision supported by three quarters of the votes cast. In Norway, the High Court of the Realm comprises both members of the Lagting and professional judges who are members of the Supreme Court. In the Republic of Vietnam, Parliament elects some of its own members as members of the special court set up to judge the President and Vice-President of the Republic.

The High Court of Justice for which provision is made under the French Constitution has the power to try the President of the Republic and ministers in the event of charges being brought against them by the National Assembly. The vote is by secret ballot, and an absolute majority of the deputies is required. The members of this High Court are elected at the beginning of each Parliament, the method of election being as follows: a President and two Vice-Presidents are elected with the support of two thirds of the votes in a secret ballot; twenty regular judges and twenty alternate judges are elected by the Assembly from among its own members, by proportional representation of the various groups; ten regular judges and ten alternate judges are chosen by the Assembly from outside its ranks, the election being subject to the support of two thirds of the votes in a secret ballot. Side by side with the High Court proper there is a Commission of Investigation, which reflects a desire to include professional judges and the Council of the Republic in the work of the High Court. This Commission consists of a chairman and two assistants, designated by the High Council of the Judiciary and six judges elected by the National Assembly from among its members by two thirds of the votes in a secret ballot. Finally, the High Court comprises a *parquet* which takes over the proceedings following the arraignment, and this is composed of a State Attorney-General and two 'Advocates-general' elected by two thirds of the votes in a secret ballot, the election being conducted by the National Assembly, either from among its own members or from outside.

(c) The third system, unlike the other two, involves no other body but Parliament proper and does not seek help from outside. The lower House is the one which initiates the charge, the upper House is the judge, and it is a parliamentary operation entirely. This is the so-called 'impeachment' procedure, which in England goes back to the sixteenth century. An accusation is made by the House of Commons before the House of Lords, which passes judgement as a court of law. The idea of the House of Lords possessing powers in this field raises no problem, since this body has preserved the judicial character which it has had from the very beginning of its history, for it remains until this day the final court of appeal in the country. As to the House of Commons and its right to bring the charges, this has been assimilated to the function of the lay justices of the various counties—the basis of all criminal proceedings. Thus the House of Commons would be, so to speak, the 'lay justice' for the whole of England.

The impeachment procedure has not been used since 1805. But if Parliament feels that impeachment is not an appropriate method of dealing with a particular problem, it can have recourse to the vote of a 'Bill of attainder'. This is a legislative measure adopted in exactly the same way as any other piece of legislation. There is no judgment; the Bill sets forth the various charges and the punishment imposed. This procedure has become obsolete, and has not been used since 1722. Admittedly it amounts to a thorough intermingling of the powers of the legislature with those of the judiciary, whose independence is after all regarded as one of the basic tenets of the Constitution. The device is not found elsewhere.

Impeachment as such has fared better outside the United Kingdom. It has been faithfully reproduced by the Constitution of the United States, where it is applicable not only to ministers but to the President, Vice-President, and all the federal officials. The initiative lies with the House of Representatives, which sets up an investigating committee, and on the strength of the latter's report can decide to bring an action for impeachment before the Senate. The latter sits as a court, and the trial takes place in private. The possible sentence must be pronounced by two thirds of the senators.

295

The impeachment procedure has been used only once against the Head of State, and in fact the person against whom the charge was made—President Johnson in 1868—was acquitted. If this practice had been resorted to more frequently, the presidential system might have turned into a parliamentary system, following the evolution of the British sytem; but it hardly seems likely that this will happen now. In Brazil, similarly, the House has authority to impeach the President and ministers, and the Senate to try them. In the Philippines, the President may be accused and tried by the same procedure—but heads of ministerial departments may not.

An unusual type of impeachment procedure is found in Burma. Here it applies only to the President. The impeachment order must be made in a resolution signed by one quarter of the members of either House, and must be agreed to by two thirds of the votes cast. When one of the Houses has thus brought the charge, the other undertakes the investigation, and by a resolution supported by two thirds of its members it can decide to remove the President from office. The impeachment procedure can be adapted for use in the situations which arise when the Parliament is of the unicameral type. This is the case with Czechoslovakia, where the impeachment of the President of the Republic, the President of the Council or the ministers is in the hands of the Presidency of the National Assembly, the latter itself investigating the case and trying the accused.

To end this brief review of the various systems under which Parliament may sit in judgement on the executive or certain of its members, mention may be made of the particular type of procedure practised in Norway and Sweden, comprising features both of political control proper and penal control. The Norwegian Storting has the right of access to the proceedings of the Councils of Ministers, and it exercises this right through the Protocol Committee of the Odelsting. In its report to the House, this committee may recommend a political penalty, but it can also recommend the impeachment of a minister. If the Odelsting upholds the impeachment charge, the minister is brought before the High Court of the Realm, made up of members of the Lagting and the Supreme Court. In Sweden, a similar dual form of control is exercised by the Constitutional Committee, which reports to Parliament, and Parliament may decide to bring members of the Government charged with illegal acts before the Arraignment Court. In fact, neither country has ever had occasion to use this procedure.

As a matter of fact, it has been the fate of all systems designed to apply judicial penalties to members of the executive to fall rapidly into disuse, and for this reason, most countries have regarded them as superfluous and have abandoned them. Indeed the use of this type of device hardly seems calculated to raise the prestige of Parliament.

CONCLUSION

Throughout this study, in attempting to describe what Parliament is, we have endeavoured to separate it from the political, economic and social context in which it functions within each country. We are fully aware that there is much that is arbitrary in this method. Any description of the various political institutions and their specific function, and any comparisons or classifications we may make, can only really serve a useful purpose if at the same time allowance is made for the special and contingent factors affecting the way they operate. But this is the price that has to be paid for trying to bring out as far as possible the analogies to be drawn in parliamentary practice as seen in the forty-one different countries. If by providing a conspectus of national experience this study has helped to show what are the constant features of parliamentary practice, despite the differences between the various political systems, it will have served its purpose.

Perhaps it will have afforded some clue to the direction in which the development of the work of Parliament is tending today. The old notion that the 'legislature' was the same as Parliament would appear to have gone by the board for the legislative function is no longer the preserve of Parliament. The initiative in legislative and financial matters has to some extent slipped out of its grasp; the practice of delegating powers has made for the curtailment of its role in the realm of law. But concurrently, the prerogatives of Parliament have shifted in the direction of control of government activity. The Government initiates and directs; Parliament controls, approves, disapproves and, now and then, inspires. Increasing powers of control in its hands, and a more skilful adaptation of the methods of exercising these powers—such are today the basic prerequisites for the development of Parliament.

INDEX

Accountability:
of Government to Parliament, 249–62; partners in conduct of public affairs, 249; primacy of Parliament, 250; dismissal of ministers and of Governments, 253; and the Presidium (USSR), 253; British tradition of, 254–5; other methods, 255; and collaboration, 255–6; and the two-party system, 256; and government instability, 256; safeguards against hasty action, 256–7; over-rigid rules of, 258. *See also* Accountability, ministerial *and* Dissolution
ministerial, 250–4, 256–8; 3 types of (personal financial, penal and political), 250–1; political, 251–3; and the Head of State, 251; and the sovereignty of the people, 251; in bicameral Parliaments, 251–2; only way of ensuring parliamentary control, 252; cabinet solidarity on major issues (the 'unanimity rule'), 252–3; in the UK, 254; and the balance between powers, 258; and 'interpellation,' 265. *See also* Accountability (of), Government to Parliament
penal, 250–1, 292
personal financial, 250–1
political, 250–1, 267, 286, 292
Accounting Office, General (USA), 281
Accounting, universality of, 210
Accounts Act, 283
Acts of Parliament:
individual, *indexed under their titles*
promulgation and publication of, 190–5; effect, date and purpose of, 191; responsibility for, 191–2; automatic, 191, 192; by Executive, 192–4; by others, 192; the 'pocket veto' (USA), 192–3; reconsideration before, 193; right of veto, 193–4; Executive's prerogative encroaching on legislative function of Parliament, 194–5

validity (constitutional) of, control over, 195–200; extent and purpose, 195; by independent body, 195–6; by Parliament itself, 196; methods of, 196–7; before promulgation, 197; and revision of the Constitution (France), 197–8; 'political' and 'legal' instruments, 198; by judicial authorities, 198–9; appeals to Privy Council, 199; by Supreme Court of Justice, 199–200; by constitutional courts, 200; by the sovereign people, 200
Agenda (parliamentary) of Order of Business, 154–60; by whom fixed, 154–5; power of Executive, 156; 'grievance days', 156; power of majority party in UK and consultation with Opposition, 157; effects on, 157; delegation of task of preparing, 158–9; planning ahead, 159; purpose of, 160
Agreement, bicameral, on legislation, 185–9, 198; efforts to reach, 185–7; joint sittings or sessions, 186; joint committees, 186–7; 'shuttle' system, exchange of messages, 187; settling the disagreement, 187–8; deadlock, 187–8; in financial matters, 188; dissolution, 188; where lower House the more powerful, 189; by qualified majority in lower House, 189; Constitutional Committee (France), 198
Albania: unicameral system in, 12; elections and electorate, 13–22 *passim*; ballot, 23–35 *passim*; candidates, 35–51 *passim*; legal position of M.P.s, 52–62 *passim*; officers and administrative services of Parliament, 62–72 *passim*; independence of Parliament, 73–103 *passim*; sittings of Parliament, 103–11 *passim*; legislative function of Parliament, 115–18 *passim*; introduction of Bills, 119–29 *passim*; delegation of legislative

299

Balance between Executive and Parliament, 258, 259

Ballot, 23–35. *See also* Voting *and* Polling

Belgium: bicameral system in, 10; elections and electorate, 13–22 *passim*; ballot, 23–35 *passim*; candidates, 35–51 *passim*; legal position of M.P.s, 52–62 *passim*; officers and administrative services of Parliament, 62–72 *passim*; independence of Parliament, 73–103 *passim*; sittings of Parliament, 103–11 *passim*; legislative function of Parliament, 115–18 *passim*; introduction of Bills, 119–29 *passim*; delegation of legislative power, 129–39 *passim*; making of laws, 139–90 *passim*

Acts of Parliament: promulgation and publication of, 150–5 *passim*; constitutional validity of, 195–200 *passim*

Budget: nature of, 204–7 *passim*; introduction and preparation of, 207–10 *passim*; and public undertakings, 210–12 *passim*; in bicameral Parliaments, 212–15 *passim*

Financial matters: rights of M.P.s in, 215–20 *passim*; procedure in, 221–33 *passim*

Appointment of Head of State and Executive, 238–49 *passim*; accountability of Government, 249–62 *passim*; machinery of control, 262–77 *passim*; financial control, 277–84 *passim*; foreign policy, control of, 284–92 *passim*; judicial functions of Parliament, 292–7 *passim*

Bicameral system: arguments for, 8; reasons for choice of, 13

In federal states: 4–7. *In non-federal states:* 7–11; origins (historical), 7–8; theory of, 8; classification of systems and relative powers of Chambers, 8–11

Bill of attainder, 295

Bills:
money, 121, 124, 125, 189; certification of, 214
parliamentary, amendments to, 170–5
parliamentary, introduction of, 119–29. *See also* Legislation, initiation of; Legislative function of Parliament; *and* Messages from Head of State

parliamentary, prior approval of, vii
private, 124
tabling of, 124

Blamont, Émile (Secretary-General of French National Assembly), v

Brazil: bicameral system in, 5; elections and electorate, 13–22 *passim*; ballot, 23–35 *passim*; candidates, 35–51 *passim*; legal position of M.P.s, 52–62 *passim*; officers and administrative services of Parliament, 62–72 *passim*; independence of Parliament, 73–103 *passim*; sittings of Parliament, 103–11 *passim*; legislative function of Parliament, 115–18 *passim*; introduction of Bills, 119–29 *passim*; delegation of legislative power, 129–39 *passim*; making of laws, 139–90 *passim*

Acts of Parliament: promulgation and publication of, 190–5 *passim*; constitutional validity of, 195–200 *passim*

Budget: nature of, 204–7 *passim*; introduction and preparation of, 207–10 *passim*; and public undertakings, 210–12 *passim*; in bicameral Parliaments, 212–15 *passim*

Financial matters: rights of M.P.s in, 215–20 *passim*; procedure in, 221–33 *passim*

Appointment of Head of State and Executive, 238–49 *passim*; accountability of Government, 249–62 *passim*; machinery of control, 262–77 *passim*; financial control, 277–84 *passim*; foreign policy, control of, 284–92 *passim*; judicial functions of Parliament, 292–7 *passim*

Budget:
and bicameral Parliaments, 212–15; generally restricted powers of second Chamber, 212–15; differential treatment 213; certification of money Bills, 214; agreement, how obtained when powers are equal, 215
and public undertakings, 210–12; dependent on Government, 210–11; independent of Government, 211–12; Parliament's right to know what is going on, 211
introduction and preparation of: 207–10; and Executive, 207; and Minister of Finance, and Cabinet, 208; and Parliament, 208–10; and

in, *and* rights of M.P.s in; Finance, control over (by Parliament)

rights of M.P.s in, 215–20; accept or reject *en bloc*, or amend?, 215; policy and technical considerations, 216; restricted and unrestricted, 216–18; British system, 218–19; power of reduction only, 218; purpose of motions to reduce expenditure, 218–19; 'balanced' proposals, 220; the Budget as an instrument of policy, 220

Financial powers of first and second Chambers, 6, 9, 11; over 'money Bills', 121

Financial Secretary to the Treasury (UK), 281

Finland: unicameral system in, 12; elections and electorate, 13–22 *passim*; ballot, 23–35 *passim*; candidates, 35–51 *passim*; legal position of M.P.s, 52–62 *passim*; officers and administrative services of Parliament, 62–72 *passim*; independence of Parliament, 73–103 *passim*; sittings of Parliament, 103–11 *passim*; legislative function of Parliament, 115–18 *passim*; introduction of Bills, 119–29 *passim*; delegation of legislative power, 129–39 *passim*; making of laws, 139–90

Acts of Parliament: promulgation and publication of 190–5 *passim*; constitutional validity of, 195–200 *passim*

Budget: nature of, 204–7 *passim*; introduction and preparation of, 207–10 *passim*; and public undertakings, 210–12 *passim*

Financial matters: rights of M.P.s in, 215–20 *passim*; procedure in, 221–33 *passim*

Appointment of Head of State and Executive, 238–49 *passim*; accountability of Government, 249–62 *passim*; machinery of control, 262–77 *passim*; financial control, 277–84 *passim*; foreign policy, control of, 284–92 *passim*; judicial functions of Parliament, 292–7 *passim*

Foreign policy: 284–92; history and current practice, 284–5. *See also* Foreign policy, control over; Foreign policy, direction of; Treaties, ratification of

control over (by Parliament), 286–9; usual means of, 286; Budget debate, 286–7; foreign policy debates, 287; questions to Foreign Minister, 287; parliamentary committees, 287–9; advisory council, 288

direction of (by Parliament), 285–6; executive's prerogative, 285; need for Parliament to be informed, 285; political accountability, 286

France, vi; bicameral system in, 10; elections and electorate, 13–22 *passim*; ballot, 23–35 *passim*; candidates, 35–51 *passim*; legal position of M.P.s, 52–62 *passim*; officers and administrative services of Parliament, 62–72 *passim*; independence of Parliament, 73–103 *passim*; sittings of Parliament, 103–11 *passim*; legislative function of Parliament, 115–18 *passim*; introduction of Bills, 119–29 *passim*; delegation of legislative power, 129–39 *passim*; making of laws, 139–90 *passim*

Acts of Parliament: promulgation and publication of, 190–5 *passim*; constitutional validity of, 195–200 *passim*

Budget: nature of, 204–7 *passim*; introduction and preparation of, 207–10 *passim*; and public undertakings, 210–12 *passim*; in bicameral Parliaments, 212–15 *passim*

Financial matters: rights of M.P.s in, 215–20 *passim*; procedure in, 221–33 *passim*

Appointment of Head of State and Executive, 238–49 *passim*; accountability of Government, 249–62 *passim*; machinery of control, 262–77 *passim*; financial control, 277–84 *passim*; foreign policy, control of, 284–92 *passim*; judicial functions of Parliament, 292–7 *passim*

Franchise, 14–18; *qualifications and disqualifications for:* sex, nationality, 15; residence, age, mental state, 16, 16*n*; education, rectitude, business integrity, 17; deprivation of, seldom permanent, 18; restrictions on, 18. *See also* Polling, Voting at elections *and* Voting systems

Fraud at elections, 33–4

207–10 *passim*; and public undertakings, 210–12 *passim*; in bicameral Parliaments, 212–15
passim
Financial matters: rights of M.P.s
in, 215–20 *passim*; procedure in,
221–33 *passim*
Appointment of Head of State and
Executive, 238–49 *passim*; accountability of Government, 249–
62 *passim*; machinery of control,
262–77 *passim*; financial control,
277–84 *passim*; foreign policy,
control of, 284–92 *passim*; judicial
functions of Parliament, 292–7
passim

Immunities of M.P.s, 52–8; origins
and *raison d'être*, 52; legal non-
accountability, parliamentary privilege, inviolability (protection
from legal process), 53–6; effects
in UK, 54; other privileges, 56
Impeachment, 251, 295–6

Independence:
administrative, of Parliament, 73–4;
meaning of, and need for, 73–4;
vis-à-vis the Executive, 74; and
the civil service, 74
financial, of Parliament, 76–8; *vis-à-
vis* the Executive, 76; audits, 77
procedural, of Parliament, 78–81
Standing Orders: scope of, 78–9;
enforcement of, 79–80; perma-
nency of, 80–1; *vis-à-vis* courts of
law, 81
of M.P.s, 52

India: bicameral system in, 6; elections and electorate, 13–22 *passim*; ballot, 23–35 *passim*; candidates, 35–51 *passim*; legal position
of M.P.s, 52–62 *passim*; officers
and administrative services of
Parliament, 62–72 *passim*; independence of Parliament, 73–103
passim; sittings of Parliament,
103–11 *passim*; legislative function
of Parliament, 115–18 *passim*;
introduction of Bills, 119–29 *passim*; delegation of legislative
power, 129–39 *passim*; making
of laws, 139–90 *passim*
Acts of Parliament: promulgation
and publication of, 190–5 *passim*;
constitutional validity of, 195–200
passim
Budget: nature of, 204–7 *passim*;
introduction and preparation of,

207–10 *passim*; and public undertakings, 210–12 *passim*; in bicameral Parliaments, 212–15
passim
Financial matters: rights of M.P.s in,
215–20 *passim*; procedure in, 221–
33 *passim*
Appointment of Head of State and
Executive, 238–49 *passim*; accountability of Government, 249–
62 *passim*; machinery of control,
262–77 *passim*; financial control,
277–84 *passim*; foreign policy,
control of, 284–92 *passim*; judicial
functions of Parliament, 292–7
passim

Indonesia: unicameral system in, 12;
elections and electorate, 13–22
passim; ballot, 23–35 *passim*;
candidates, 35–51 *passim*; legal
position of M.P.s, 52–62 *passim*;
officers and administrative services of Parliament, 62–72 *passim*;
independence of Parliament, 73–
103 *passim*; sittings of Parliament,
103–11 *passim*; legislative function
of Parliament, 115–18 *passim*;
introduction of Bills, 119–29 *passim*; delegation of legislative
power, 129–39 *passim*; making of
laws, 139–90 *passim*
Acts of Parliament: promulgation
and publication of, 190–5 *passim*;
constitutional validity of, 195–200
passim
Budget: nature of, 204–7 *passim*;
introduction and preparation of,
207–10 *passim*; and public undertakings, 210–12 *passim*
Financial matters: rights of M.P.s
in, 215–20 *passim*; procedure in,
221–33 *passim*
Appointment of Head of State
and Executive, 238–49 *passim*;
accountability of Government,
249–62 *passim*; machinery of
control, 262–77 *passim*; financial
control, 277–84 *passim*; foreign
policy, control of, 284–92 *passim*;
judicial functions of Parliament,
292–7 *passim*
Inquiries, parliamentary, 272–5, 278;
'interpellation', and 'question in
the House', 272; investigating,
272; legislative committees, 272–
73; parliamentary decisions, and
the classic parliamentary system,
and political accountability, 273;

PARLIAMENTS